Duke
BASKETBALL

I0792529

Duke BASKETBALL

A Pictorial History

Lewis Bowling

THE History PRESS

Published by The History Press
Charleston, SC 29403
www.historypress.net

Cover design by Marshall Hudson.

All images courtesy of Duke Archives unless otherwise noted.

First published 2008
Second printing 2010

Manufactured in the United States

ISBN 978.1.59629.467.7

Library of Congress Cataloging-in-Publication Data

Bowling, Lewis.
Duke basketball : a pictorial history / Lewis Bowling.
p. cm.
ISBN 978-1-59629-467-7
1. Duke University--Basketball--History--Pictorial works. 2. Duke Blue Devils (Basketball team)--History--Pictorial works. I. Title.
GV885.43.D85B69 2008
796.323'6309756563--dc22
2008013967

CONTENTS

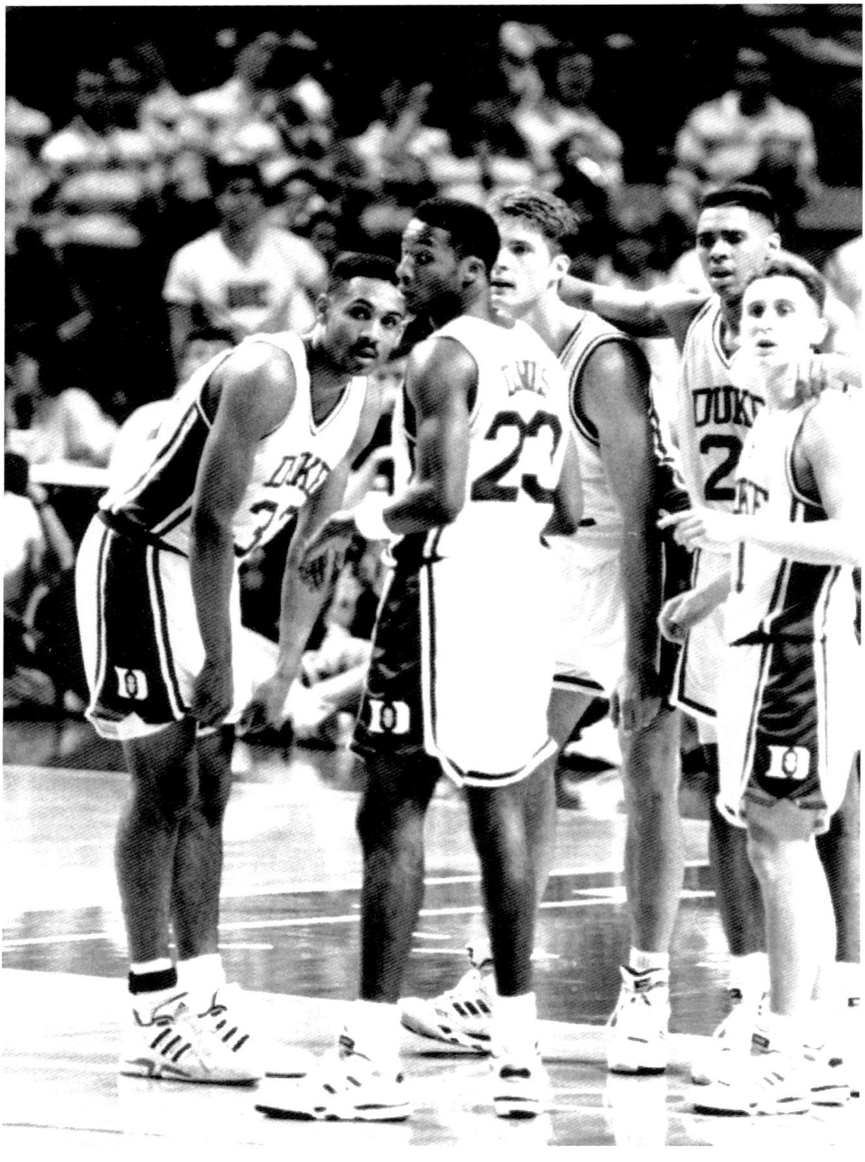

From left to right are Grant Hill, Brian Davis, Christian Laettner, Antonio Lang and Bobby Hurley in 1992.

FOREWORD

There weren't any lights on, but I stepped inside the big oak doors anyway. I could make out the scoreboard and a few banners hanging from the rafters. It hit me: I was standing in one of the greatest sports venues in the history of sports. The "kid from the cotton mill hill" was inside Cameron Indoor Stadium for the very first time. I had a feeling of awe. I was near the very spot where Dick Groat, Jeff Mullins, Art Heyman, Jack Marin, Bob Verga, Steve Vacendak, Mike Lewis, Randy Denton and all the greats of Duke University basketball had played. I had no idea that I would ever have the privilege of broadcasting almost every dribble and shot of the Blue Devils over the next thirty-plus years. That first occasion was Monday, September 13, 1975. I had come to Cameron to cover football coach Mike McGee's press luncheon in what is now the media room. I had just arrived in Durham and begun my career at WDNC radio.

Duke basketball was not foreign to me. Growing up as a sports fan in Albemarle and working for a local radio station for eight years had given me a good background for what has followed. I listened to the radio accounts of the Blue Devils from Add Penfield, Woody Woodhouse and Ed Higgins as Howard Hurt, Joe Belmont, Ronnie Mayer, Bobby Joe Harris and others played the best of the best. There were not a lot of televised ACC games until the 1960s and '70s, so radio was my only connection to Cameron.

In 464 of the last 468 games that have been played in Cameron, I have had the best seat in the house to call the game on the Duke Radio Network. I have climbed up and down the eight steps of that yellow wooden ladder that takes me to my perch in the "Crowsnest" at least four times per game, and sometimes more.

Every time I walk into Cameron Indoor Stadium, I have a tremendous feeling. I don't care whether it's for a Duke/Carolina game with the ACC title on the line, or a visit to the Sports Information or Iron Dukes office; it's still a trip to Cameron. I've talked to people who have driven *fourteen* hours to get to Duke to see their very first game in Cameron and paid way over face value for the tickets. But to look into their eyes and see the expressions on their faces tells me that a lot of people take Cameron for granted. It's not just to see a basketball game. It's to be in one of the most hallowed arenas in the United States and witnessing, firsthand, the Cameron Crazies standing the entire game, and the pep band playing "Devil with the Blue Dress On" and seeing the Blue Devils emerge from the locker room to a tumultuous roar. It's the clever messages taped to the forehead of the Blue Devil mascot. It's PA announcer Dr. Art Chandler and his patented, "Here comes DUKE!!!" It's the Crazies' chants. It's "air-ball," "ugly t-shirt," "start the bus," "no points—four fouls," "sweat Gary sweat" and the famous "ahhhhhhhhh see ya" when an opposing player fouls out. It's "Viking," "Mullet-man" and the grad students. It IS Duke basketball in Cameron Indoor Stadium.

Since 1975, I've seen twelve jerseys retired to the rafters. I've seen eleven Final Four banners and twelve ACC Tournament flags hung there. And yes, I've witnessed *three* NCAA Championship banners being unveiled.

Cameron Indoor Stadium is about more than championships. It's about people. It's about every player who has put on a Duke jersey and stepped on that floor since 1940. It's not just the all-Americans. It's the players down the bench who don't get the headlines. It's the walk-ons who work their fannies off every day in practice to make the all-Americans better and make the team better too. That's what Cameron Indoor Stadium is. Cameron is sweating in February when it's eighteen degrees outside. Cameron is popcorn and Cokes and hot dogs and pizza and Chick-fil-A. It's screaming until your throat hurts and your head aches from the cacophony of 9,314 Crazies trying to out-yell, out-clap and out-stomp each other.

Cameron Indoor Stadium is also home to the Duke women's basketball, volleyball and wrestling teams. It has hosted some of the biggest names in show business and the music world, including Bob Hope, Perry Como and the orchestras of Glenn Miller, Benny Goodman, Duke Ellington, Les Elgart and Louis "Satchmo" Armstrong. Presidents and presidential hopefuls have graced the stage in Cameron. The Duke Children's Classic Celebrity Show brought Frank Sinatra, Dinah Shore, Glen Campbell, Chet Atkins, the McGuire Sisters, Tennessee Ernie Ford and Pat Boone. Rock bands like the Grateful Dead, the Turtles, Bruce Springsteen, the Allman Brothers, Eric Clapton, Simon and Garfunkel, Ike and Tina Turner, Earth, Wind and Fire and a host of others have played to a packed house. Eugene Ormandy and the Philadelphia Orchestra played Cameron, as did the BBC Symphony Orchestra and Leontyne Price.

Even with all this diversity, when you think of Cameron Indoor Stadium, you think about basketball. As the Duke victory total heads toward eight hundred in the building that was conceived on the back cover of a pack

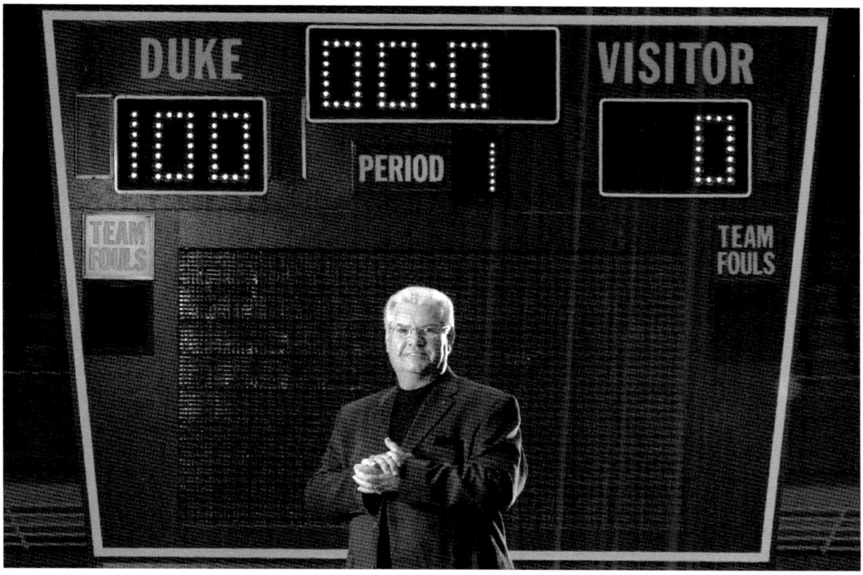

Bob Harris.

of matches, it's the "big" games that stand out. It's beating John Wooden's UCLA dynasty in 1965. It's beating Michigan's "Fab 5" in '92. It's all the great wins over UNC. It's Dick Groat putting forty-eight on the 'Heels in '52, "Tinkerbell" Banks's jumper over Perkins in '81, Robby West's jumper from the key in '72, Fred Lind's sixteen points off the bench in '68, Art Heyman going out in style with forty in '63, the 87–81 win in Vic Bubas's last home game and Jeff Capel's half-court shot to send the 1995 game to a second overtime. Who can ever forget Johnny Dawkins blocking David Rivers's last-second shot to preserve a Blue Devils victory over Notre Dame in '86? How about NBC's Al McGuire with a pith helmet, chair and whip proclaiming the Crazies "a zoo"?

Cameron Indoor Stadium means something different to everyone who has ever sat, or stood, in the building. I even remember one night in 1978 when I almost fell out of the Crowsnest! But that's another story. You have to experience Cameron on a cold winter night to know what I'm talking about. No words, or even pictures, as great as these are, can truly tell the story of Cameron Indoor Stadium. Come and experience it for yourself—if you can find a ticket.

Bob Harris
"Voice of the Duke Blue Devils"
1975–present

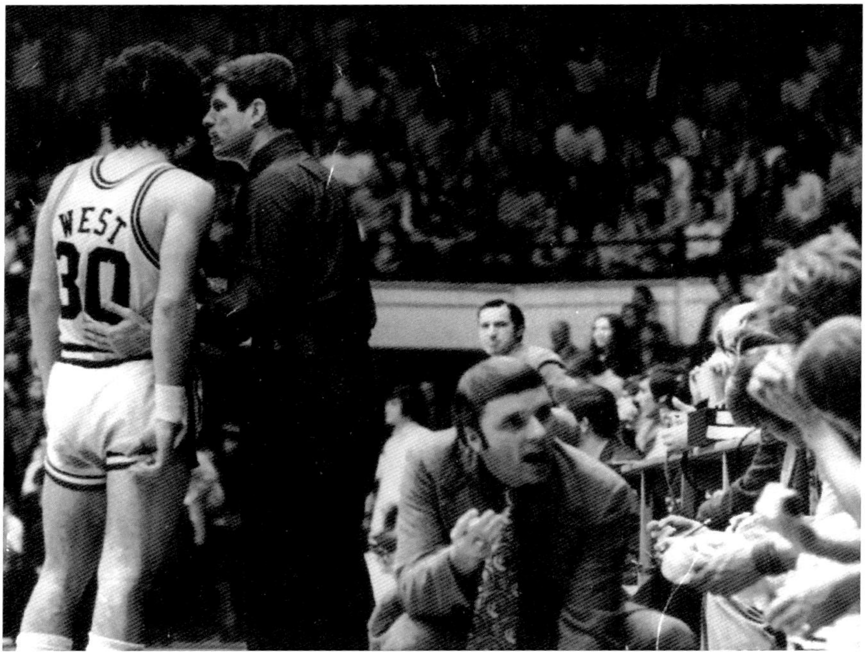

Bucky Waters talks to Robby West just before West hits the winning shot with no time on the clock to beat UNC in 1972. Hubie Brown, Duke assistant coach, is shown kneeling down facing the camera, and just above Brown's head is UNC Coach Dean Smith.

FOREWORD

Written history in sports is very available. Especially in our great tradition of college basketball in North Carolina, we have been blessed by many talented writers with strong loyalties to "particular universities." They have given us wonderful detail on the passion and excellence of the hoops history in our area. This well-written history will not cease, and that's a good thing. Lewis Bowling is taking Duke basketball to the visual level, which will be received with great enthusiasm by young and, well, more mature fans of the Blue Devils.

The photos of those who have put talent, inspiration and perspiration into Duke hoops will be seen in this book by many for the first time. Thanks to Bowling's superb effort, what were once mere names will become history in action. Coach Mike Krzyzewski's twenty-eight years leading Duke are simply incredible and one of the greatest runs of success in all of sports. He came in 1980 and there is no reason it cannot be continued. As you peruse this book, you will be reminded of his early seasons, players and games as Bowling brings them back in photos. Yes, men's basketball trunks were very short for a very long time, and I never heard of women objecting.

Duke basketball was good—sometimes very good—before 1980. Coaches like Vic Bubas, Eddie Cameron, Bill Foster, Hal Bradley, Cap Card and Gerry Gerard will be more than names to Duke fans through this pictorial. Even Duke assistant coaches like Red Auerbach, Chuck Daly and Hubie Brown are in the Naismith Basketball Hall of Fame.

Most of all, though, it is about the players. Yes, we are proud of and enjoyed following those who have made basketball a career beyond college. The great percentage of Duke basketball players, however, end their basketball life in a Duke uniform, but move on to successful careers in many professions and pursuits all over the world that have continued to bring pride to Duke University and its basketball heritage. The best way to evaluate a university is to assess what the graduates do with the rest of their lives. Duke basketball players keep winning.

I was blessed with ten years on the Duke basketball staff: six years as an assistant to a great Vic Bubas and four years as the head coach. But my history with Duke basketball goes back to my high school days, when I first saw Dick Groat—yes, #10 was my hero. But, ironically, I was recruited to North Carolina State by Hall of Fame Coach Everett Case in 1954, the first year of existence for the Atlantic Coast Conference. As an opponent, as a Duke coach and as a television broadcaster, I have seen Duke basketball up close and personal for over fifty years. Duke basketball is about winning, great people, nearly perfect graduation rates and very loyal fans—fans who are probably outnumbered in their own area code by Tar Heel and Wolfpack alumni and fans.

As head coach of West Virginia University, I played the bad guy who beat Duke two out of three—once when Duke was number one nationally and again when Duke was on its way to its third Final Four of four years. But my best good guy role was being the coach of the Blue Devils the day Duke wanted to honor the legendary coach and athletic director Eddie Cameron by renaming Duke Indoor Stadium, the now iconic Cameron Indoor Stadium. The date was January 22, 1972. The opponent was number three University of North Carolina and our Blue Devils were fourth in the ACC. Look for the picture about the last-second 72–70 victory on that Cameron Stadium dedication in this book. The photo shows me walking senior Robby West to the scorer's table just before he hit the winning shot with no time on the clock. In the photo are two Hall of Fame personalities. See if you can identify them. (Hint: Robby West and I are not the answers!)

Enjoy this photo history as I have. Duke basketball from December 1905 to 2008 is a heritage you can feel proud to pull for—on and off the court. Pictures are better than words if you weren't there; and if you were around to enjoy the history in person, I know you will welcome the memories. Enjoy, again I say, enjoy!

Bucky Waters
Duke Basketball Coach, 1969–1973
Sports Broadcaster

ACKNOWLEDGEMENTS

The majority of the pictures in this book came from the Duke University Archives, and I am most grateful to Tim Pyatt and Tom Harkins for their assistance. This book could not have been done without their help and willingness to make available the archives' resources to me. Tim and Tom both went beyond the call of duty, as I had to get some pictures rescanned, and they gave me what I needed in spite of their busy schedules. Both of these men are a credit to Duke University.

The Duke Sports Information Office also made pictures available to me. I appreciate their assistance, and a special thanks goes to Jon Jackson, the associate director of athletics at Duke. Duke Photography also was very helpful in assisting me.

Bob Harris has been the "Voice of the Blue Devils" since 1974, and he most graciously wrote a foreword for this book. I have been listening to Mr. Harris on the radio broadcasting Duke basketball and football games for many years. He is such a big part of the Duke basketball tradition, and it is a real pleasure to have him be a part of this book.

Bucky Waters, a former coach of Duke basketball, also wrote a foreword. Coach Waters has been a pleasure to get to know. I have always enjoyed his television broadcasting, but he is even more engaging and friendly in person. Coach Waters's basketball knowledge is far superior to mine, needless to say, so his help was greatly appreciated.

My wife, Beth Harward Bowling, just may qualify as the most avid Duke basketball fan around. She sometimes gets so excited or agitated during games that I have to go to another room to watch them. Beth did the typing for this book, and much of the editing. I love you girl.

Also, I would like to thank Lee Handford and Hilary McCullough of The History Press, as they helped me tremendously as my editors.

John Roth of the Duke Radio Network and *Blue Devil Weekly* authored a book in 2006 called *The Encyclopedia of Duke Basketball*. This book is a must-have for any serious Duke basketball fan, with more information in it than any other book ever published on Blue Devil basketball. With John's gracious permission, his book was a great reference for me, especially regarding player statistics.

GoDuke.com, with its Duke basketball database, also served as a good source of information for me.

Add Penfield, former radio voice of Duke basketball and football, was a good person to turn to for advice. Mr. Penfield, through our phone conversations and his mailing of information to me, was a big help. I would recommend to any Duke fan to visit the Duke Archives and read Mr. Penfield's manuscript of his long association with Duke. I included excerpts of it in my book on the legendary football coach at Duke, Wallace Wade.

About halfway into writing this book I learned I had cancer, so publication was delayed as I was treated with chemotherapy. With good medical care and good fortune, I am now in remission. A special thank you goes to Dr. James Hathorn of Regional Cancer Care in Durham and formerly of Duke University Hospital.

INTRODUCTION

It is well nigh a certainty that Trinity is to have another game added to her list of athletic sports in the near future. The game in question is basket ball, one of the most fascinating and most intensely interesting indoor games known today. Next to football probably it holds the constant attention of the spectators more than any other game. The play is extremely fast and vigorous.

Many preparations have been made within the last few days in the gymnasium with the view of starting practice as soon as examinations are over. Iron guards have been fastened around the electric globes and detachable goals have been constructed.

Basketball should appeal to a larger number of students than does base ball. Yet not everyone is a successful basket ball player, for everyone does not possess great activity, nerve and endurance, the three prime essentials of a good player.

So basketball at Trinity, now Duke University, began as reported in the campus newspaper, the *Trinity Chronicle*, back in 1906. Wake Forest came to Durham to play Trinity in its home gymnasium, known as the Ark, and beat Duke 24–10.

Since the introduction of basketball to the Duke campus by Wilbur "Cap" Card, the Blue Devils have established themselves as one of the premier programs in the nation. Duke has won three national championships and played in fourteen Final Fours, and at the time of this book going to press, the men had won 1,849 games against 810 losses, including an outstanding home court record of 825–184.

Cap Card, the father of Duke basketball, served as the first basketball coach at Duke, and won 30 games against 17 losses from 1905 to 1912. Still called Trinity, Card's best team was in 1908–09, winning 8 and losing only 1. Eddie Cameron became coach in 1928, and from then until 1942 Cameron's teams won 226 games with 99 losses, with three conference championships. In 1941–42, Duke went 22 and 2 in Cameron's last year as coach. Cameron Indoor Stadium was dedicated in Coach Cameron's honor in 1972.

Another successful era followed from the 1942–43 season through 1950 under Gerry Gerard. Duke was 131–78 during that time, and won two conference championships, highlighted by a 21–6 team in 1945–46. Harold Bradley succeeded Gerard as Duke coach in 1950, and Duke won 167 games with 78 losses through 1959, with a 24 and 6 record and a final national ranking of twelfth in 1951–52, and an 18–7 mark and finishing tenth in the final rankings of 1957–58.

Duke really became one of the premier programs in the country upon the arrival of Vic Bubas as coach in 1959. From then until 1969, Duke was 213–67 with four ACC Tournament championships and played in three Final Fours. Duke played UCLA for the national title in 1964. Bucky Waters succeeded Bubas, and Duke continued to win. The Blue Devils were 63–45 under Coach Waters, and won 20 games during the 1970–71 season. Bill Foster led Duke to another Final Four in 1977–78, when Duke played Kentucky for the national title. Foster was 113–64 with two ACC Tournament titles during his reign from 1974–80.

In 1980, a man now known worldwide as Coach K was named as Duke's coach. Mike Krzyzewski is now a legend on the Duke campus and anywhere basketball is played. He has led Duke to ten Final Fours and three national titles. Coach K, at the time this was written, had won 803 games with 267 losses over his career, with a 69–20 record in the NCAA Tournament. His 69 NCAA wins are the most in history.

Many great players have played for Duke through the years, such as Duke's first All-American, Bill Werber, to 2006 national player of the year J.J. Redick.

The Duke women's basketball teams, from the guidance of Coach Debbie Leonard to Gail Goestenkors to present coach Joanne P. McCallie, have also contributed greatly to the tradition of Duke basketball.

Many of the players and coaches who have been connected to Duke over the years are included on the following pages. Whether it be 1905, the first year of Duke basketball, or 2008, Blue Devil basketball has a history second to none.

Chapter 1
HOME COURTS

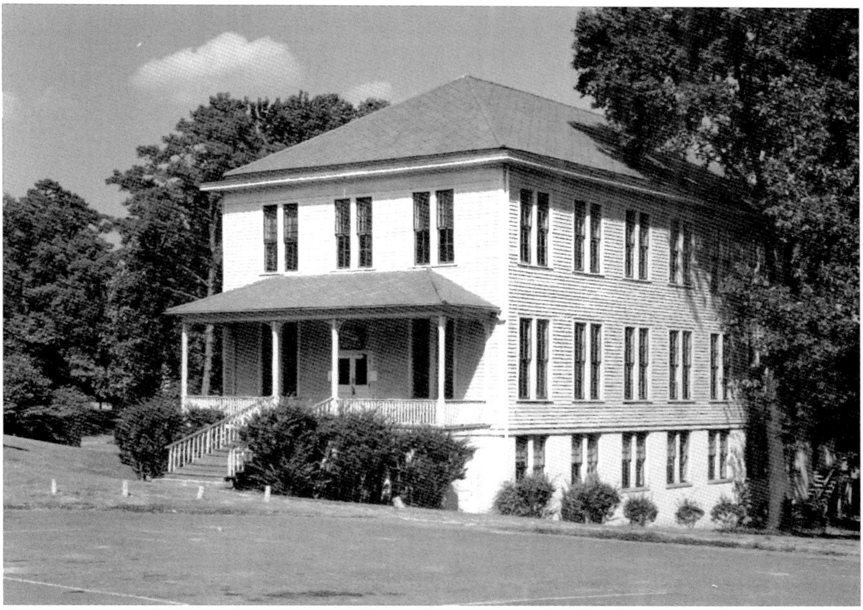

Trinity College, now Duke University, played its first basketball game on campus at the Angier B. Duke Gym, nicknamed the Ark. Duke lost that game to Wake Forest 24 to 10, but many victories and championships have been won by the Blue Devils since. The playing surface at the Ark was only thirty-two feet by fifty feet.

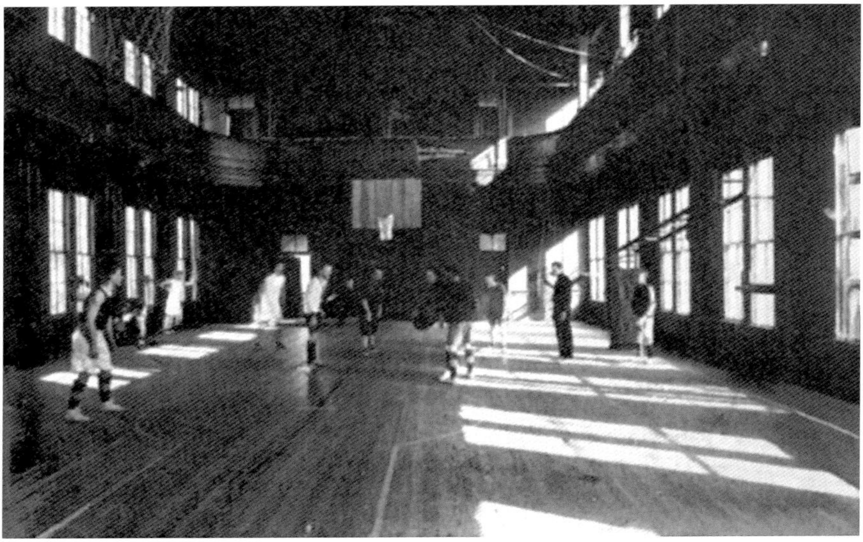

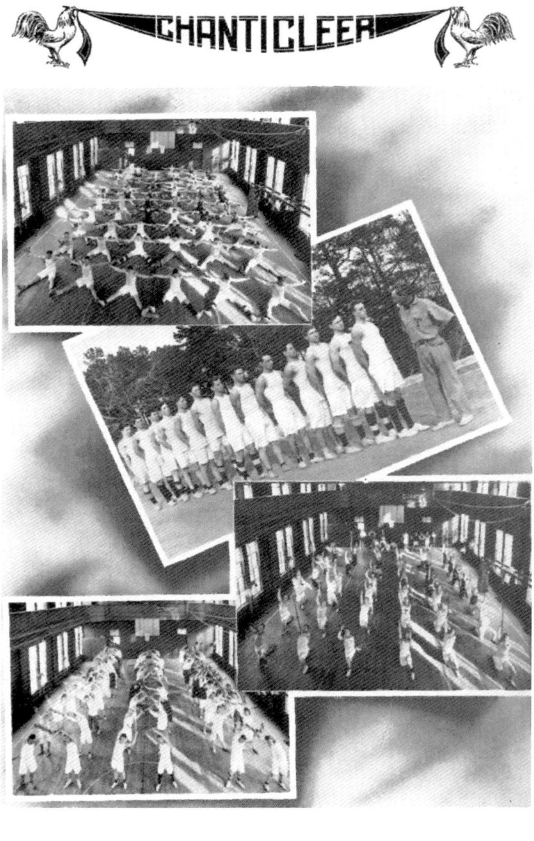

Above: Cap Card practices his basketball team inside the Angier B. Duke Gym in 1912. Trinity, now Duke University, played Wake Forest on March 2, 1906, in its first intercollegiate basketball game. Duke captain T.G. Stem and teammate C.R. Claywell scored a team high 4 points apiece. Stem later became a prominent member of the Duke Athletic Council and mayor of nearby Oxford, North Carolina.

Left: Physical education students at Trinity College exercise inside the Ark, Duke's first basketball home court. These pictures are from 1912. The Ark still stands on Duke's East Campus.

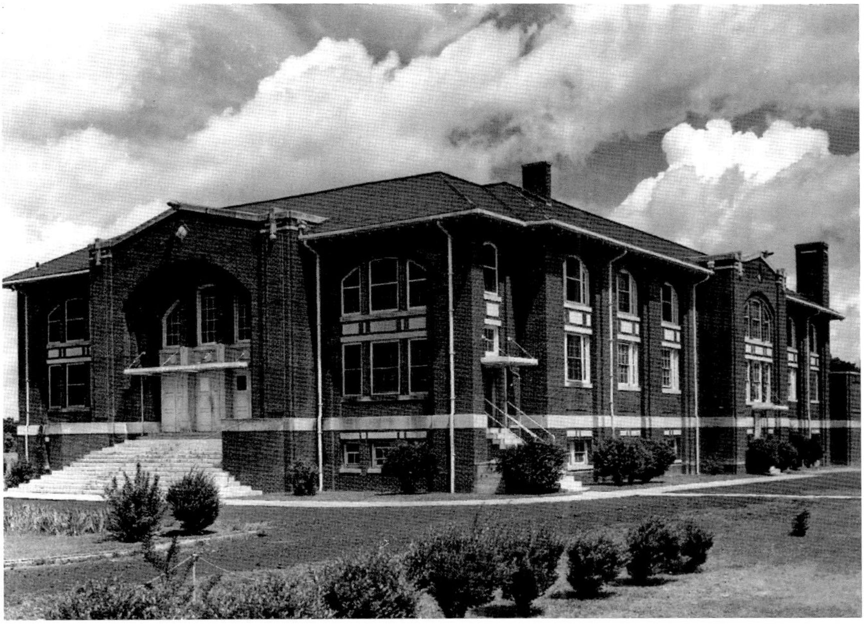

Alumni Memorial Gym served as Duke's home basketball arena from 1924 to 1930. It was named in honor of Duke alumni who died in World War I. Today the gym still stands as a proud testament to the past on Duke's East Campus.

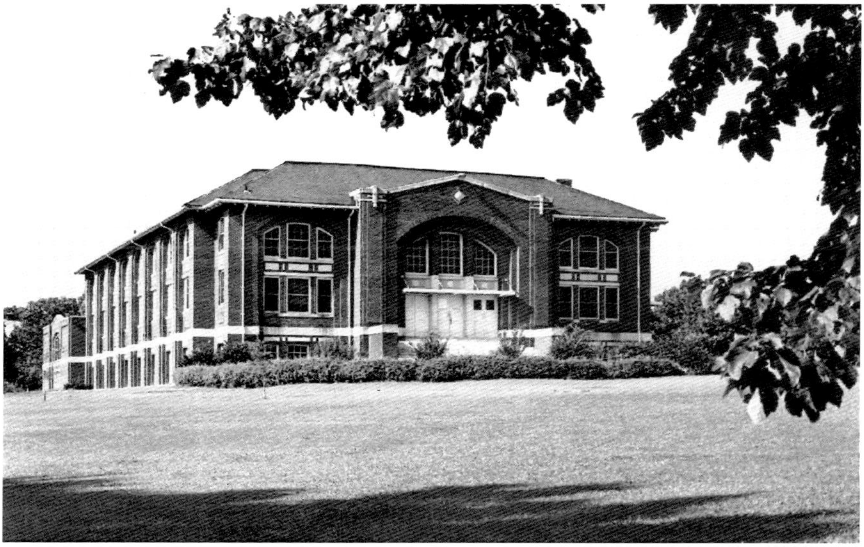

The Alumni Memorial Gym held a little over two thousand fans, including an upstairs balcony.

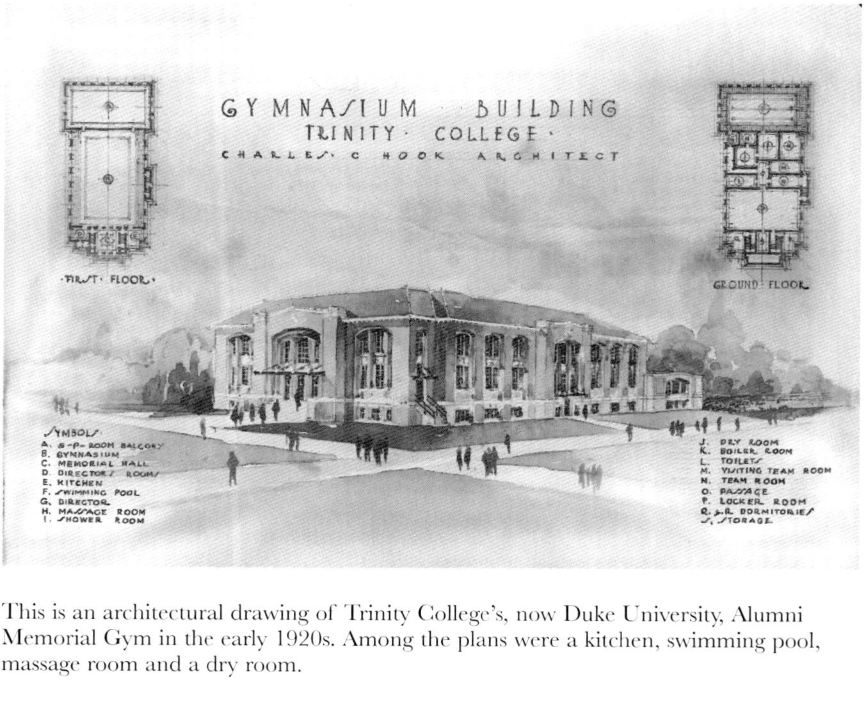

This is an architectural drawing of Trinity College's, now Duke University, Alumni Memorial Gym in the early 1920s. Among the plans were a kitchen, swimming pool, massage room and a dry room.

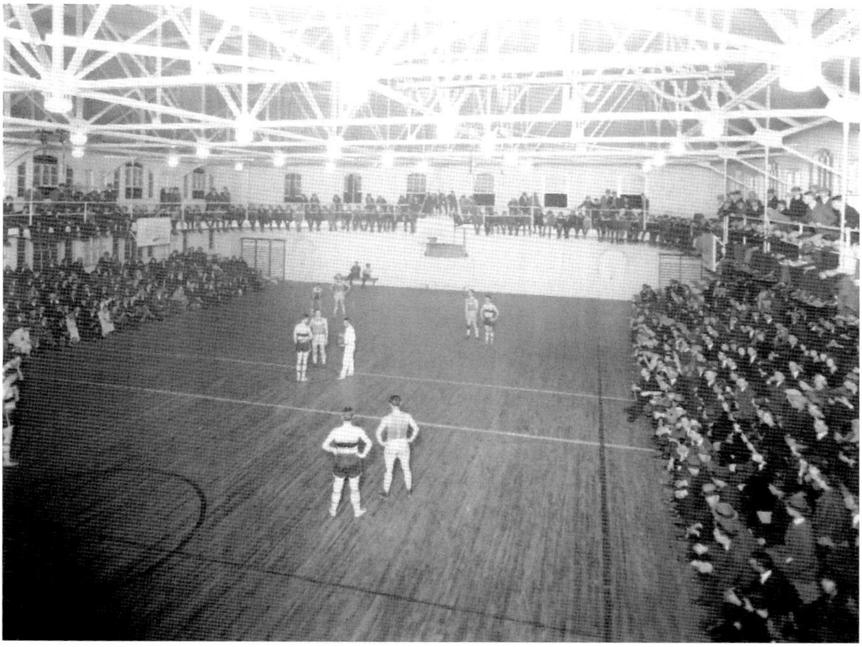

Duke is playing North Carolina State in Alumni Memorial Gym in 1924. This home court facility opened on Duke's East Campus in 1924, and served as Duke's home facility until Card Gym opened in 1930 on the West Campus. *Courtesy of Duke Sports Information.*

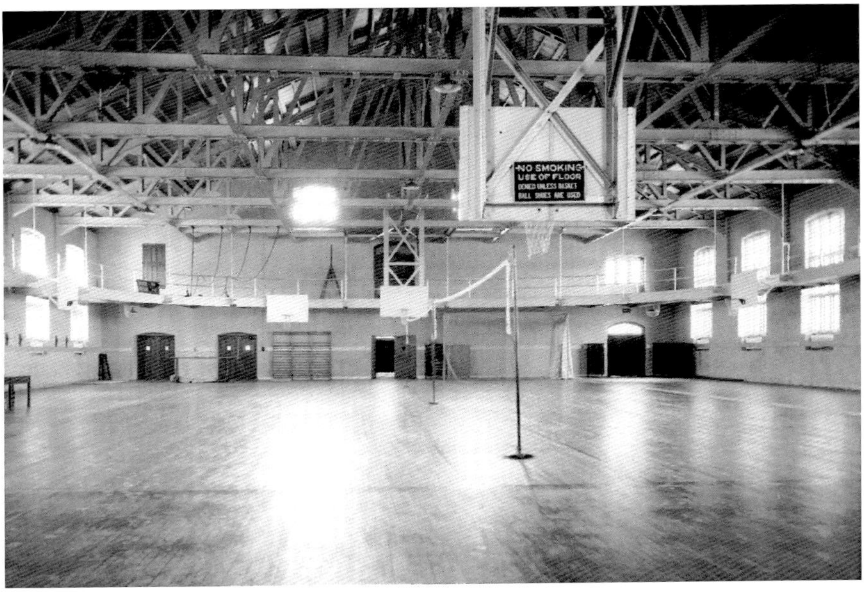

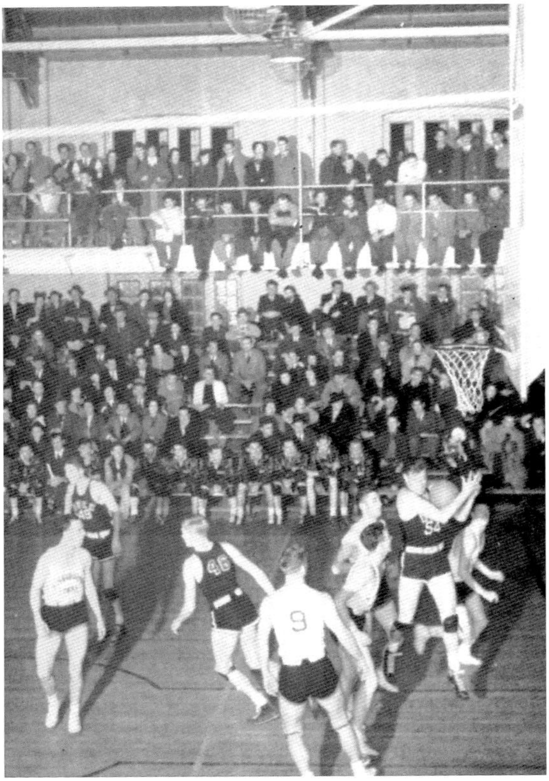

Above: The interior of Alumni Memorial Gym.

Left: Game action inside Card Gym in 1938. This gym opened in 1930 and the last game played there was in 1939. The gym was named in honor of Wilbur "Cap" Card, who was Duke's first basketball coach in 1905. The facility was called Duke Gym until being named after Card in 1958.

Opposite top: An aerial view of the 1942 Rose Bowl football game in Durham. The game was held on the Duke campus because of concerns that the West Coast was vulnerable to enemy attack during World War II. Directly above the football stadium is Cameron Indoor Stadium, and just to the right of Cameron is Card Gym. In the upper left is Jack Coombs Field, and in the upper right is Duke Chapel.

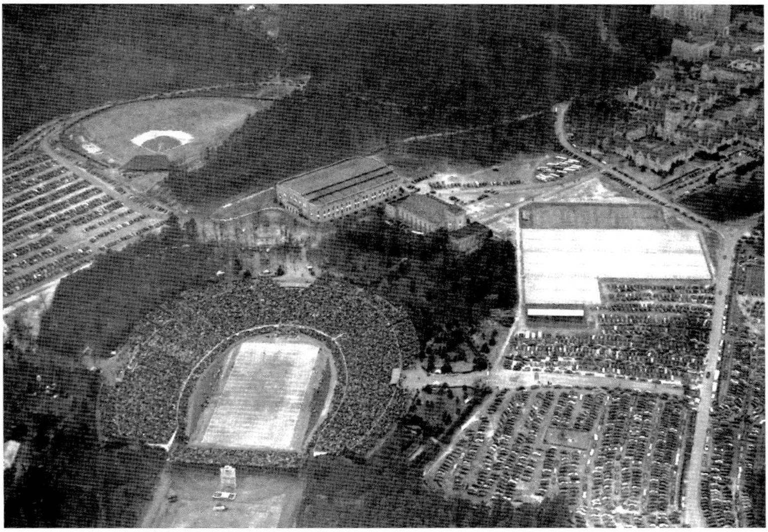

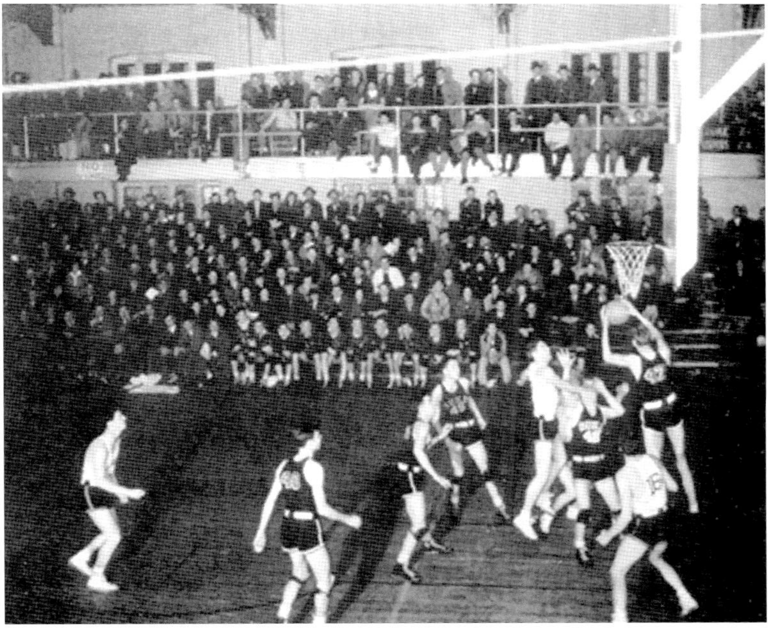

Lang Hobgood of Duke, number 47, grabs a rebound in a 1938 game in Duke Gym, now called Card Gym. Hobgood stood six feet, six inches, and was from Durham. The leading scorer for the 1937–38 team was number 40 in the picture, Ed Swindell, the second player from the left. Swindell averaged 8.6 points a game, and he was also from Durham. The 1937–38 team finished 15 and 9 and won the Southern Conference Tournament under coach Eddie Cameron. Swindell scored a team high of 14 points in the tournament title game over Clemson.

Chapter 2

CAMERON INDOOR STADIUM

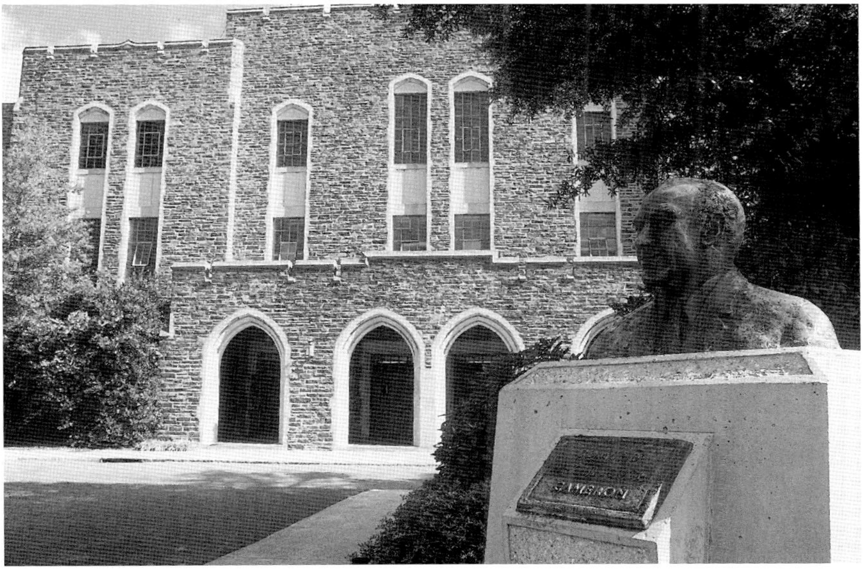

A statue of Eddie Cameron stands in front of the arena named for him, Cameron Indoor Stadium. *Courtesy of Duke Sports Information.*

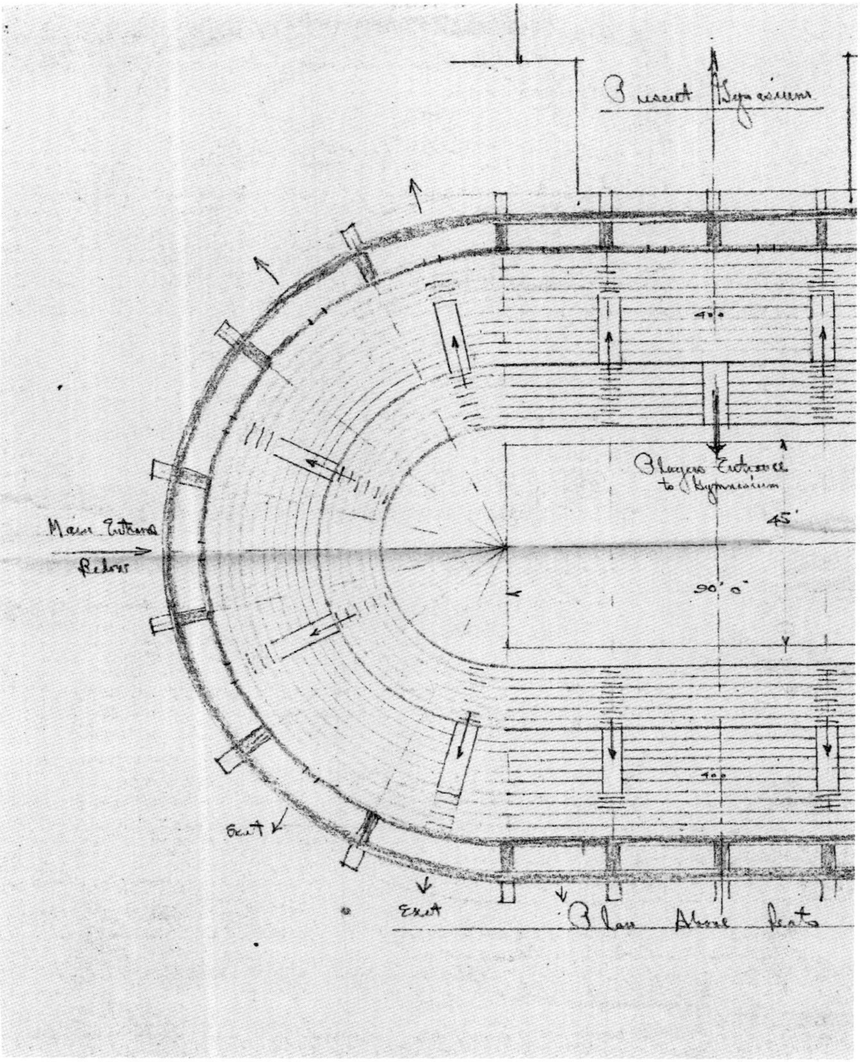

Here is a floor plan of Cameron Indoor Stadium. According to a report from 1940, "Base for the maple playing floor are five-inch concrete slabs, cresoted wood subflooring, and waterproofing paper."

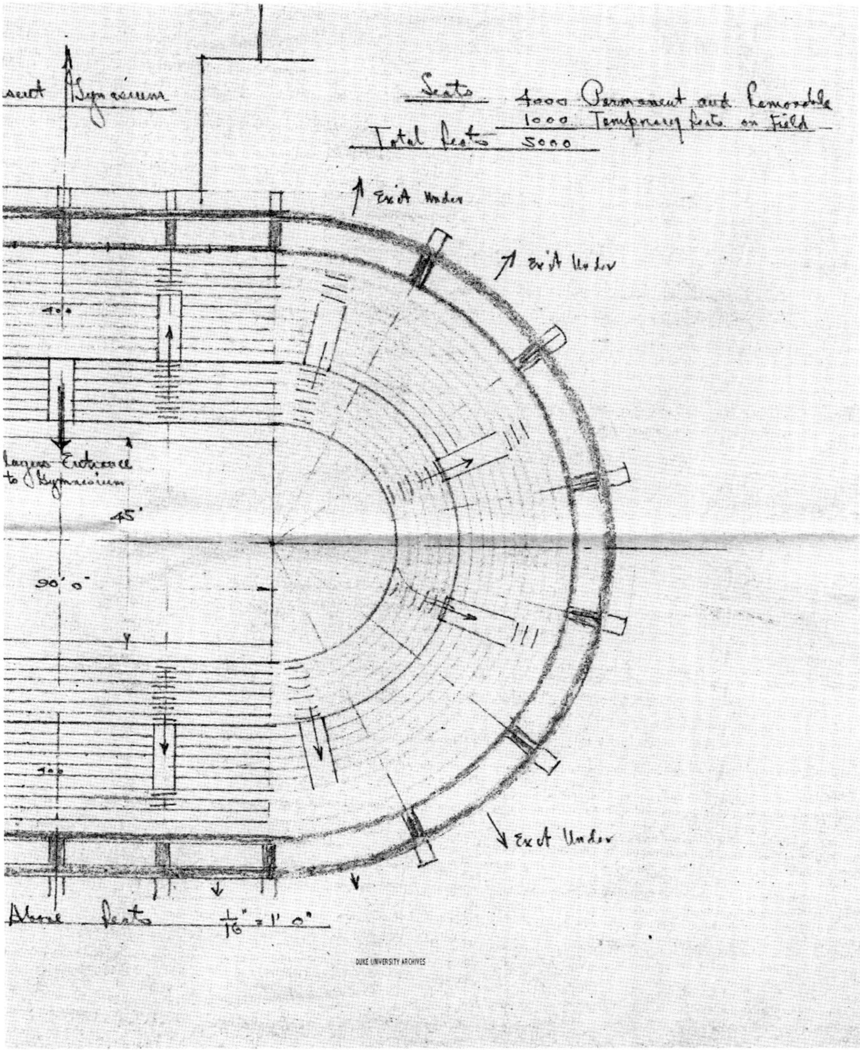

The other half of the floor plan for Cameron Indoor Stadium is shown. A report from 1940 stated, "Despite its large volume, the building can be readily and comfortably heated by a combination of radiators and unit heating, with thermostat controls. The electrical features of the new gym include superb lighting by the use of 42 1,000watt lights."

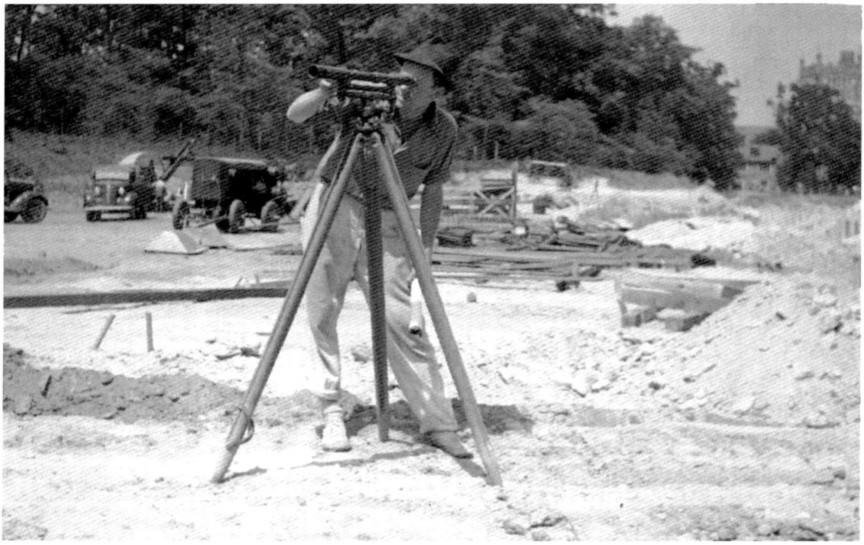

Construction started on Cameron Indoor Stadium in 1939 with money earned from Wallace Wade's 1939 Rose Bowl football team. The building of Cameron cost $400,000 and was opened on January 6, 1940, in a win over Princeton.

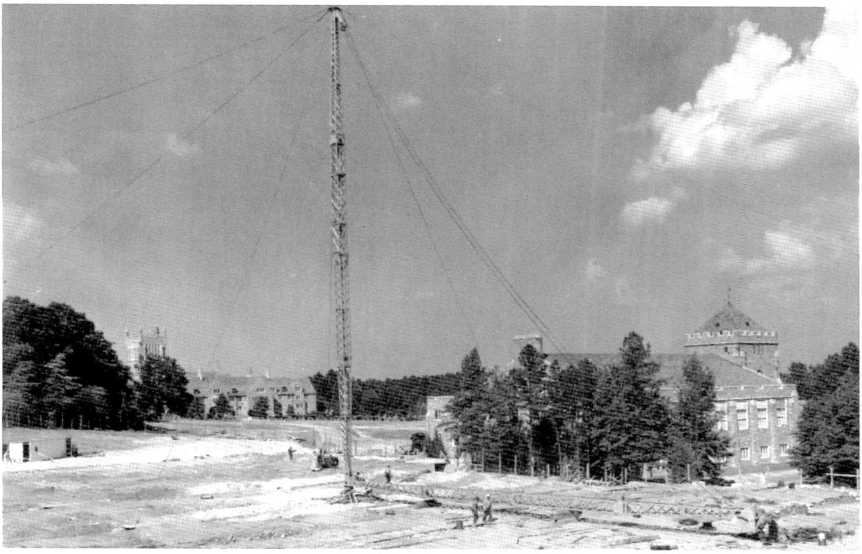

This sacred ground would soon hold the building that is now known worldwide, Cameron Indoor Stadium. Card Gym, where Duke played basketball from 1930 to 1939, can be seen on the right.

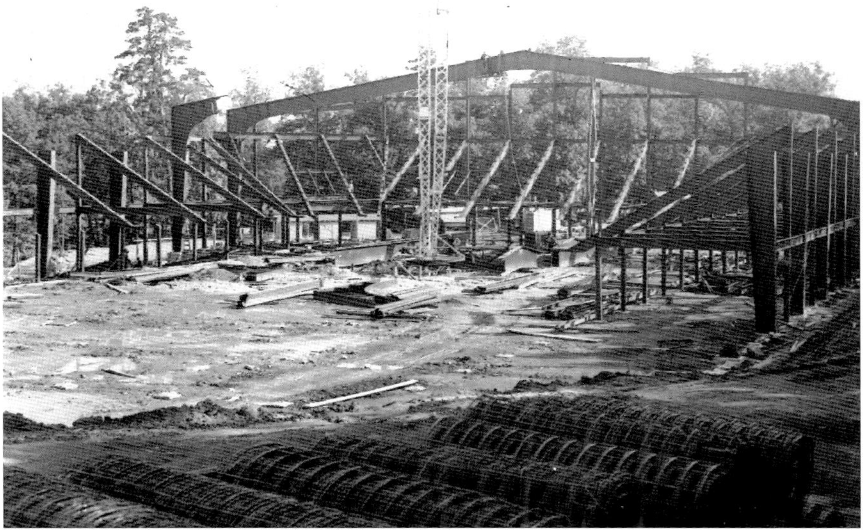

Steel beams are in place as construction of Duke Indoor Stadium, new named Cameron Indoor Stadium, continues in 1939.

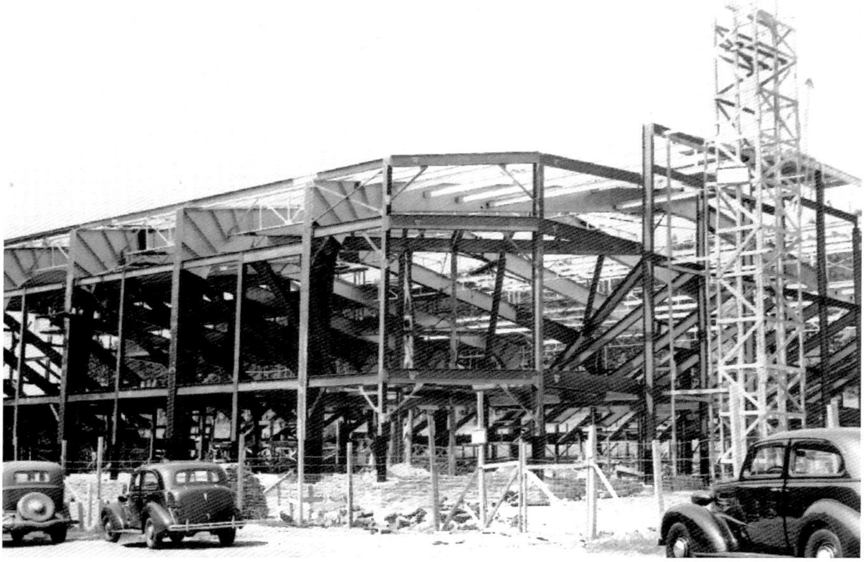

Construction on Cameron Indoor Stadium is moving right along in 1939.

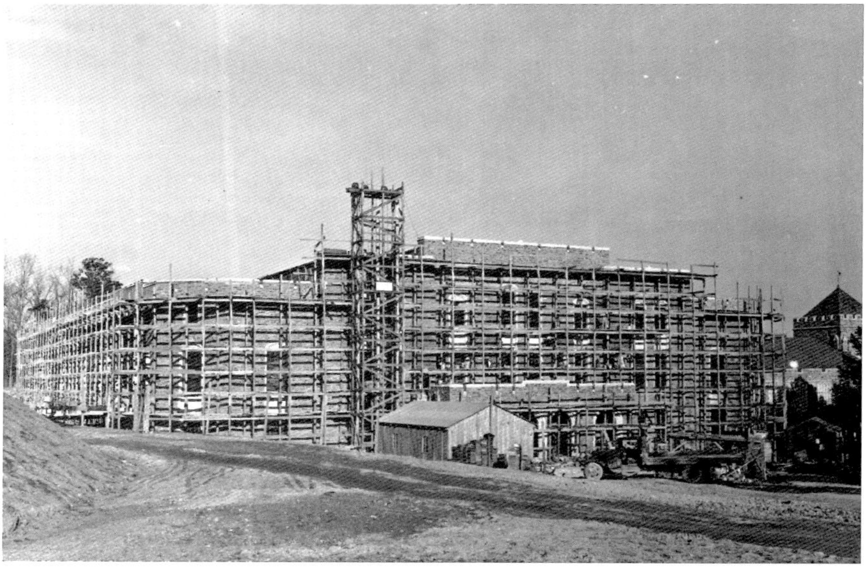

The intimidating presence of Cameron Indoor Stadium is taking shape from this shot of 1939. Today, to the left from this view, stands the Michael W. Krzyzewski Center for Athletic Excellence.

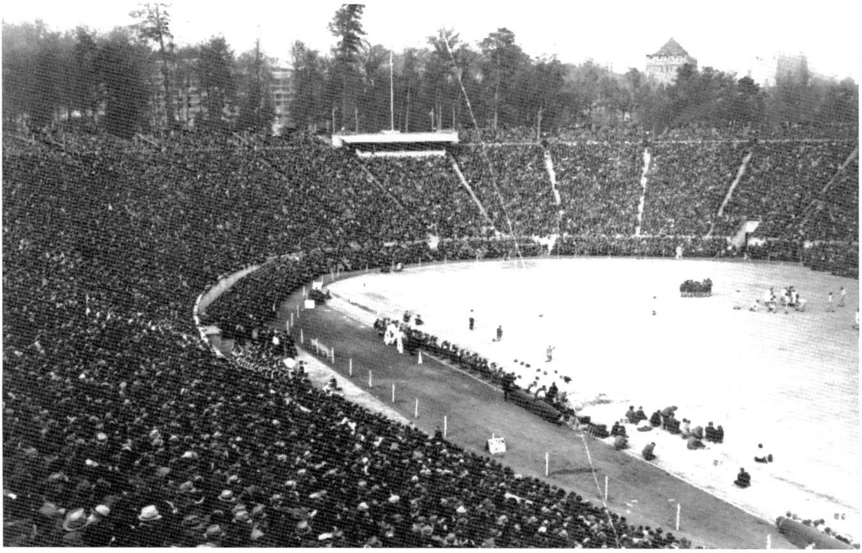

A Duke football game takes place in 1939. In the upper left of this picture, you can see the progress of Duke Indoor Stadium being built.

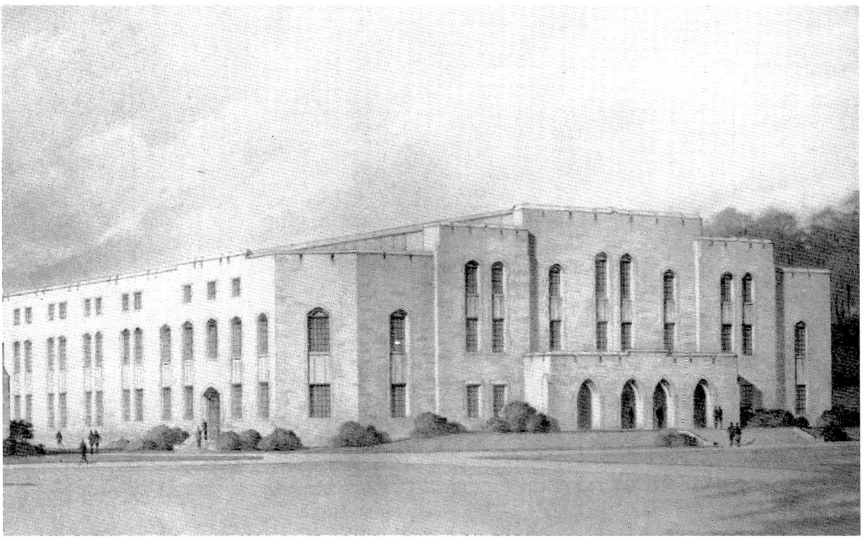

Here is an architectural drawing of Duke Gymnasium, which came to be known as Duke Indoor Stadium and is now Cameron Indoor Stadium. The first game was in 1940, and the first sellout of 8,800 was in 1946 for a game against University of North Carolina.

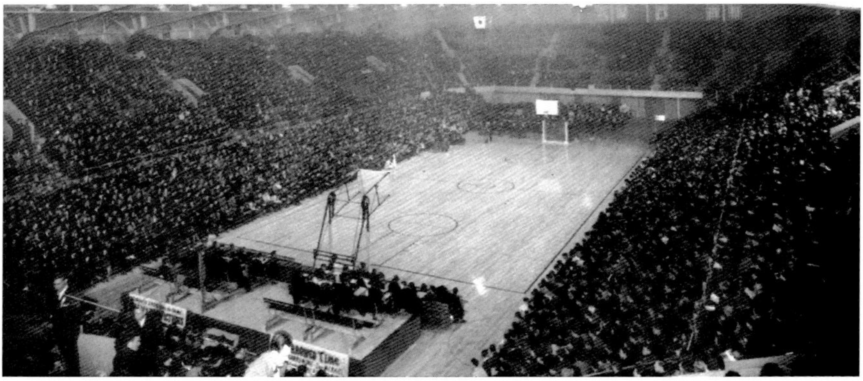

A 1940s' look into the interior of Cameron Indoor Stadium.

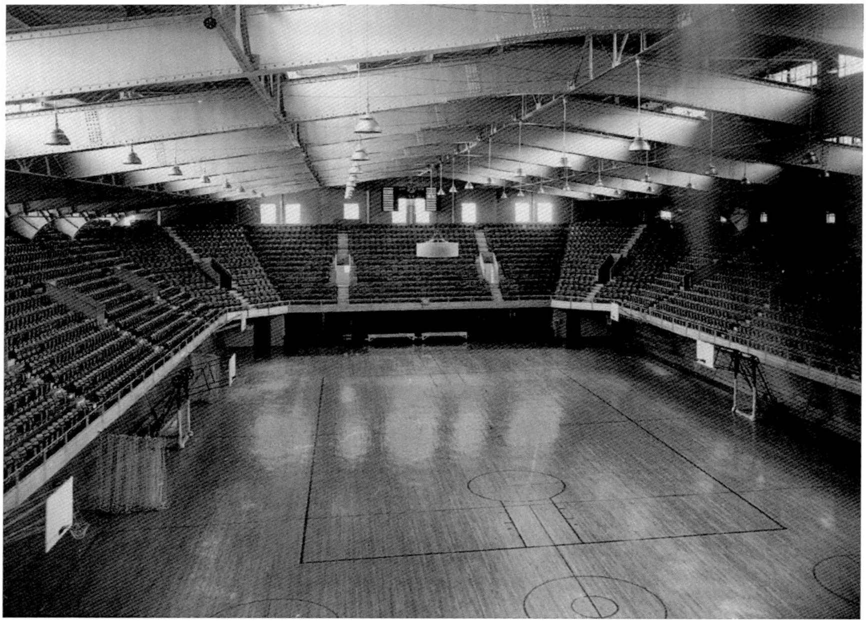

You are now looking inside Cameron Indoor Stadium sometime in the 1940s. There is no better atmosphere in college basketball than in the confines of this home court facility of the Duke Blue Devils.

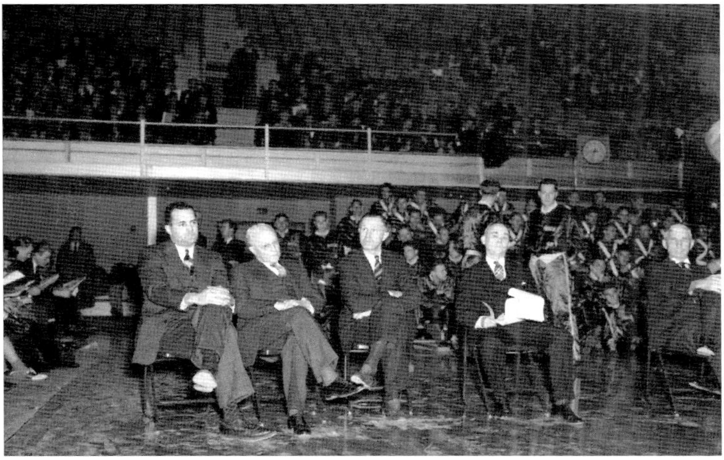

Seated second from the left is Robert Flowers, who became president of Duke University in 1941; third from the left is Wallace Wade, legendary football coach and athletic director at Duke; fourth from the left is William Wannamaker, who played a crucial role in Duke's rise to academic and athletic excellence; and fifth from the left is Cap Card, Duke's first basketball coach. This scene is from the dedication of Duke Indoor Stadium, now Cameron Indoor Stadium, in 1940.

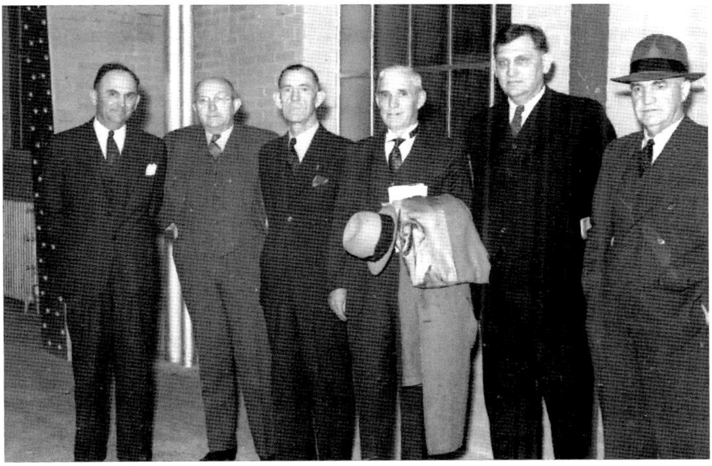

This is a reunion of the first basketball team at Duke, then Trinity, at the opening of Duke Indoor Stadium, now Cameron Indoor Stadium, in 1940. Duke basketball fielded its first team in 1905, winning 2 games with 3 losses. The third man from the left is T.G. Stem, who served as captain of the first two Duke basketball teams in 1905–06 and 1906–07. The man holding the hat is Wilbur "Cap" Card, the first basketball coach in Duke history, who won 30 games against 17 losses from 1905 to 1912.

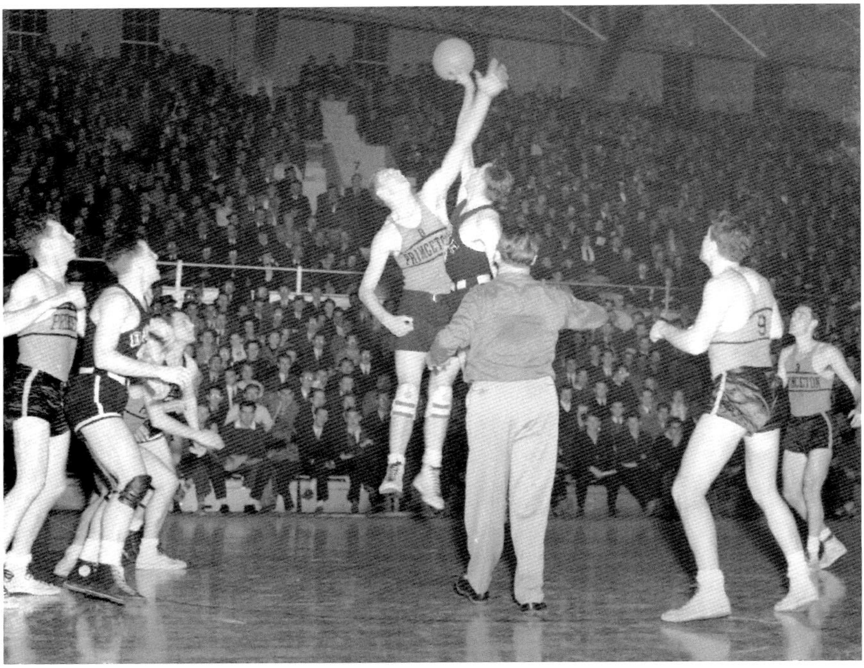

A crowd of eight thousand attended the first game in Cameron Indoor Stadium in 1940 as Duke beat Princeton 36 to 27. The facility was then known as Duke Gymnasium and Duke Indoor Stadium, and was in 1940 the largest gym south of Philadelphia. Glenn Price, a five-foot, ten-inch player from Beaver Falls, Pennsylvania, scored the first 5 points of the game and finished with a team high of 13. Price was a second team all-conference choice in the 1939–40 season and served as co-captain of the 1940–41 team that won the Southern Conference Tournament under coach Eddie Cameron.

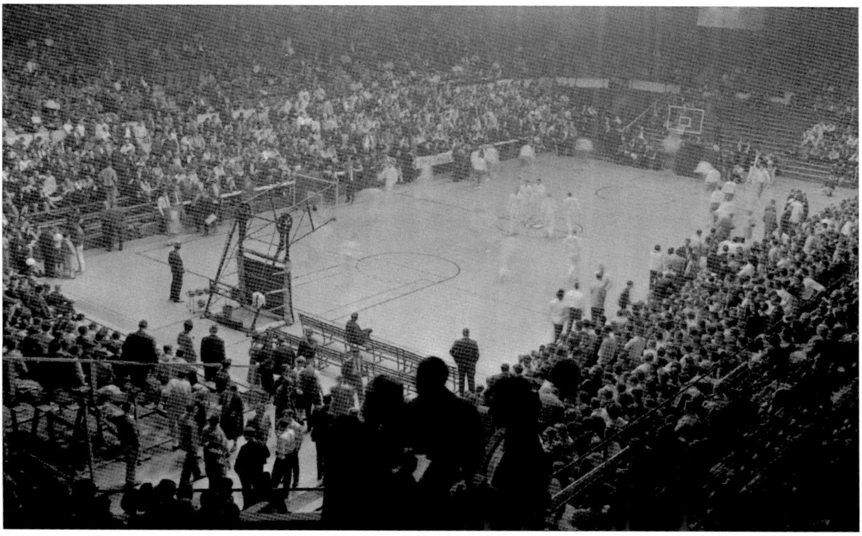

This is a view inside Cameron Indoor Stadium shortly after it opened in 1940.

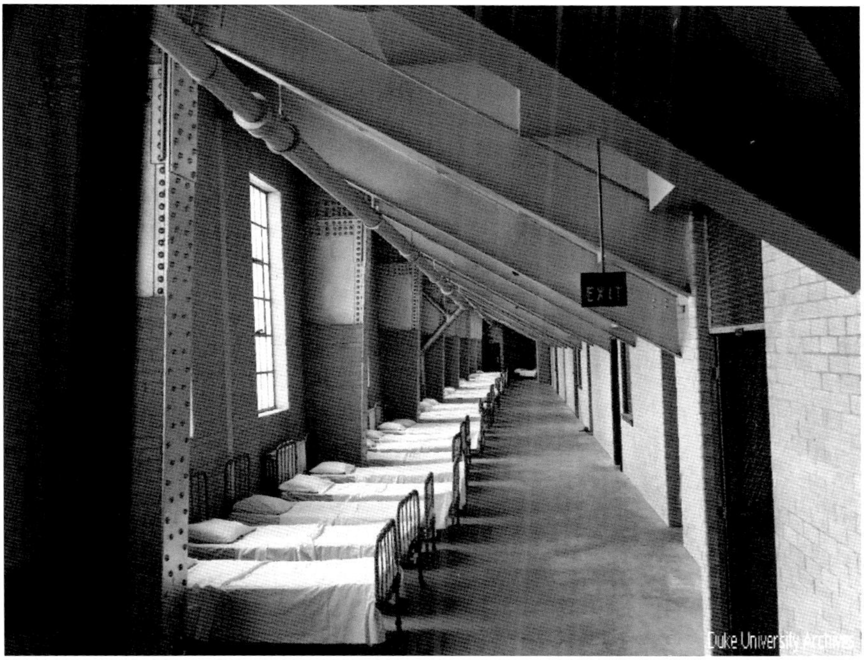

These beds were placed inside Cameron Indoor Stadium back in the 1940s. Cameron through the years has been used for different functions, such as student registration, concerts, graduation ceremonies and speeches.

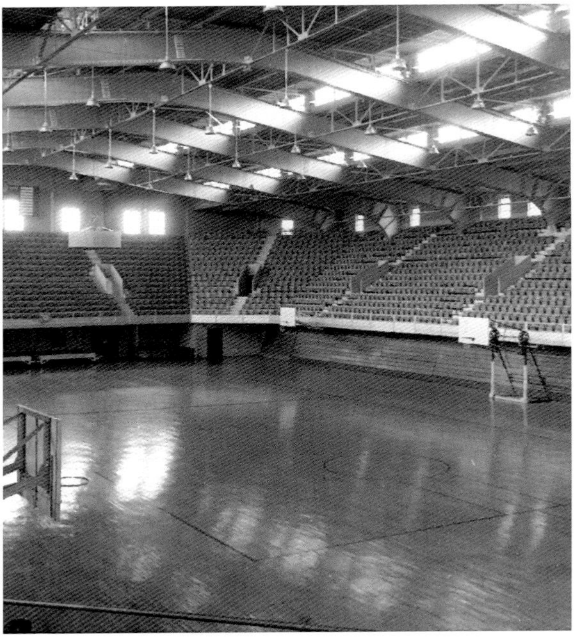

This is a scene from 1941 inside Cameron Indoor Stadium, then called Duke Indoor Stadium. The 1941–42 team, coached by Eddie Cameron, won 22 and lost only 2, while winning the Southern Conference Tournament. Three members of this team were from local Durham High School: Cedric Loftis, his brother Garland and Bob Gantt. In the 1942–43 season, these three were joined by Gordon Carver, another player from the state champion Durham High School program. Bill McCahan made first team all-conference and went on to play professional basketball for Syracuse and Major League baseball for the Philadelphia Athletics.

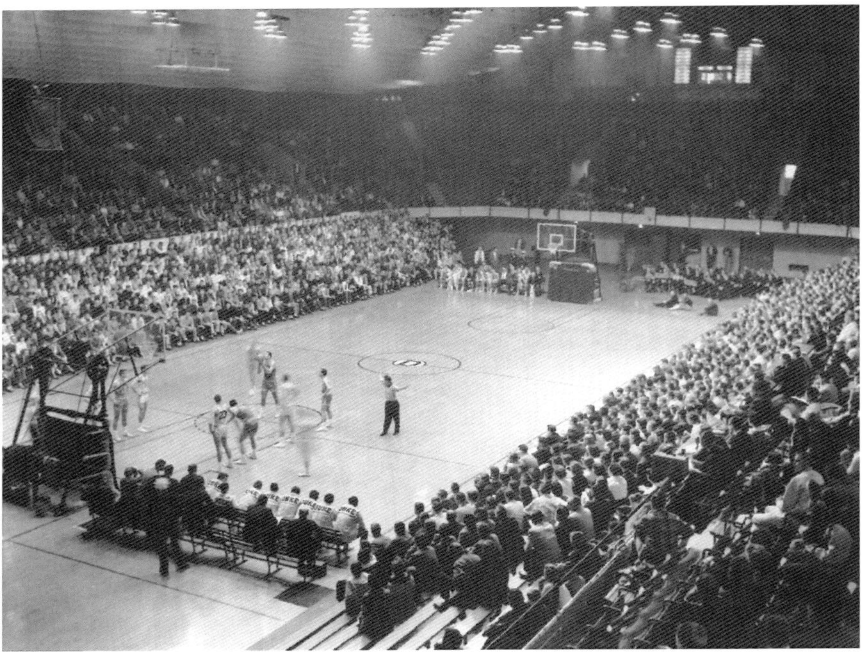

This is action from a 1960 game inside Cameron Indoor Stadium. Notice where the teams sat during games.

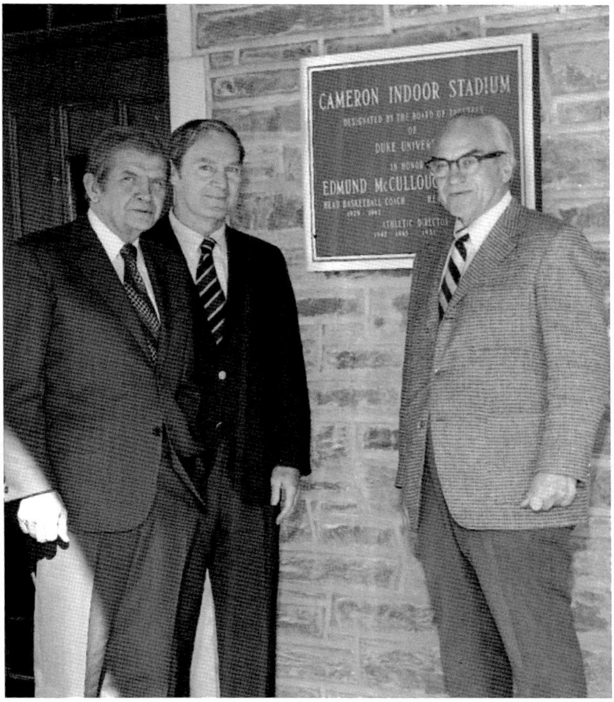

Cameron Indoor Stadium was dedicated in Eddie Cameron's name in 1972. On the left is Terry Sanford, who was Duke's president from 1969 to 1985. In the middle is Carl James, who replaced Eddie Cameron as Duke athletic director in 1972. On the right is Cameron, one of the most revered figures in Duke athletic history. This picture was taken during the 1972 dedication ceremonies.

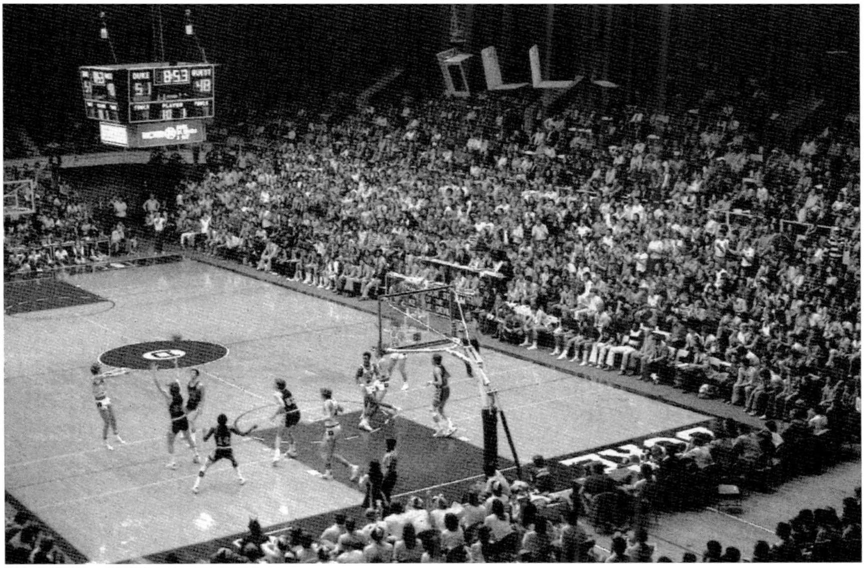

This is game action from the late 1970s inside Cameron Indoor Stadium. Big Mike Gminski can be seen near the basket with his side turned to the camera.

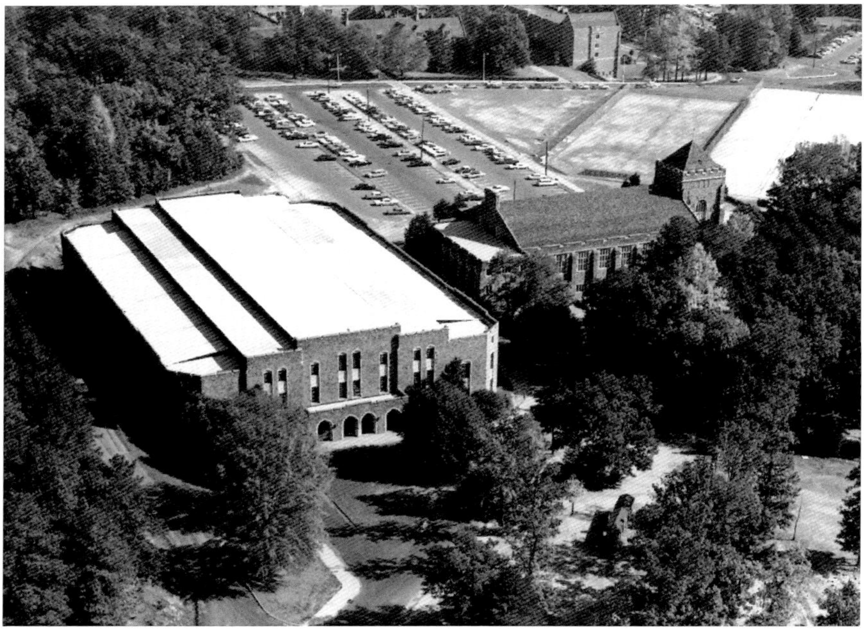

Shown here is an aerial view of Cameron Indoor Stadium to the left and Card Gym to the right. Cameron Indoor Stadium is recognized as one of the most famous sporting venues in America. Card Gym was Duke's basketball home court from 1930 to 1939 and held around 3,500 people. Card Gym is still used as an athletic and physical education facility.

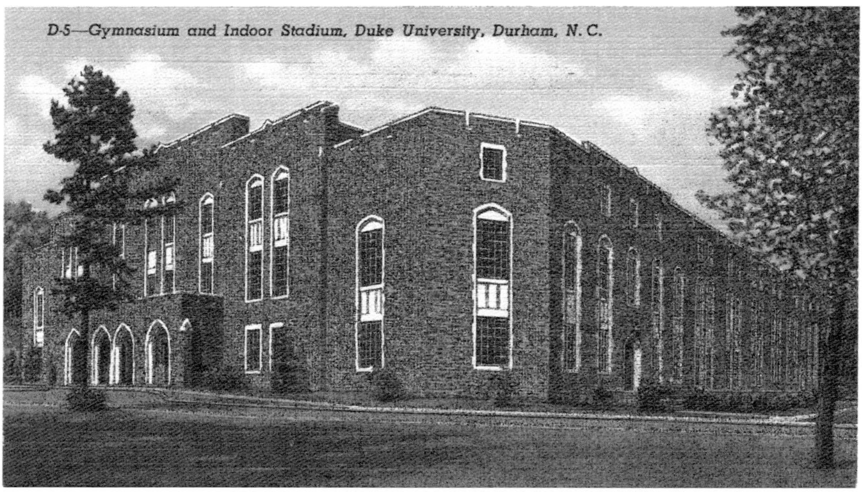

This is a postcard drawing of Cameron Indoor Stadium. *Courtesy of the author.*

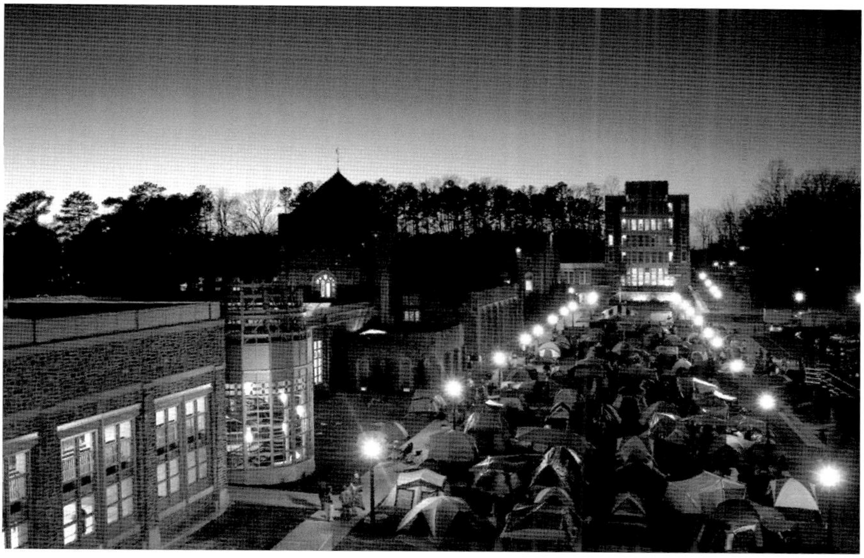

During basketball season, one will see tents around Cameron Indoor Stadium as far as the eyes can see. These belong to Duke students camping out for the next home game of their beloved Blue Devils. This tradition is known as Krzyzewskiville, or K-ville. *Courtesy of Duke Photography.*

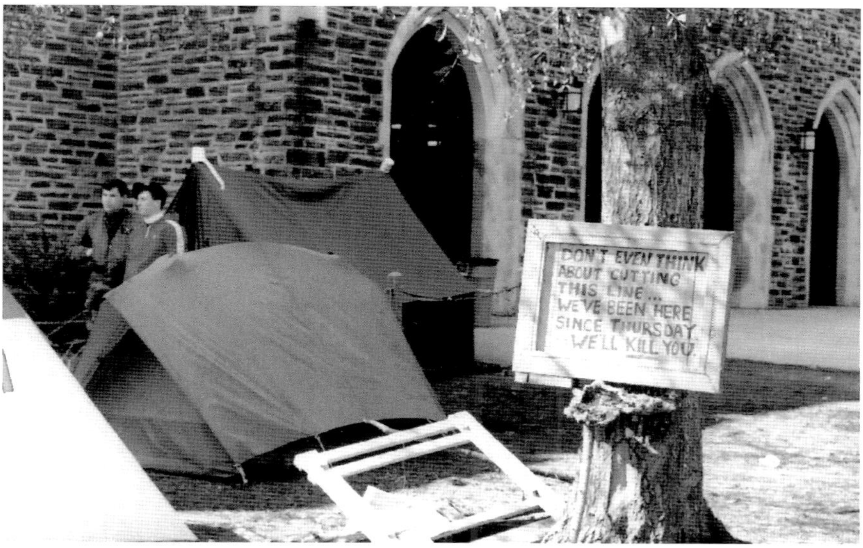

This scene is part of Krzyzewskiville, where students camp out in tents for the opportunity to cheer the Blue Devils in Cameron Indoor Stadium. *Courtesy of Duke Photography.*

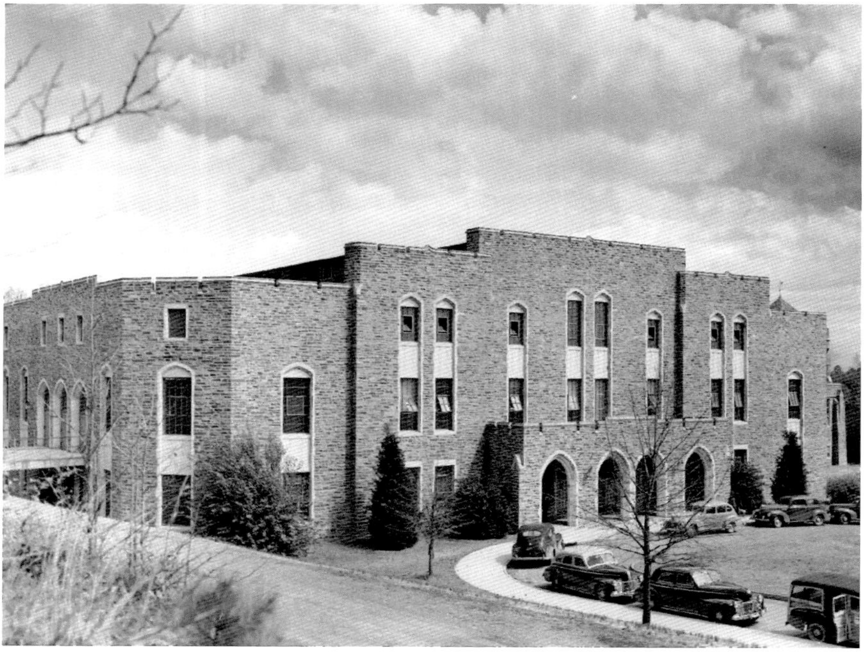

Cameron Indoor Stadium in the 1940s. Duke basketball teams are hard to beat at home, due in large part to their loyal fans and students, who pack the arena each game. The arena was opened in 1940 as Duke Indoor Stadium and was renamed Cameron Indoor Stadium in 1972 in honor of Eddie Cameron. The playing floor was dedicated as Coach K Court in 2001 to honor current Coach Mike Krzyzewski.

Chapter 3

CAP CARD TO COACH K

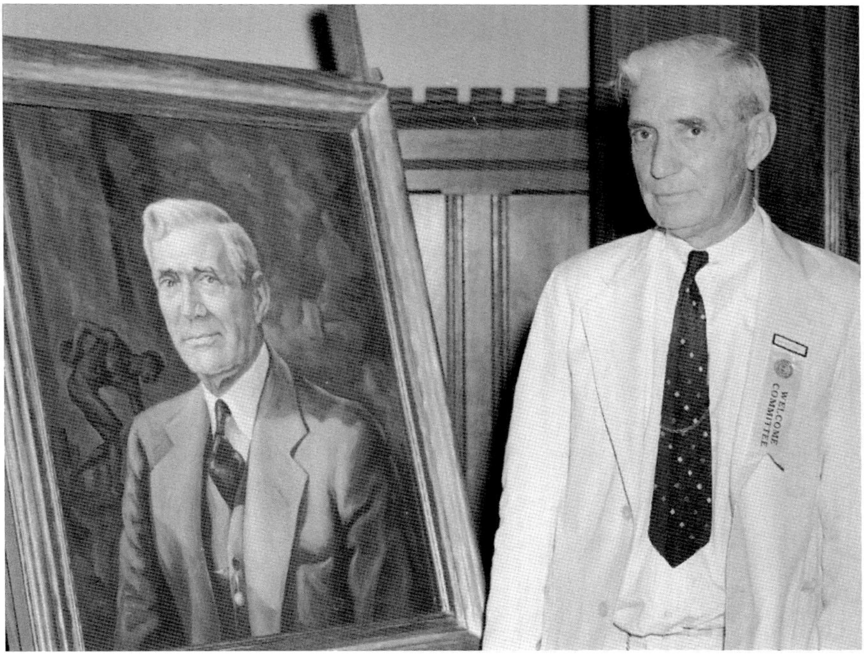

Wilbur "Cap" Card stands next to a portrait unveiling of himself. Card was Duke's first basketball coach and one of the leaders who established college basketball in North Carolina. Card was a standout baseball player for Duke, then named Trinity College, and after being selected captain of the 1899 team, became known as Cap. Along with being instrumental in starting several sports at Duke, Card was director of physical education. He died in 1948 at the age of seventy-four. Card Gym, located next to Cameron Indoor Stadium and at one time the home court for Duke basketball, was named for Card in 1958.

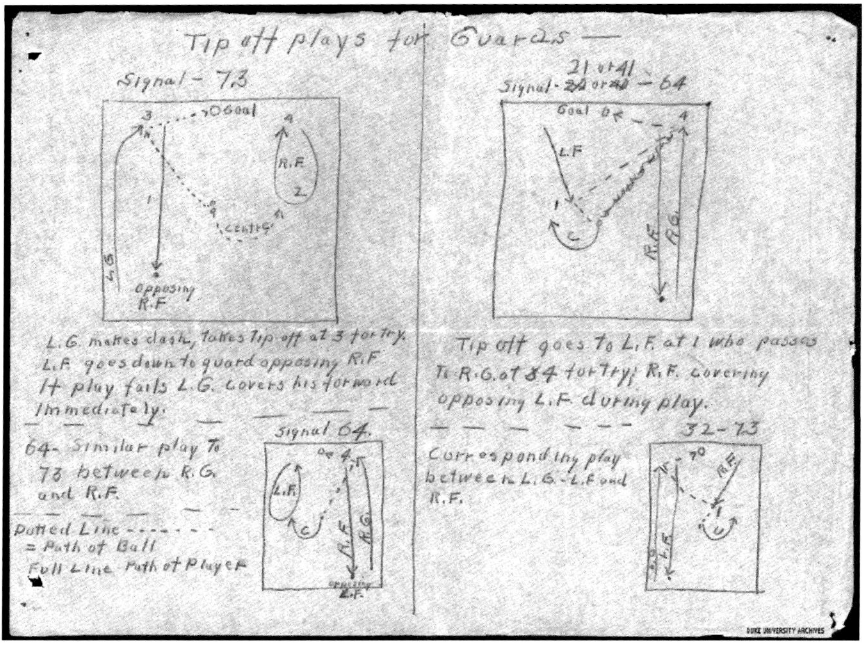

These tipoff plays for guards were diagrammed by Cap Card, Duke's first basketball coach from 1905 to 1912.

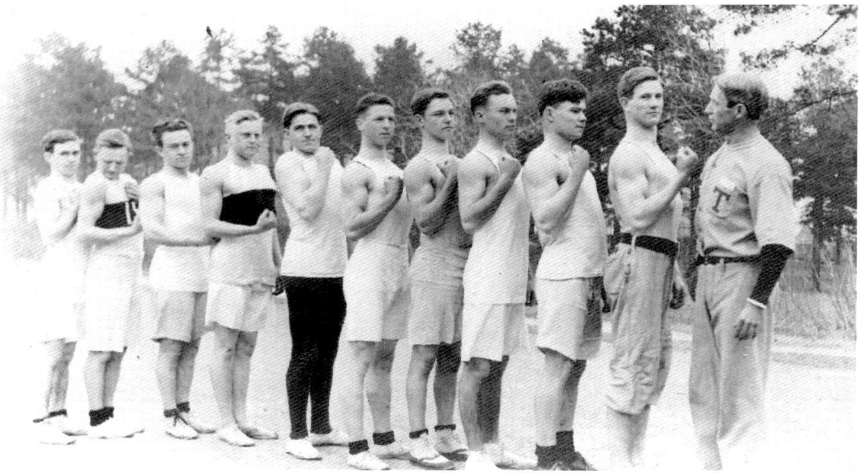

Wilbur "Cap" Card, far right, stands outside with some of his physical education students at Trinity College, now Duke University.

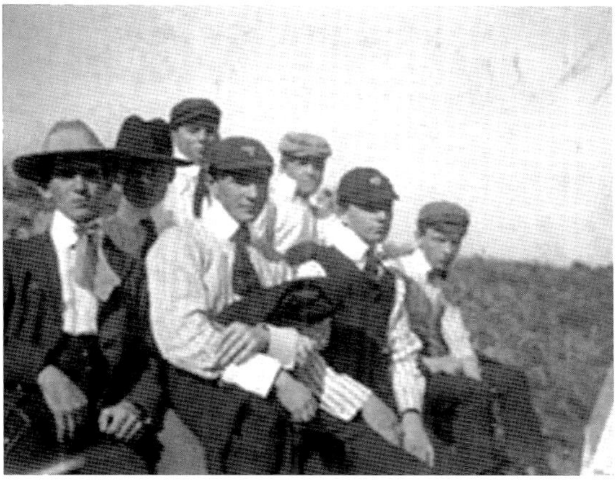

Along with being Duke's first basketball coach, Cap Card, shown here with some of his players and students, played many roles on the Duke campus. He started Duke's track and field program and also was director of the Angier B. Duke Gymnasium.

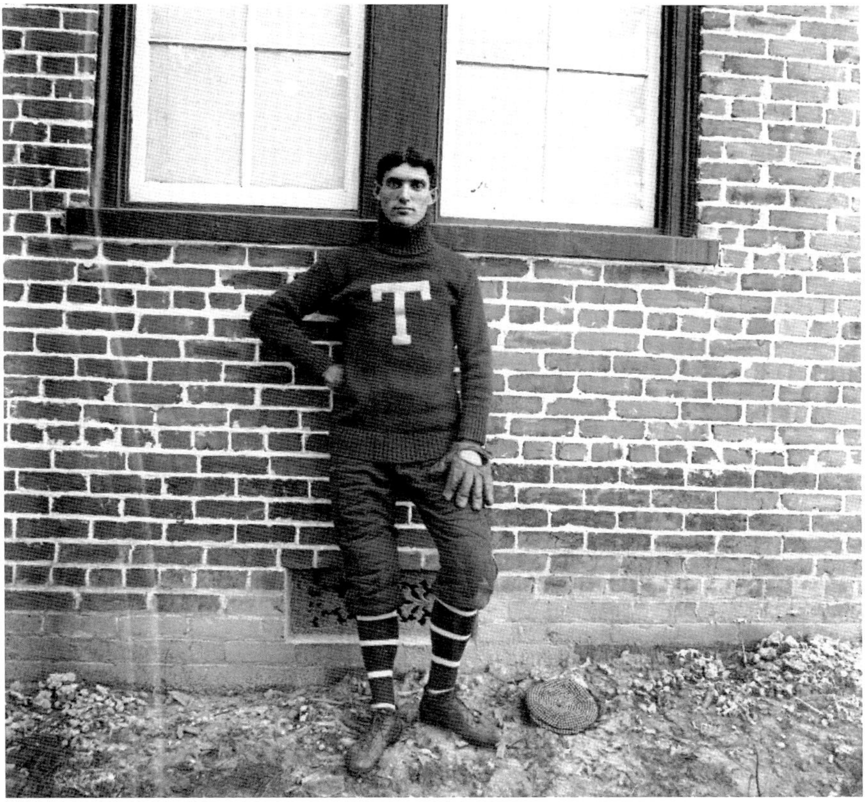

Wilbur "Cap" Card is shown here in his Trinity baseball uniform in 1898. He was selected as team captain in 1899, and he then became known as Cap. Card is known as the "father of intercollegiate basketball in North Carolina," as Duke and Wake Forest played the second intercollegiate game in the state in 1906, and he was instrumental in popularizing the sport.

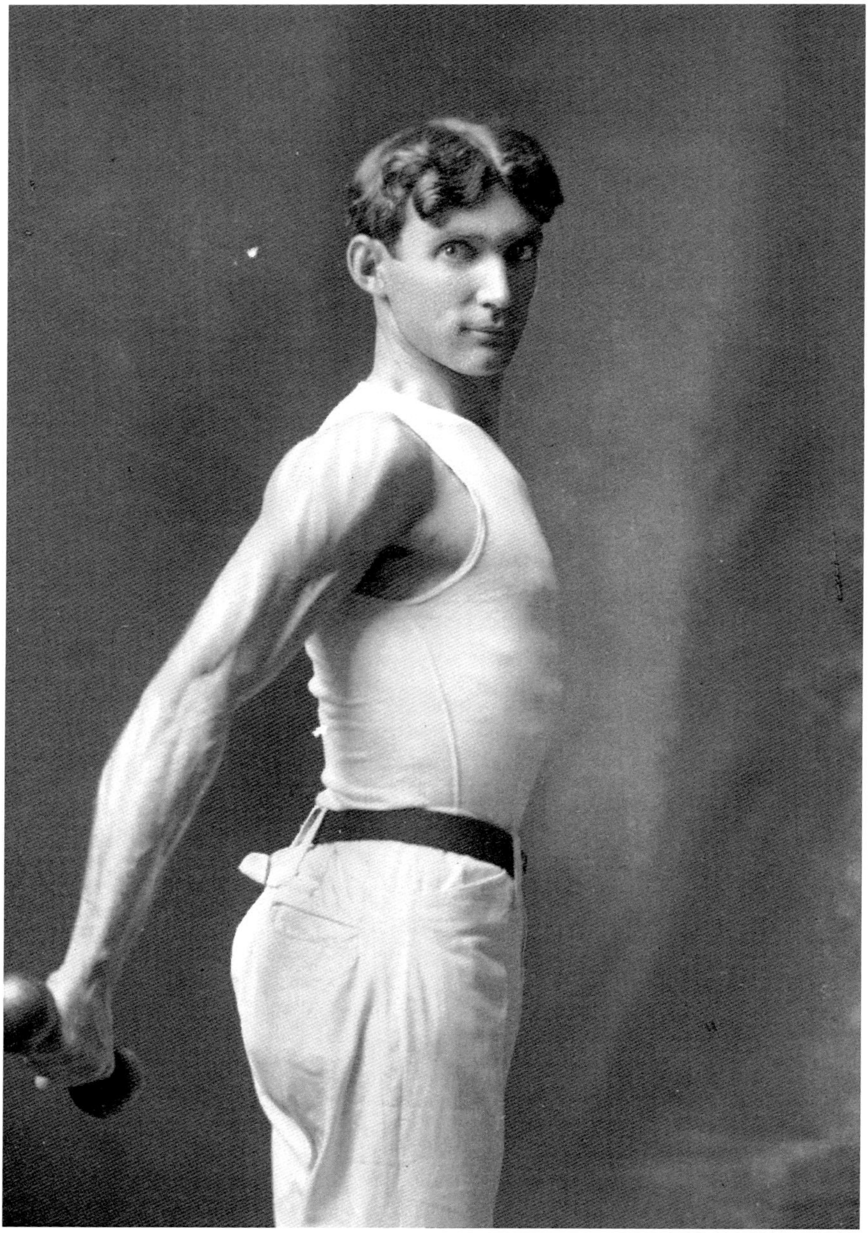

Cap Card is shown in the very early 1900s flexing his muscles with a dumbbell. In his role as director of Trinity's Angier B. Duke Gymnasium, Card emphasized physical fitness for Duke students and took meticulous measurements of their strength, endurance and body girth, such as chest and arm circumference. As Duke's first basketball coach, Card won 30 and lost 17 over his seven seasons from 1905 to 1912.

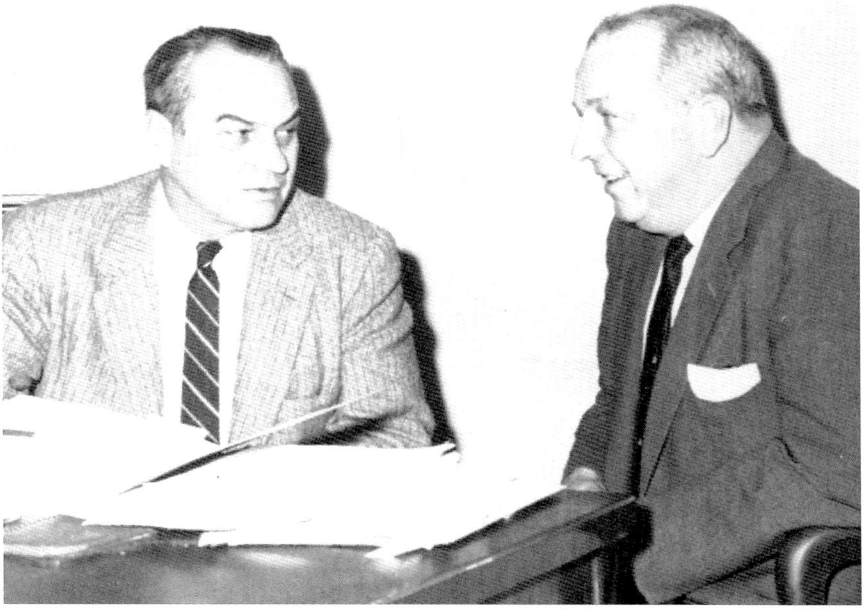

Shown are Eddie Cameron on the left and Ted Mann on the right. Cameron won 226 games as head basketball coach at Duke from 1928 to 1942, and served as athletic director from 1946 to 1972. From 1942 to 1945 he also was head football coach, compiling a record of 25–11–1, which included a victory over Alabama in the 1945 Sugar Bowl and a 5 and 0 mark against rival UNC. Duke Indoor Stadium was renamed Cameron Indoor Stadium in 1972. Ted Mann was sports information director at Duke from 1931 to 1966, doing as much as anyone to gain national recognition for Duke's athletic programs.

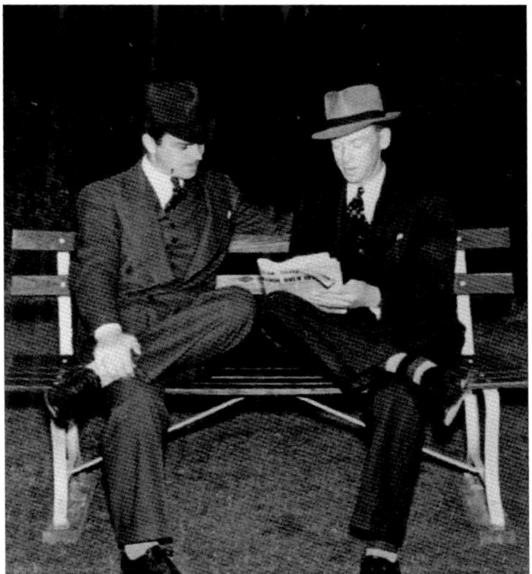

Eddie Cameron, on the left, won 226 games as Duke's basketball coach from 1928 to 1942 and held the record for most wins in Duke history until Coach Mike Krzyzewski passed him in 1990. Herschel Caldwell was a coach at Duke from 1930 until 1971. One of his jobs was coaching freshman basketball. Caldwell was a star football player at Alabama in the 1920s, playing for legendary coach Wallace Wade. Both Wade and Caldwell left Alabama for Duke.

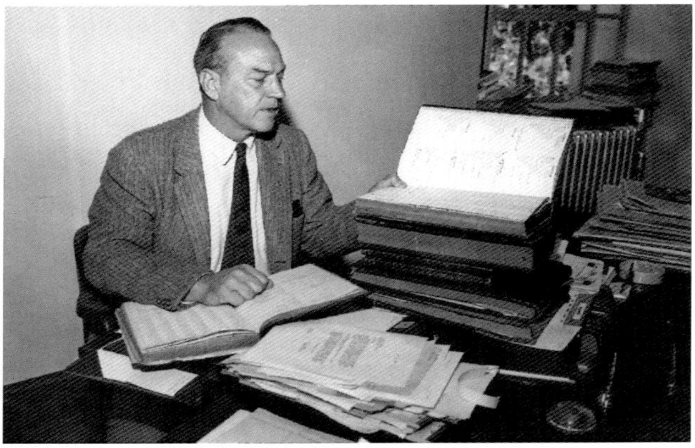

Eddie Cameron is shown behind his desk during his days at Duke. Perhaps the most famous college basketball arena in the world, Cameron Indoor Stadium, was named in his honor in 1972. From Irwin, Pennsylvania, few individuals have contributed so much to the Duke athletic tradition.

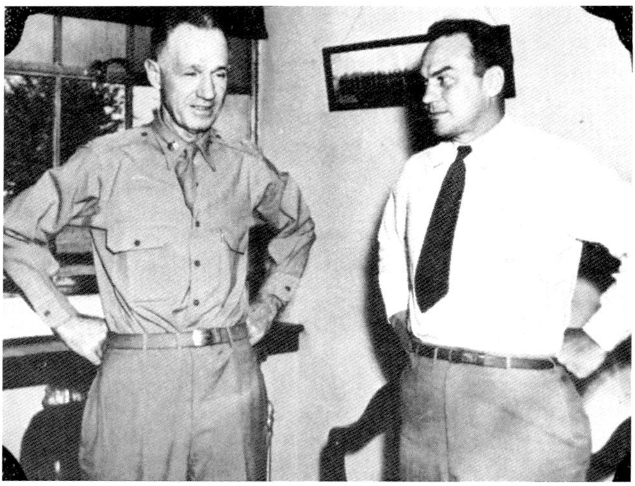

Wallace Wade, on the left, and Eddie Cameron, on the right, are two of the most legendary figures in Duke history. Coach Wade won 110 games as Duke football coach while losing 36, and took Duke to two Rose Bowls, in 1939 and 1942. Funds from the 1939 Rose Bowl started the construction of Cameron Indoor Stadium. Eddie Cameron was a very successful basketball and football coach at Duke. Cameron also served as athletic director at Duke from 1946 to 1972. Wade is shown here in a military uniform. He resigned from Duke in 1942 to serve in World War II, eventually becoming a lieutenant colonel. Cameron took over for Wade as football coach.

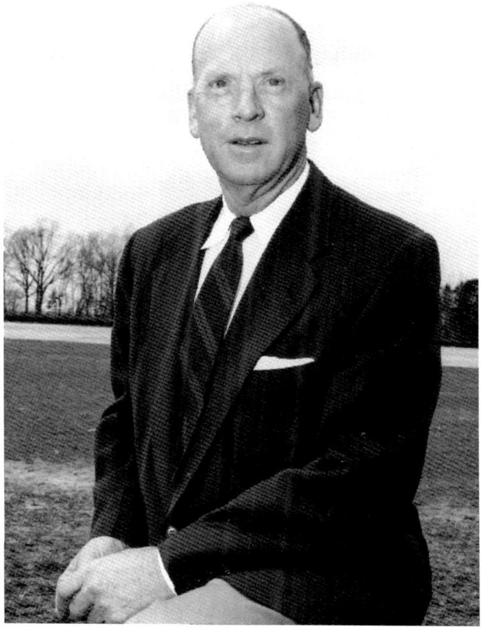

Herschel Caldwell served as an assistant football coach and freshman head basketball, baseball and football coach during his forty-one years at Duke, from 1930 to 1971. During his time as freshman football coach, his record was 46–9–5. Caldwell is now in the Duke Sports Hall of Fame.

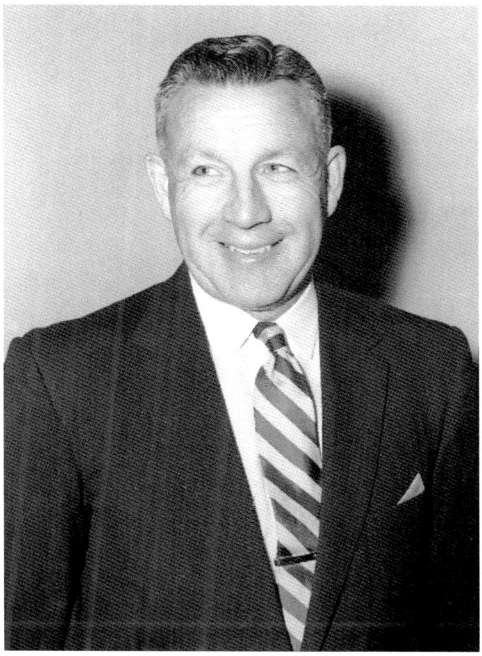

Harold Bradley was Duke basketball coach from 1950 to 1959, and compiled an impressive record of 167 wins with 78 losses. He was the first Duke basketball coach to take a team to the NCAA Tournament, with the Blue Devils losing to Villanova in the first round in 1955. Bradley was successful in all of his college head coaching jobs, going 50–18 at Hartwick College and 125–73 at Texas.

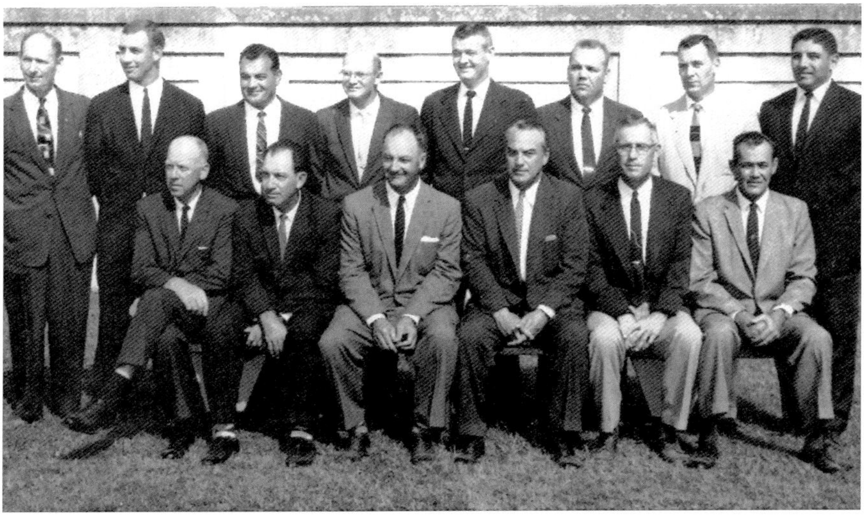

Some of the coaches for different sports at Duke in 1959 are shown. *Standing, left to right*: Howard Steele, Doug Knotts, Carmen Falcone, Bob Monfort, Marty Pierson, Tommy O'Boyle, Carl James and Bill Recinella. *Seated, left to right*: Herschel Caldwell, Clarence "Ace" Parker, Bill Murray, Eddie Cameron, Bob Cox and Bob Chambers.

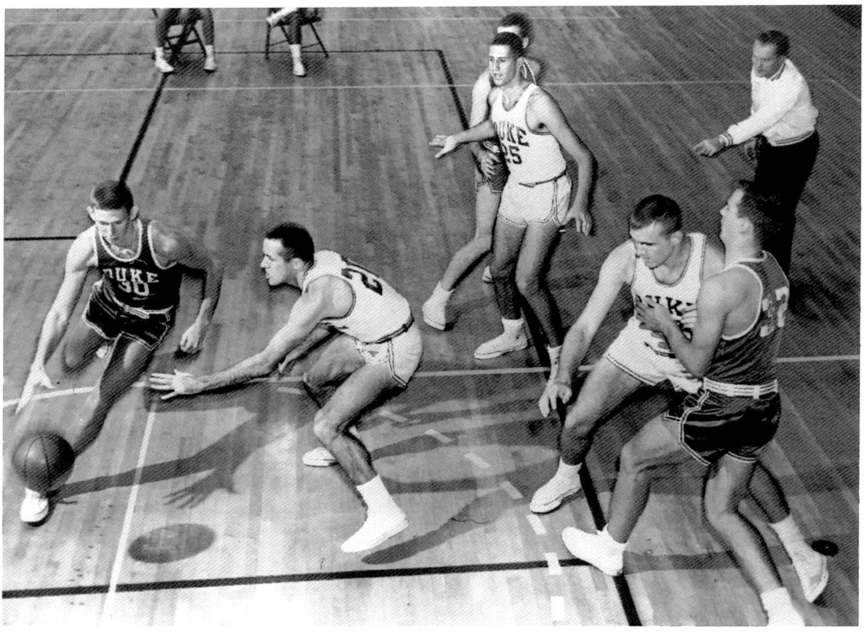

Coach Vic Bubas directs a practice during the 1961–62 season. Duke finished 20 and 5 and ranked number ten in the country.

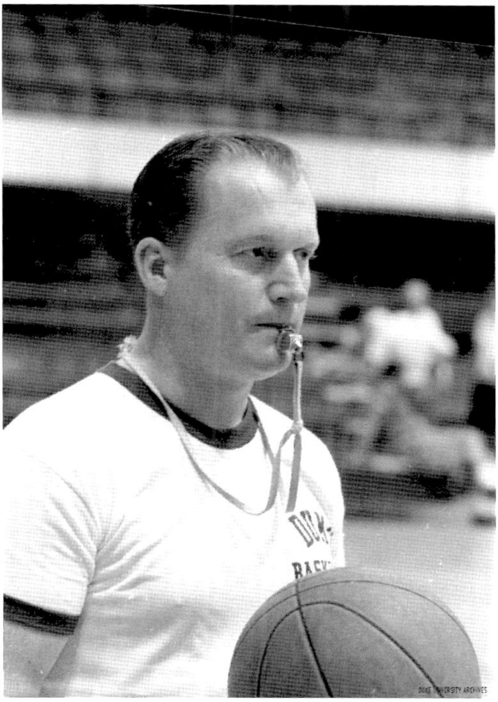

Right: Vic Bubas is shown here during the 1960s during his tenure as Duke basketball coach. Before coming to Duke in 1959, Bubas had been an all-conference player and then served as an assistant coach for Everett Case at North Carolina State. Case was a good coach to learn under, as he won an amazing 1,103 games as a high school and college coach, losing only 209.

Below: During this action from a Vic Bubas basketball clinic, number 11 is setting a screen for his teammate, number 9, so that he can get around his opponent.

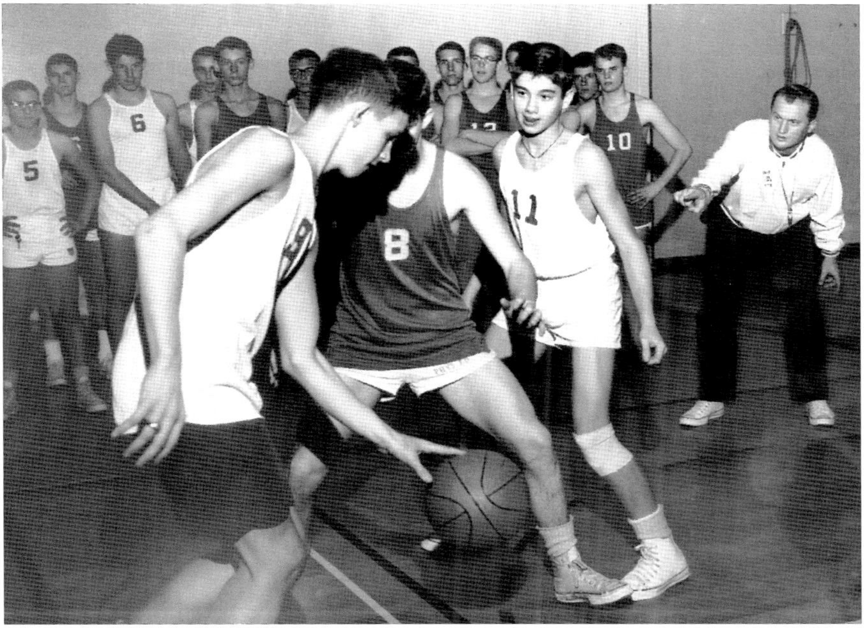

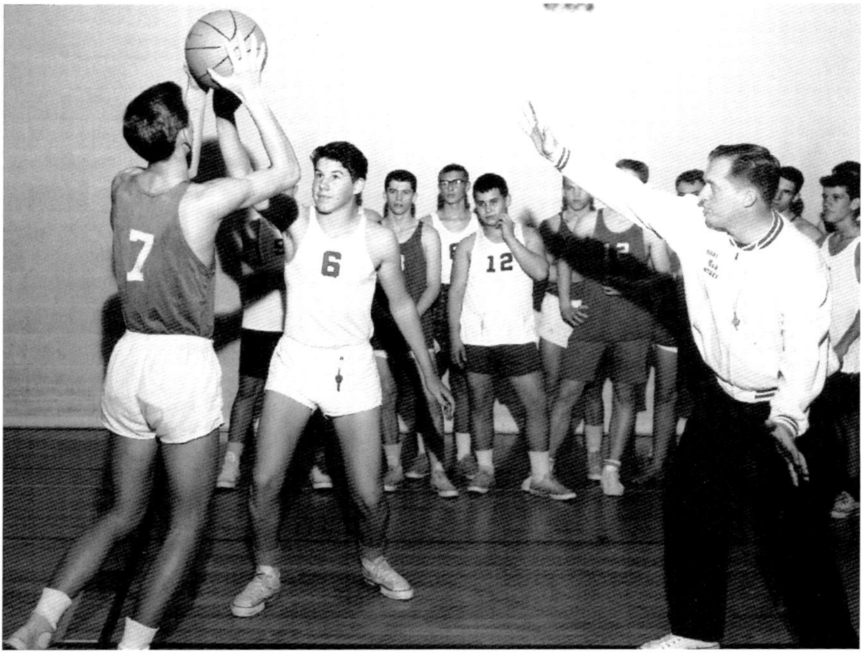
7
6
12

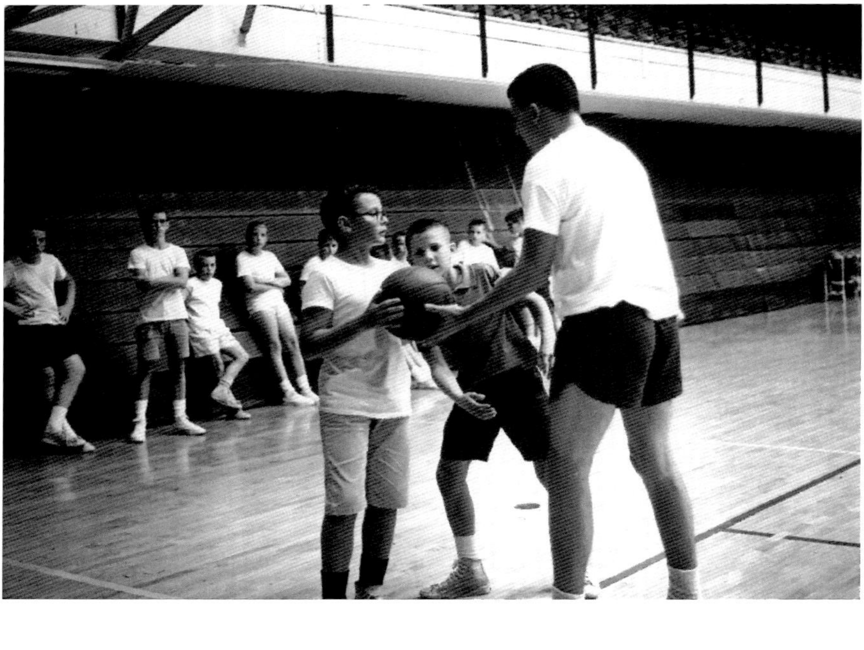

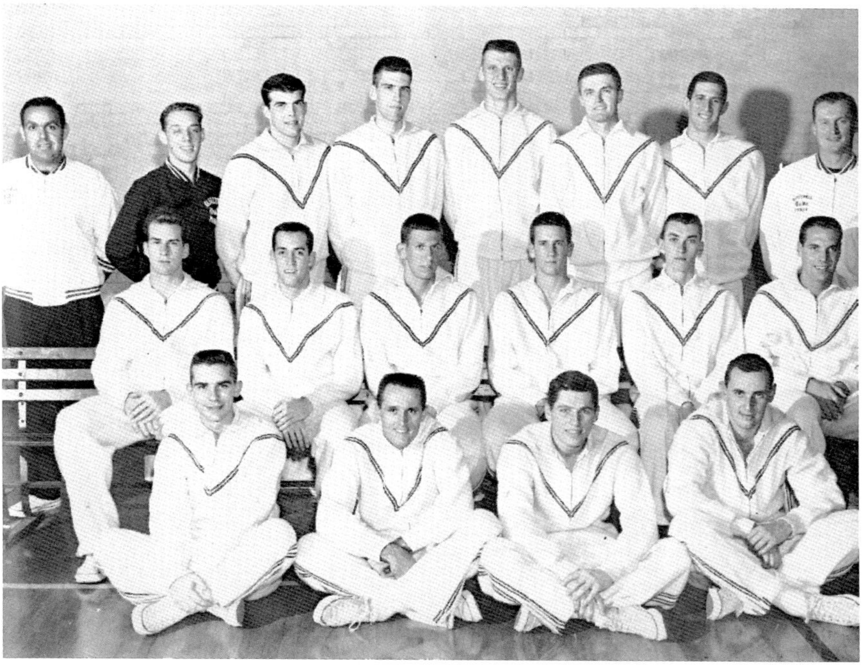

Above: Coach Vic Bubas is shown on the back row, far right, with his 1962 team.

Opposite top: Vic Bubas conducts his summer basketball clinic at Duke University in the 1960s. Here he shows a young man how to play defense.

Opposite bottom: With dreams of being the next star player for Duke, such as Mike Lewis, Art Heyman or Jeff Mullins, some young boys practice basketball fundamentals at a Vic Bubas basketball clinic in the 1960s.

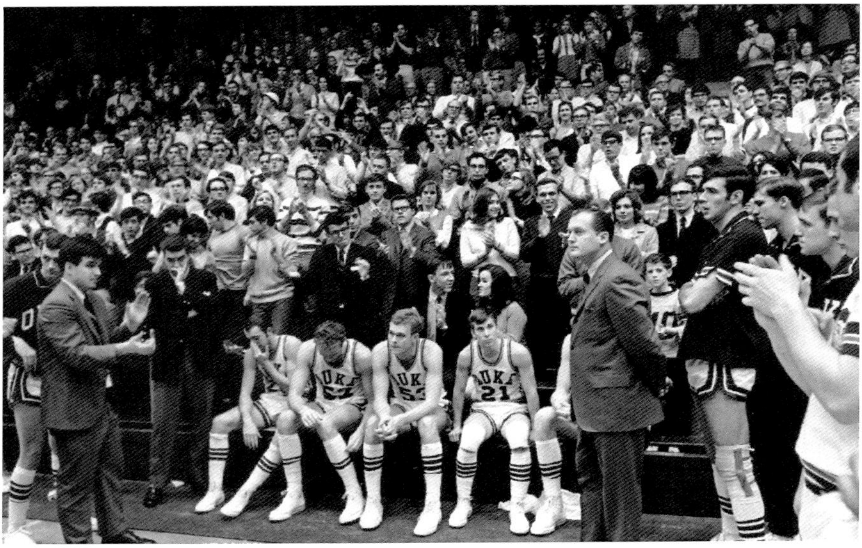

Vic Bubas is shown coaching his last home game at Duke in 1969. Athletic Director Eddie Cameron hired Bubas in 1959 from North Carolina State, where he was an assistant. The hire turned out to be a good one, as Bubas was 213 and 67 with four ACC Tournament titles and three Final Fours. The concourse at Cameron Indoor Stadium is named in Coach Bubas's honor. After coaching, Bubas became commissioner of the Sun Belt Conference.

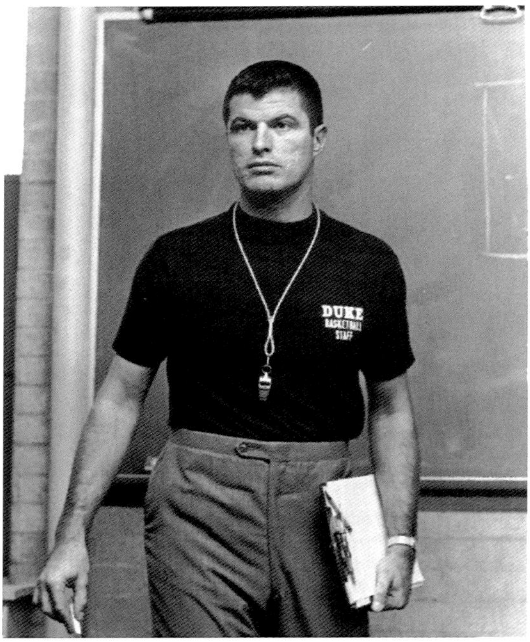

Bucky Waters is shown here during his time as Duke basketball coach. Coach Waters was Duke head coach from the 1969–70 season to 1972–73, and was 63 and 45. His 1970–71 team won 20 and lost 10. Waters had played for the great Everett Case at North Carolina State, and was taught also by assistant coach Vic Bubas. When Bubas was named Duke coach in 1959, he brought Waters to Durham as an assistant coach, where Waters helped Duke reach two Final Fours. West Virginia hired Waters as its head coach in 1965, and he was outstanding there, going 70–41. West Virginia, under Waters, beat Duke in 1966 when the Blue Devils were ranked number one in the nation.

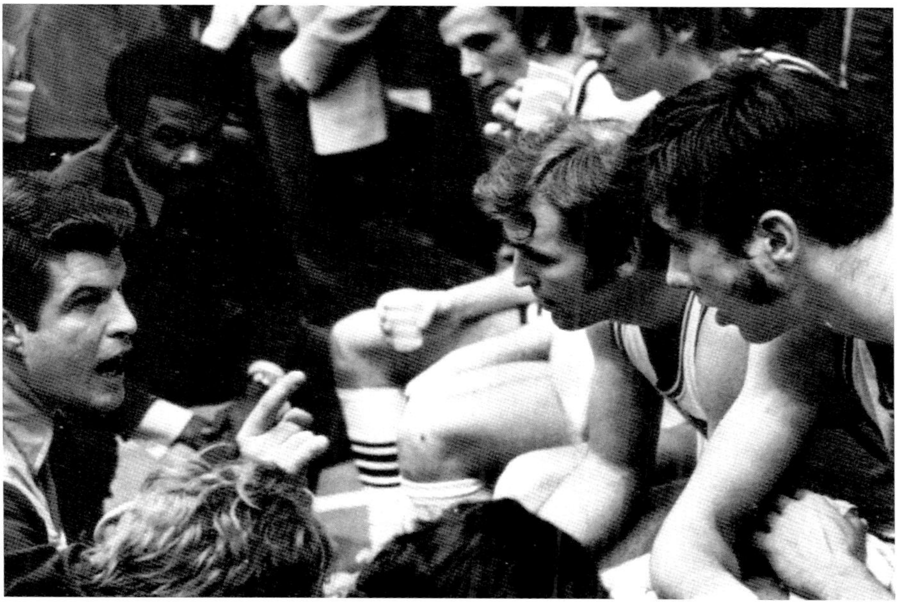

Coach Bucky Waters talks to his team during a break in play. Waters compiled a record of 63 and 45 from 1969 to 1973. Also shown is Jim Lewis, who Waters hired as the first black assistant basketball coach in Duke history. Lewis had played for Waters at West Virginia in the 1960s. Lewis later became head coach of the women's team at George Mason and Fordham, and also was coach of the WNBA's Washington Mystics.

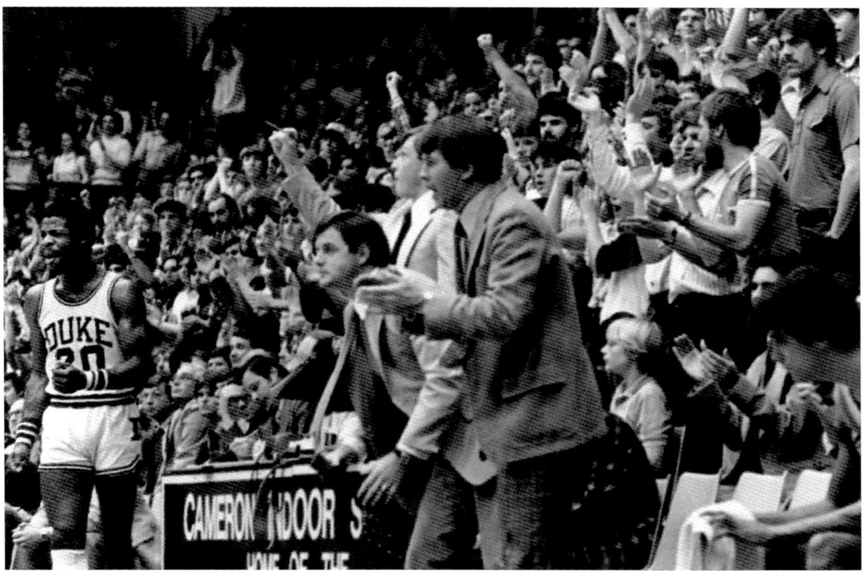

Coach Bill Foster and Gene Banks, facing the camera with fists clenched, celebrate a play in 1979.

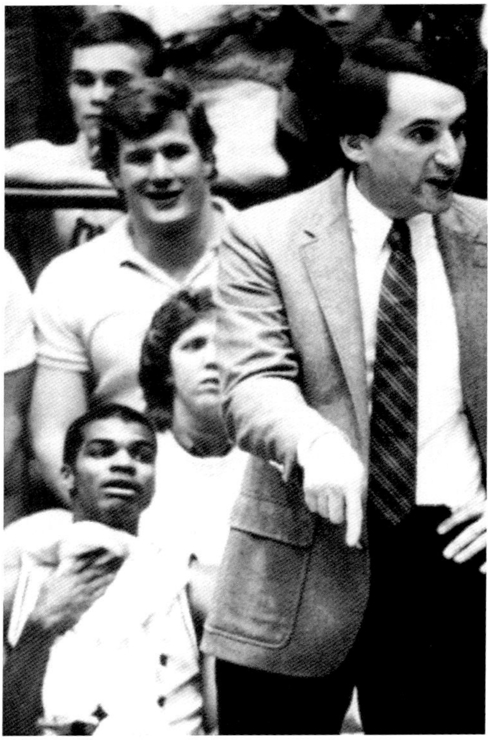

Left: Coach K is shown in 1985 pointing to the basketball. Tommy Amaker is seated on the bench to the left of Coach K. The 1984–85 team was Coach K's fifth team at Duke, and it won 23 and lost 8. Duke beat Pepperdine in the first round of the NCAA Tournament and then lost to Boston College in the second round. Johnny Dawkins made first team All-America while scoring 18.8 points per game. Mark Alarie averaged 15.9 per game.

Below: Coach Mike Krzyzewski is shown on the sidelines during a game in 1986. Coach K's numbers are staggering, his teams having won 3 national championships, played in 10 Final Fours and having won 10 ACC Tournament championships. Coach K's win-loss record after the 2007–08 season was 803 wins and 267 losses, and his 69 NCAA Tournament wins were the most in history.

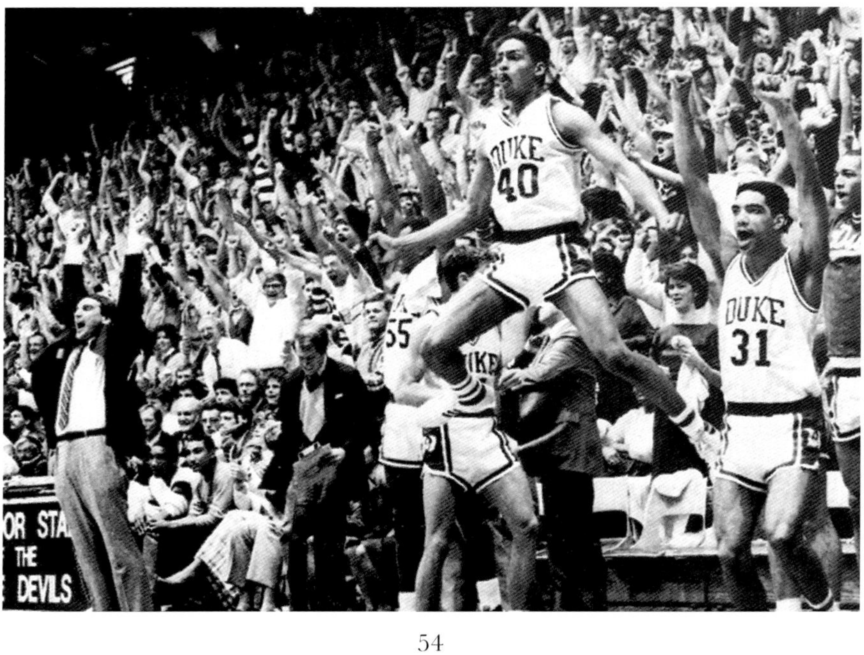

Right: Shown here in the early stage of his Duke career, Coach K had some rocky years during his first three years from 1980–81 to 1982–83. Duke won 17 and lost 13 in his first year, won 10 and lost 17 in his second year and won 11 and lost 17 in his third year. In his fourth year of 1983–84, Duke won 24 games and has been the nation's best program since that time.

Below: Coach K directs practice during the 1980s. Before coming to Duke in 1980, Coach K had played for legendary coach Bobby Knight at Army, playing point guard and serving as captain as a senior in 1969. He later became head coach at Army, where he won 73 games with 59 losses in 5 years.

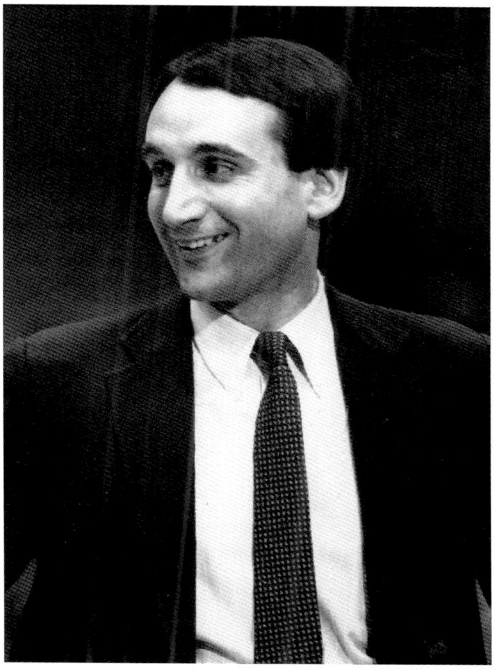

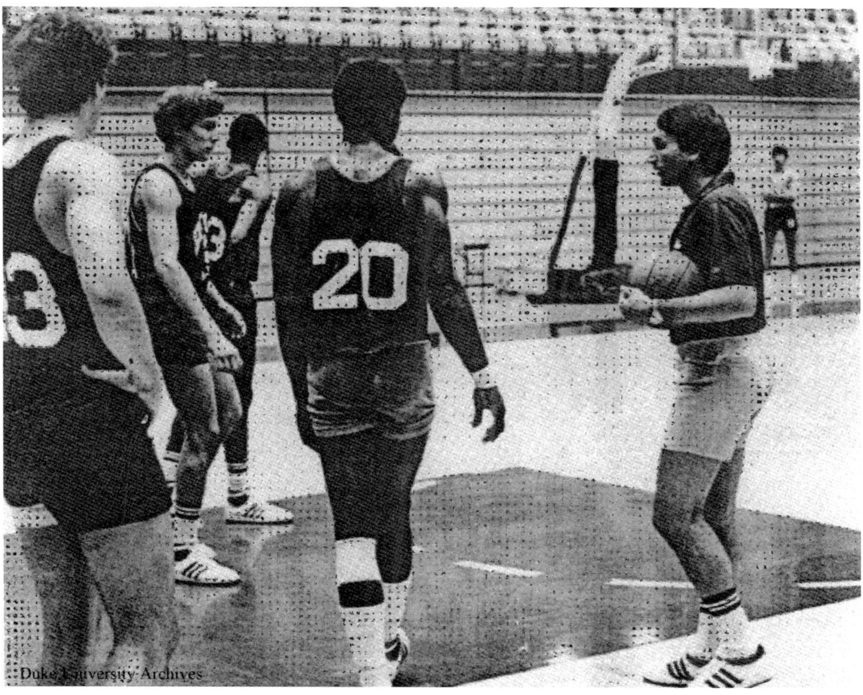

Duke University Archives

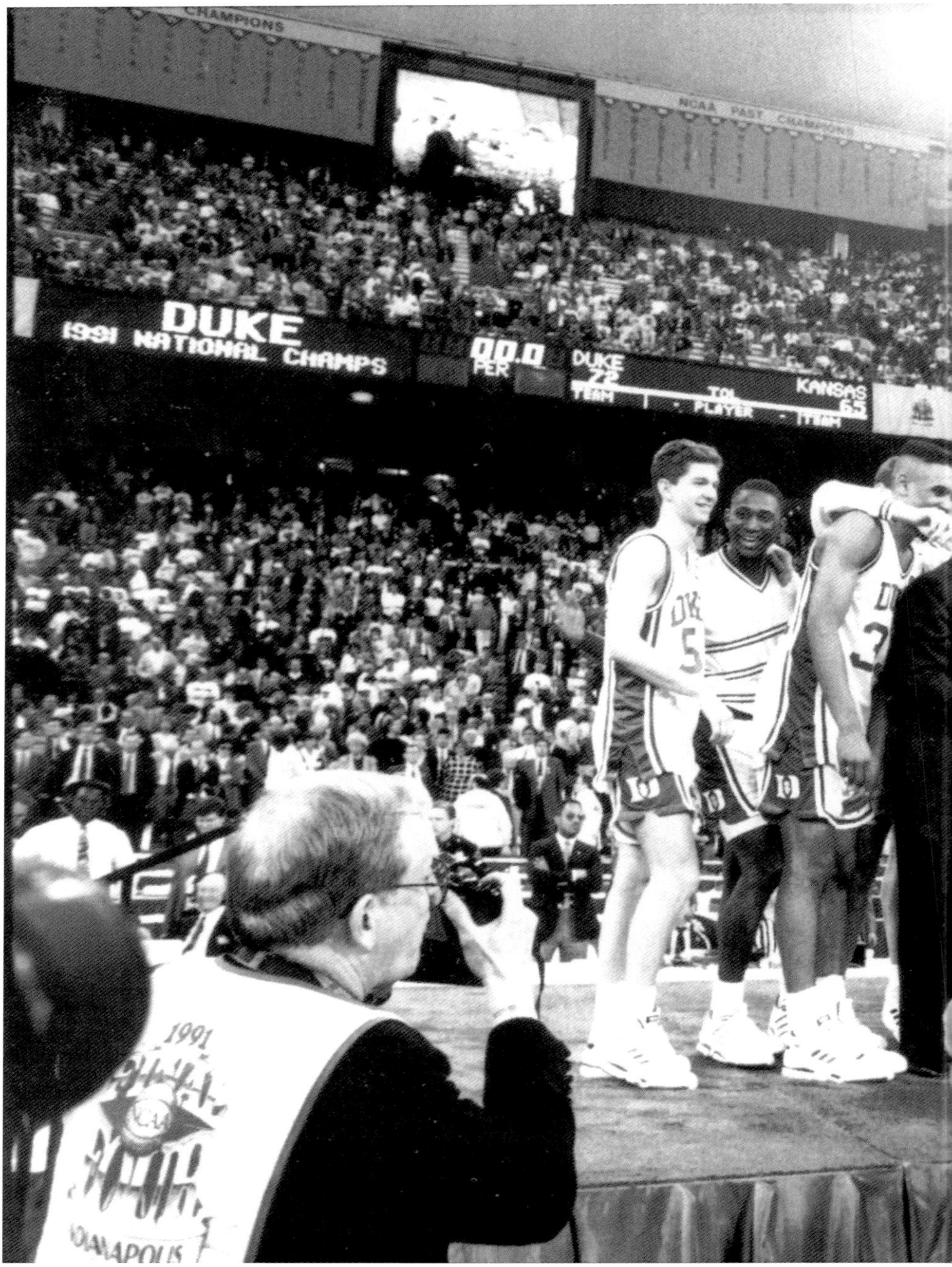

Duke defeated Kansas in 1991 for the national title 72 to 65 in Indianapolis. Christian Laettner scored 18 points in the victory. Laettner led Duke for the season in points, rebounds, field goal percentage, steals and blocked shots, leading Duke to a 32 and 7 overall record. *Courtesy of Duke Sports Information.*

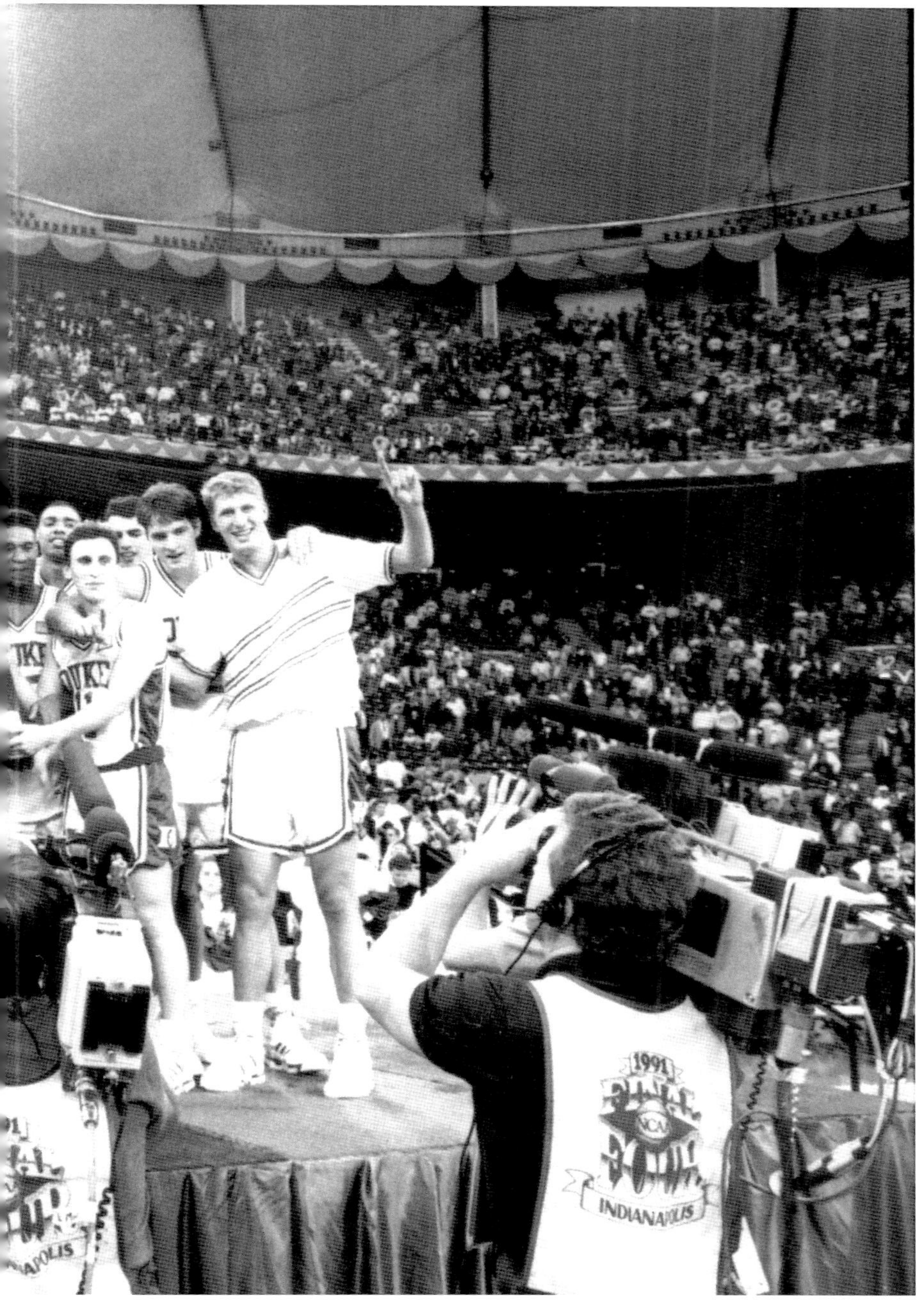
1991
INDIANAPOLIS

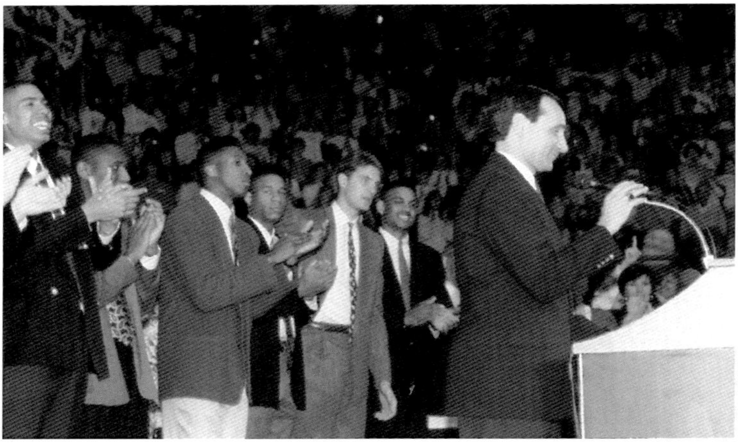

Coach Mike Krzyzewski and his 1991 national championship team return home to celebrate with their fans. Mickie Krzyzewski, Coach K's wife, is shown just below Coach K's right arm, at the side of the podium. Duke beat Northeast Louisiana, Iowa, Connecticut, St. John's, University of Nevada Las Vegas and then Kansas in succession to win the 1991 NCAA Tournament. Kansas was coached by Roy Williams at the time, and now Coach Williams is at Duke's arch rival, the University of North Carolina at Chapel Hill. *Courtesy of Duke Sports Information.*

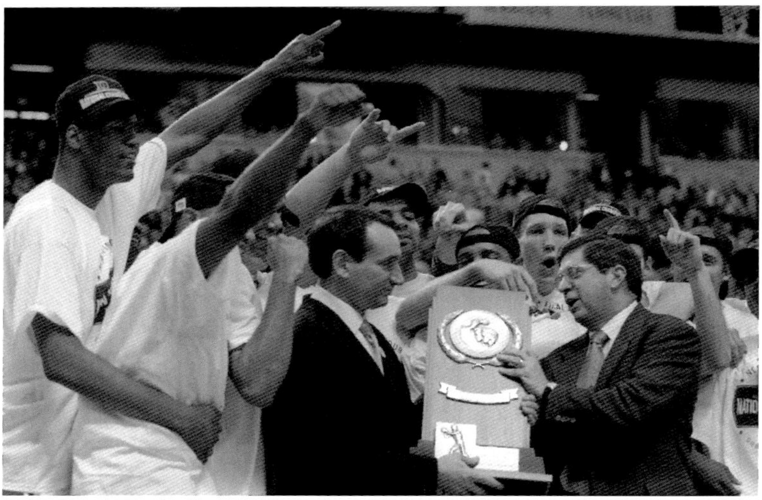

The Duke Blue Devils celebrate their national championship game victory over Arizona in 2001. Mike Dunleavy scored 21 points in the 82–72 victory. Duke beat Monmouth, Missouri, UCLA, Southern Cal and Maryland in the 2001 NCAA Tournament before playing Arizona. Jason Williams led the team in scoring with 21.6 points per game, followed by Shane Battier at 19.9. This was Coach Mike Krzyzewski's third national title at Duke. *Courtesy of Duke Sports Information.*

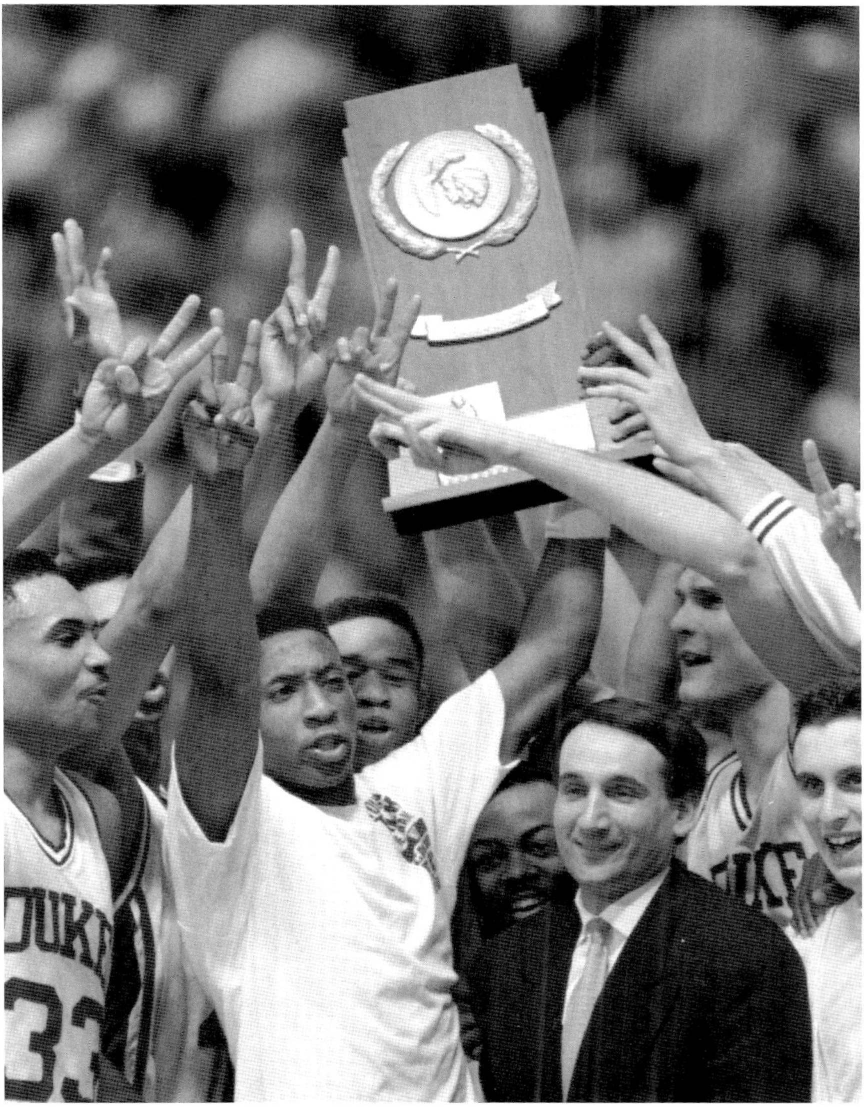

In 1992, Duke repeated its 1991 national championship with a 71 to 51 victory over Michigan in Minneapolis. This team finished 34 and 2. Christian Laettner averaged 21.5 points and 7.9 rebounds a game to win national player of the year honors. In a game against Kentucky for the NCAA Tournament Regional Final, Laettner made 10 of 10 field goals and finished with 31 points. *Courtesy of Duke Sports Information.*

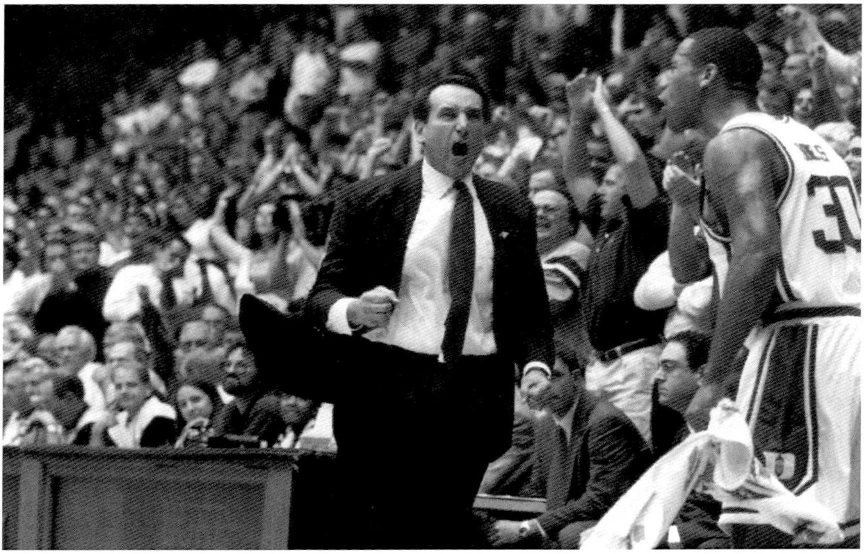

Coach K fires up his team and the Cameron Crazies during a 2002 game. Dahntay Jones is standing up also, showing a little emotion of his own. A transfer from Rutgers, Jones led Duke in scoring in the 2002–03 season and also made the all-ACC defensive team. Jones was a member of the Sacramento Kings of the NBA during the 2007–08 season.

Chapter 4

PLAYERS

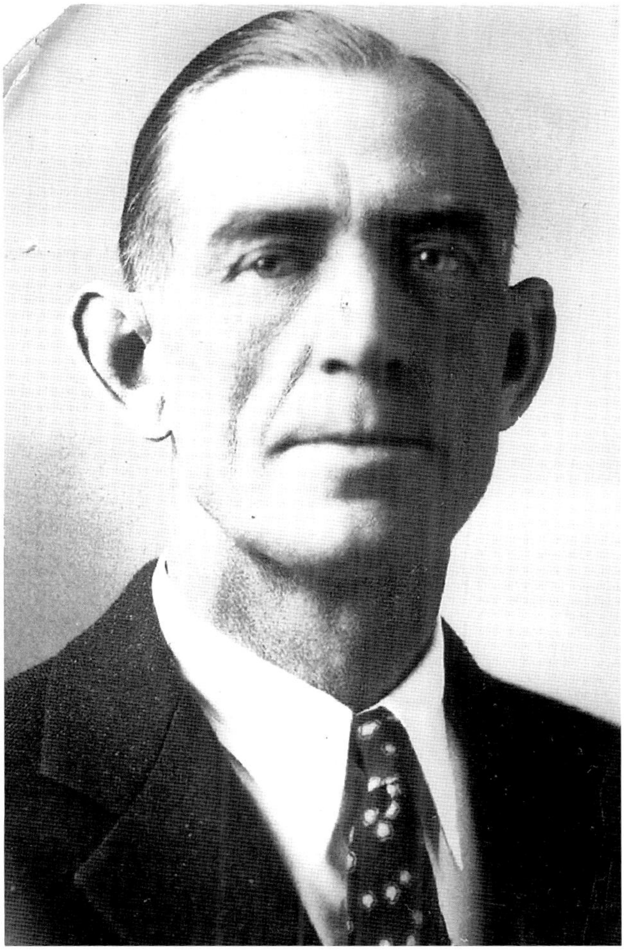

Thad Stem was the captain of the first two Duke teams. Duke was then called Trinity. Stem scored four of the ten points in Trinity's first intercollegiate game against Wake Forest in 1906. Stem later became a lawyer and a member of the Duke Athletic Council, and also mayor of nearby Oxford, North Carolina. *Courtesy of the author.*

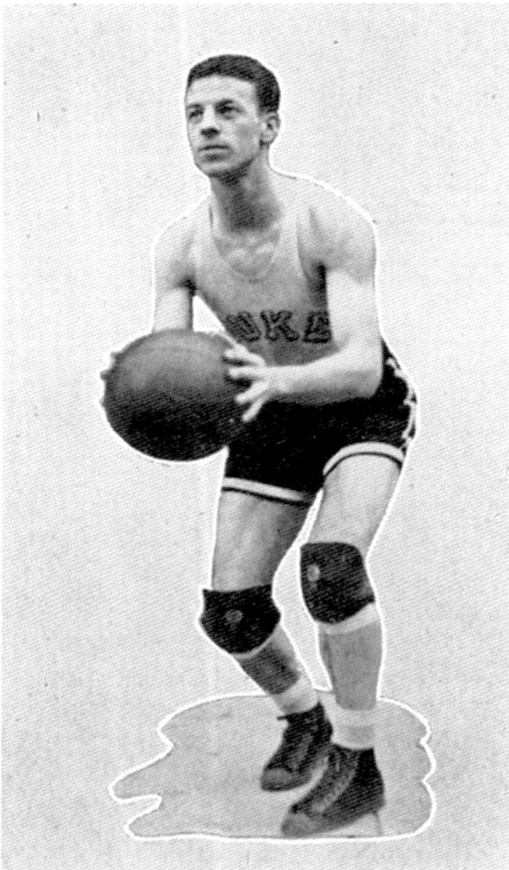

Left: The first player in the history of Duke basketball to earn All-American, Bill Werber played from 1927 to 1930. Duke won 18 and lost only 2 games in the 1929–30 season when Werber was a senior playing for Coach Eddie Cameron. As a shortstop, Werber also starred for the Duke baseball team before signing with the New York Yankees. Werber went on to an eleven-year career in the Major Leagues, including a world championship with the Cincinnati Reds in 1940.

Below: Bill Werber and Joe Croson were two of the great early players in Duke basketball history. Croson is considered Duke's first outstanding "big man," standing six feet, four inches. Croson was the leading scorer for Duke in his three varsity seasons from 1928–29 to 1930–31.

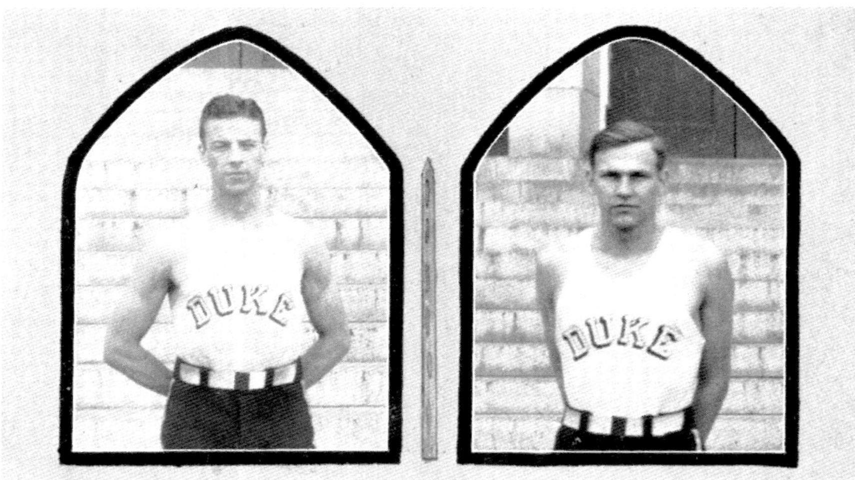

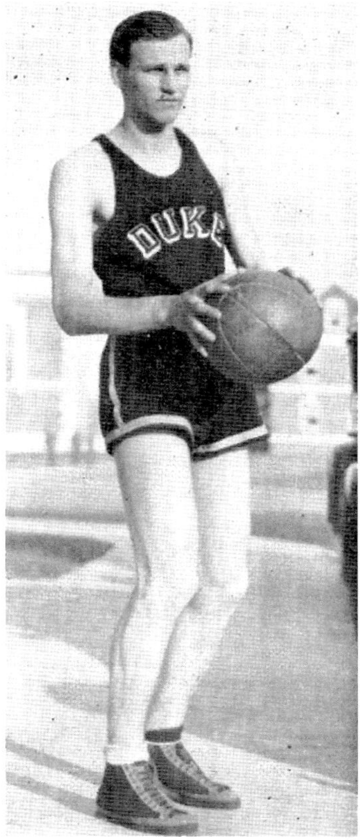

Joe Croson came to Duke from McKinley Tech, in Washington, D.C. Perhaps Croson's best game was in 1929, when he scored 15 of the 36 points Duke scored to break a long losing streak to University of North Carolina. Croson was Duke's top scorer during the 1929–30 season, as Coach Eddie Cameron's team finished 18 and 2. The starting lineup during 1929–30 featured Croson, Bill Werber and Harry Councilor; all three had been teammates in high school at McKinley Tech.

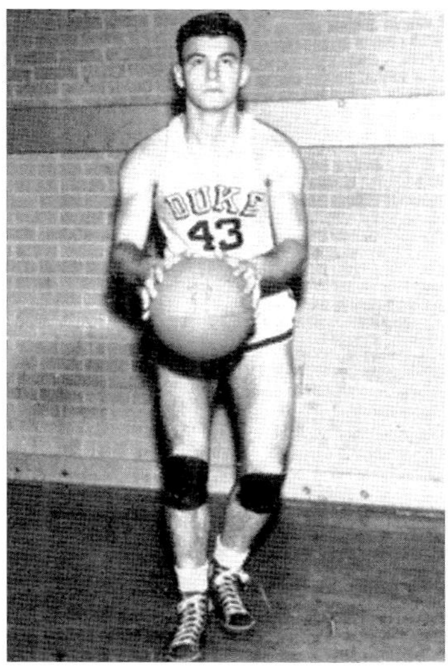

Bill Mock was Duke's second All-American, accomplishing the honor during the 1939–40 season, as he was the leading scorer for Eddie Cameron's 19 and 7 squad. Mock also played on the 1940–41 team that won the Southern Conference Tournament and finished 14 and 8. Mock was a tall player for his time, at six feet, two inches. He came to Duke from Altoona, Pennsylvania.

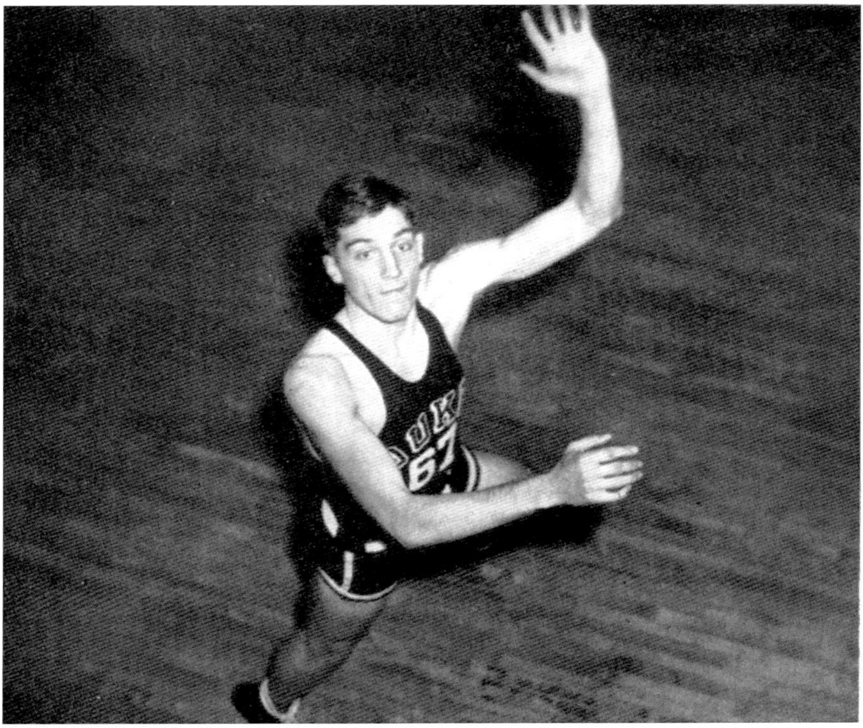

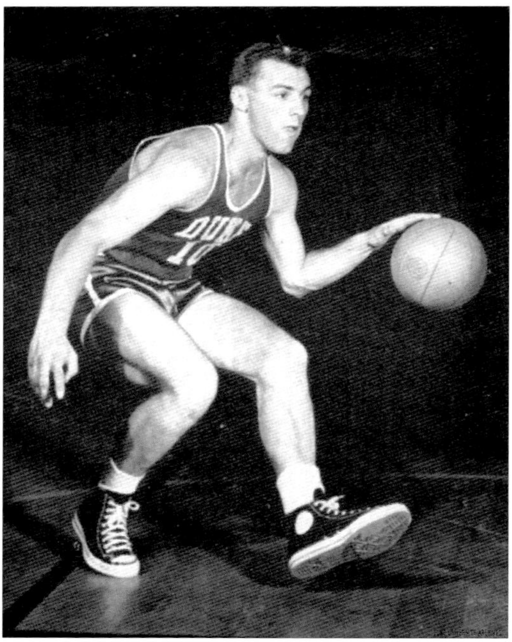

Above: Gerry Gerard was coach of Duke in the 1945–46 season, when the Blue Devils went 21 and 6 and won the Southern Conference championship. The leading scorer on that team was Ed Koffenberger, shown in this photo. Koffenberger played on the varsity from 1944 to 1947, and was Duke's all-time scoring leader upon graduation. He made All-American in his last two years, and was the first player in Duke history to score 30 points in a game.

Left: Here is Dick Groat, who once scored 48 points in 1952 against UNC and had 46 in a game versus George Washington, also in 1952. In a 1951 game against Davidson, Groat made 17 of 17 free throws.

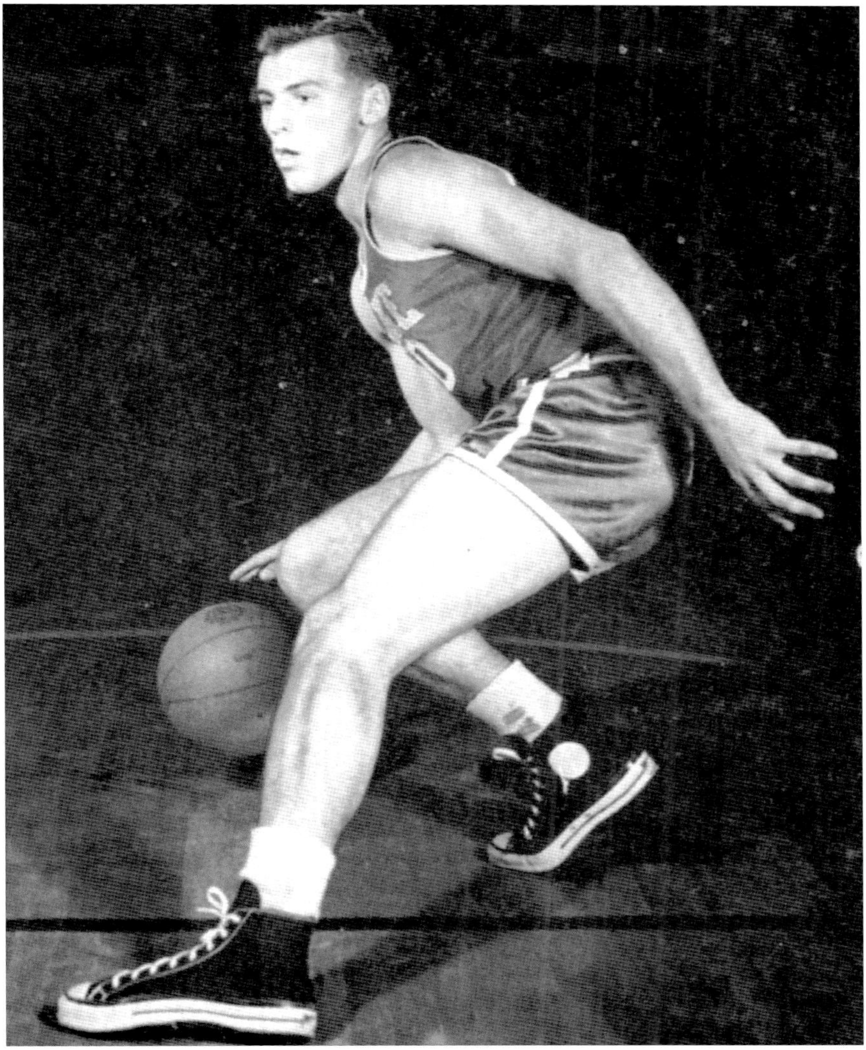

Dick Groat was the first athlete at Duke to have his jersey retired. His 26 points per game in 1951–52 are the third highest average for a season in Duke history, behind J.J. Redick's 26.8 in 2005–06 and Bob Verga's 26.1 in 1966–67. As a senior, Groat finished second in the nation in scoring and led the country in assists. His senior year of 1951–52 has to rank as one of the best years in Duke basketball history, as along with his 26 points a game, Groat also averaged over 7 assists and 7 rebounds per game. He scored 48 in his final home game against UNC. In baseball Groat led the Blue Devils to the College World Series. He signed contracts to play both major league baseball and in the NBA. Groat averaged 12 points a game in his rookie year with the Fort Wayne Pistons of the NBA, after being the third pick of the draft. He signed for $10,000. It was in baseball that Groat spent most of his career, and what a career it was. He won an MVP award, led the National League in hitting one year with a .325 average, made 5 All-Star teams and was on two World Series winning teams.

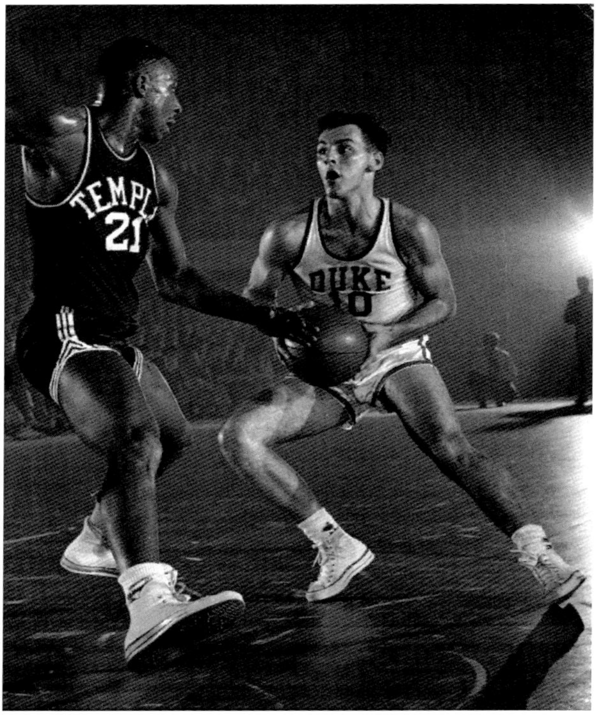

Samuel Sylvester of Temple guards Dick Groat of Duke at Duke Indoor Stadium, now called Cameron Indoor Stadium, in a 1951 game. Sylvester became the first black player to play in Cameron. He was given a loud ovation upon being taken out of the game. Groat, Duke's All-American player, scored 33 as Duke won the game.

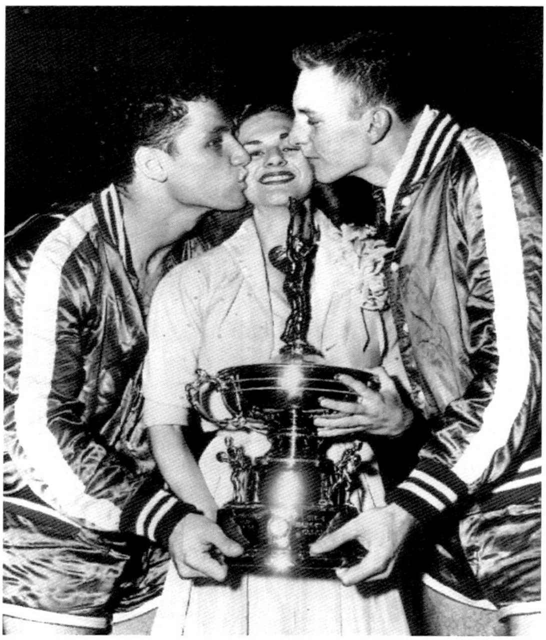

Bernie Janicki, on the right, and Rudy D'Emilio, on the left, kiss the queen of the Dixie Classic Tournament, Pat Godwin. Janicki could rebound a basketball perhaps as well as anyone in Duke history. He averaged 11.1 boards a game during his three varsity years from 1952 to 1954. During his sophomore year, he averaged 16 rebounds a game, setting a school record for one game by hauling down an incredible 31 rebounds against North Carolina. Janicki could also score, averaging 16.8 points a game in 1953. Janicki played for Duke teams that won 64 games against 20 losses under Coach Harold Bradley, finishing number twelve in the nation in the final rankings in 1952. Rudy D'Emilo was first team All-ACC in 1954.

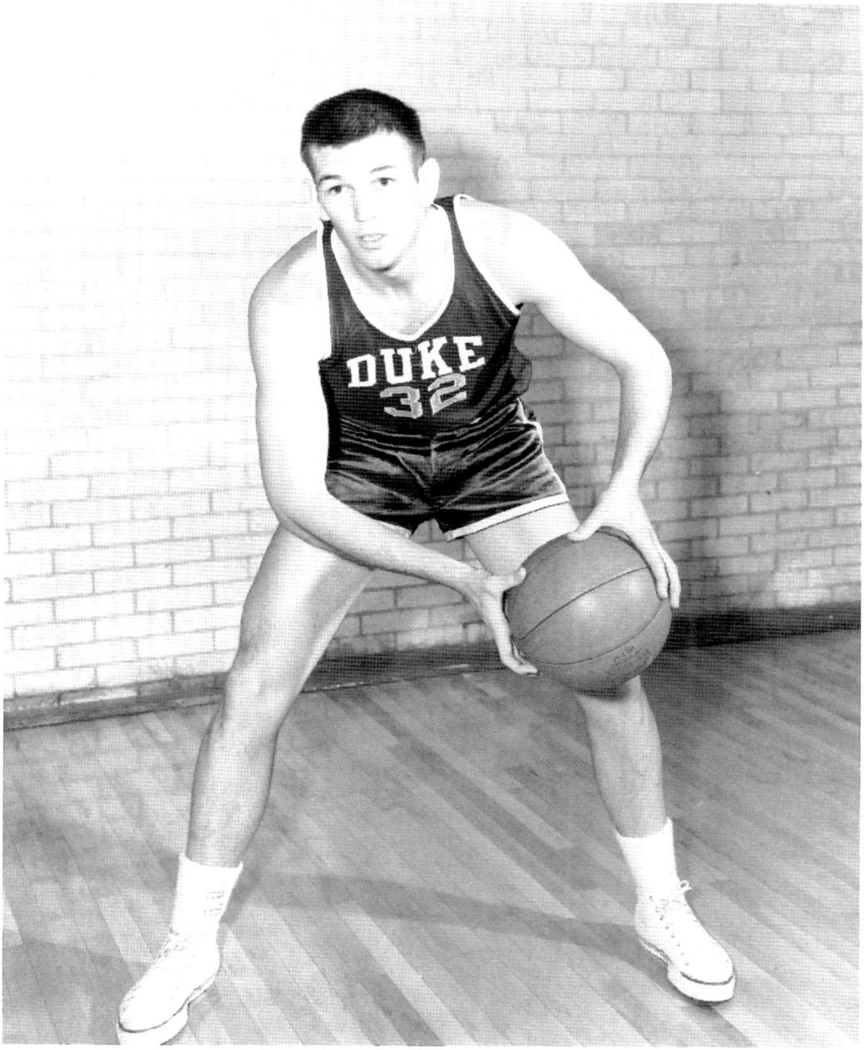

Lefty Driesell is known as one of the great college basketball coaches, but he once played basketball for Duke. Driesell played for Duke from 1950 to 1954. Lefty scored a career high 19 points against Vanderbilt in 1954, as that year's team (1953–54) went 22 and 6 and finished fifteenth in the nation under coach Harold Bradley. In a forty-one-year coaching career, Driesell won 786 games against 394 losses. He is the only coach to win at least 100 games at four different schools. Those schools were Davidson, Maryland, James Madison and Georgia State. *Courtesy of Duke Sports Information.*

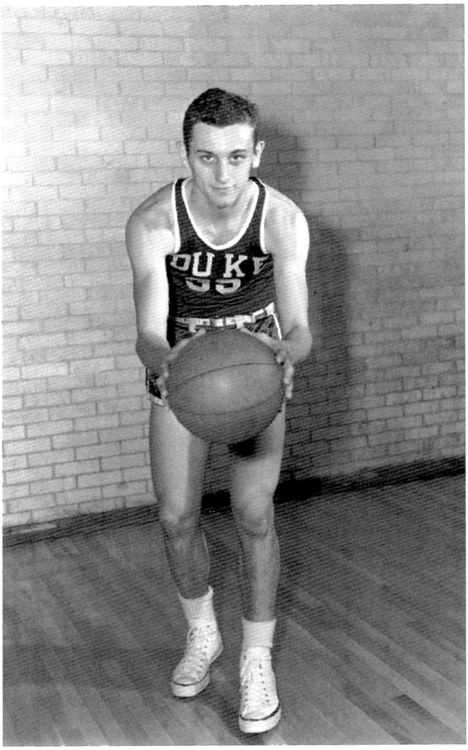

Ronnie Mayer was a key player on Harold Bradley's Duke teams of the mid-1950s. From 1953–54 to 1955–56, Duke won 61 games with 21 losses, and Mayer had season scoring averages of 12.9 in 1953–54, 21.7 in 1954–55 and 22.1 in 1955–56. He scored 38 against Maryland in his senior season. Mayer could also rebound, averaging 9.1 for his career, with the 12.4 per game in 1954–55, his best. *Courtesy of Duke Sports Information.*

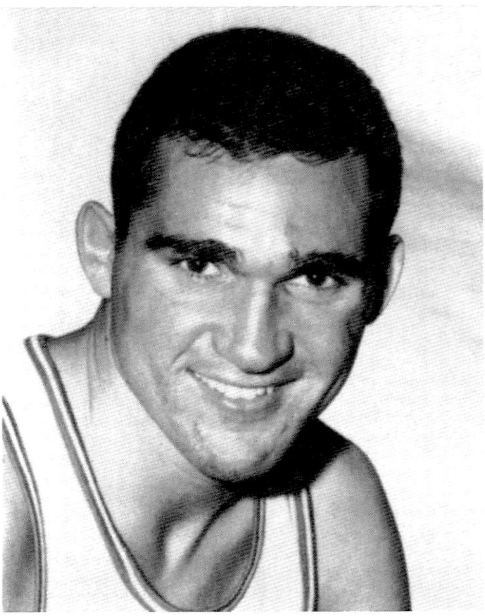

Howard Hurt, from Beckley, West Virginia, played for Harold Bradley at Duke in Bradley's last year as coach in 1958–59. The next year, playing for Coach Vic Bubas, Hurt scored 13.4 points a game as Duke won the ACC Tournament. In 1960–61, Hurt averaged 12.3 a game as Duke went 22 and 6 and finished tenth in the nation. Hurt was captain of both the 1959–60 and 1960–61 teams.

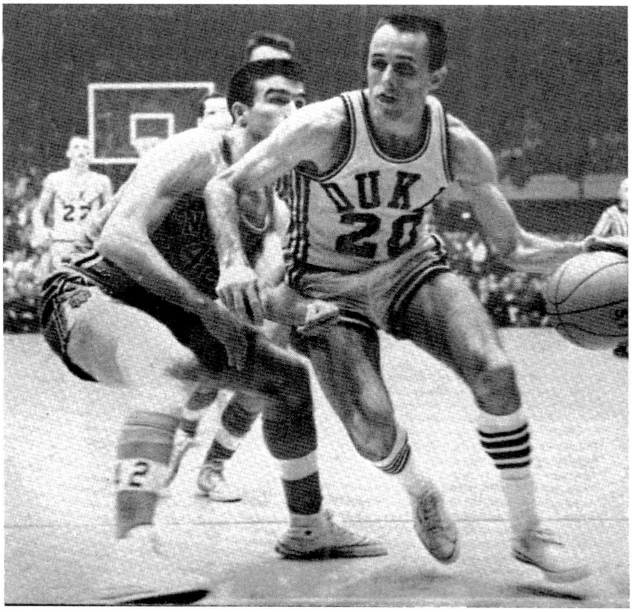

Jack Mullen was twenty-four years old when he first played for the Duke varsity basketball team in 1959. Mullen had been in the navy, making the All-Navy team in 1958. Not a prolific scorer, Mullen had perhaps his best game in 1962 against arch rival UNC, scoring 17 points on 7 of 8 shots. The 1959–60 team, coached by Vic Bubas, won the ACC championship and reached the Elite Eight of the NCAA Tournament.

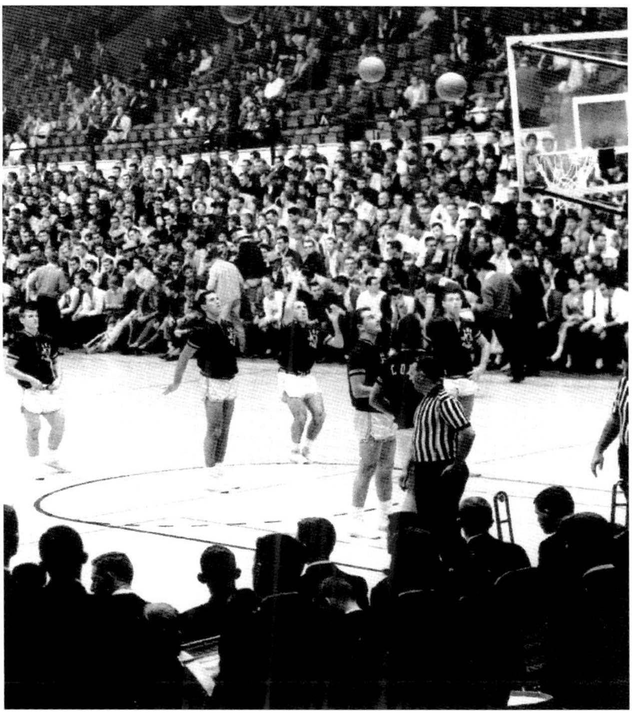

Art Heyman shoots a free throw. Heyman averaged 25.1 points and 10.9 rebounds a game during his career at Duke from 1960–61 to 1962–63, and will always rank as one of the best players to ever wear the Blue Devil uniform. Duke was 69 and 14 in his three varsity years, and won an ACC Tournament and played in a Final Four.

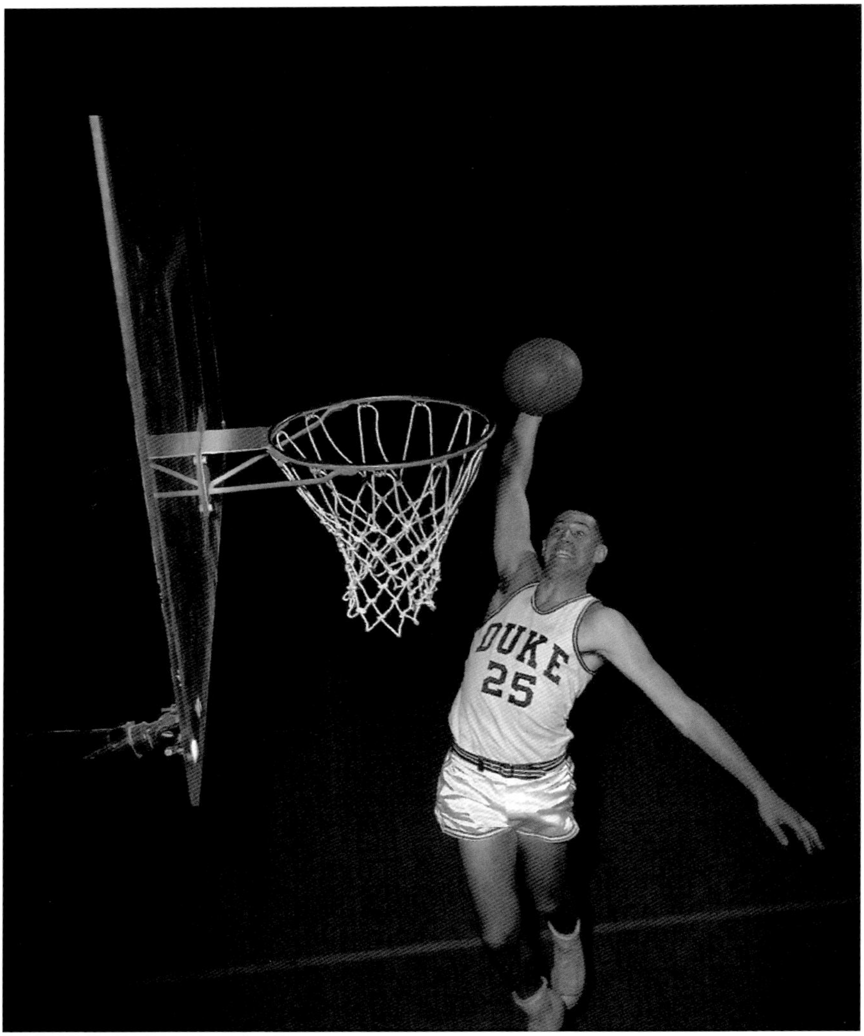

The numbers speak for the caliber of player Art Heyman was. In 1960–61, Heyman averaged 25.2 points a game as Duke went 22 and 6 and finished number ten in the nation. In 1961–62, Duke was 20 and 5, again finishing tenth in the nation, as Heyman scored 25.3 a game. During the 1962–63 season, Duke won 27 and lost 3 and reached the Final Four, along with winning the ACC Tournament Championship. Heyman averaged 24.9 a game, and saved his best for his final home game in a victory over North Carolina, scoring 40 points and pulling down 24 rebounds.

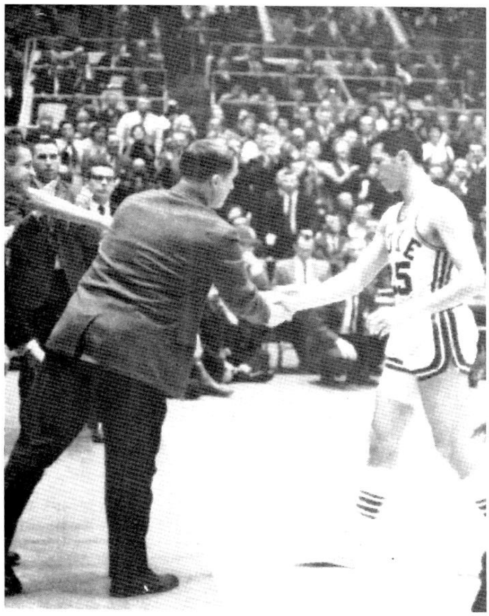

Art Heyman is shown with Coach Vic Bubas in 1963. Heyman was national player of the year for the 1962–63 season, and had the first triple-double in Duke history in the 1963 ACC Tournament against Virginia, when he had 21 points, 18 rebounds and 10 assists. Vic Bubas's record as coach at Duke from the 1959–60 season to 1968–69 speaks for itself: four ACC Tournament titles, three Final Fours and played for the national title in 1964, losing to John Wooden's UCLA team. Overall, Bubas won 213 games and lost 67.

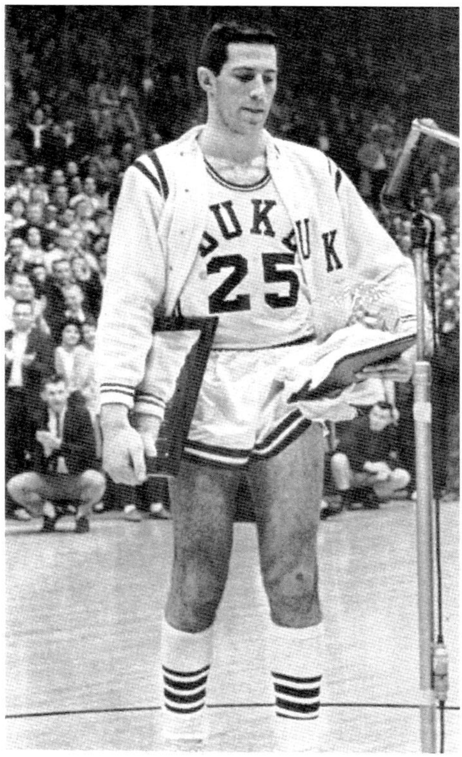

During the 1962–63 season, Art Heyman led Duke to a 27 and 3 record and the Final Four. Heyman averaged 10.8 rebounds a game and won national player of the year honors. Heyman was the first Duke player to be drafted number one by the NBA, where he made the all-rookie team. Later in his career, he switched leagues to the ABA (American Basketball Association), where he scored 20.1 points a game in 1968 for the Pittsburgh Pipers.

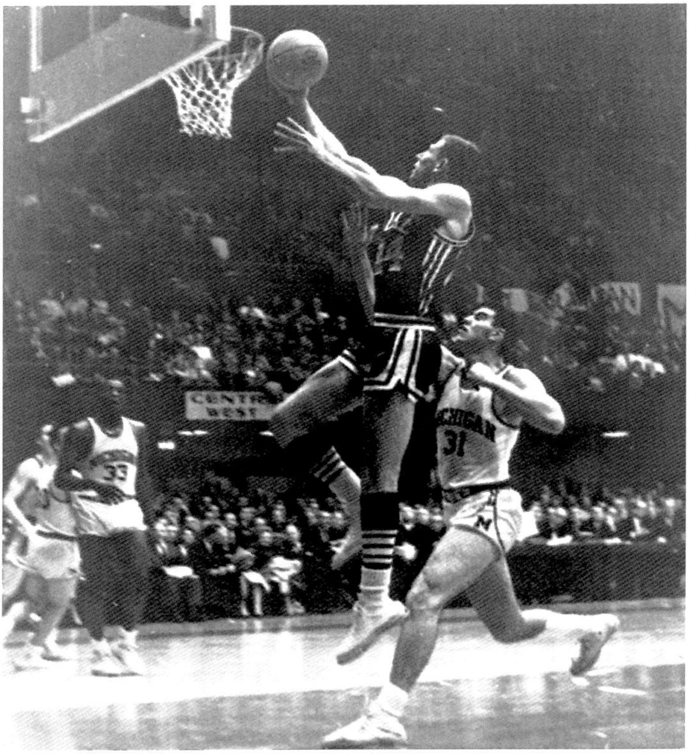

Above: Jeff Mullins epitomized consistency during a Duke varsity career that spanned from 1961 to 1964. Mullins scored in double figures in all 86 games of his career, and averaged 21.9 points in those games. He also averaged 9 rebounds a game, and this at a height of six feet, four inches. In his senior year he was ACC player of the year. He still holds the Duke record for most points in a NCAA tournament game, scoring 43 in 1964 against Villanova. Duke won 73 games with 13 losses in his three varsity seasons, with two Final Four appearances. After college, Mullins was the fifth draft pick in the NBA, made three All-Star teams and his teams reached the playoffs in ten of his twelve years. He later became head coach at UNC-Charlotte.

Opposite top: Winning was a habit for Jack Marin. During his varsity career, from 1963 to 1966, Duke won 72 games with only 14 losses. Duke won two conference tournament championships and went to two Final Fours, and finished third in the nation in 1963–64, tenth in 1964–65 and second in 1965–66. Marin was an All-American his senior year, and averaged 14.9 points and 8.1 rebounds a game for his career. The six-foot, six-inch Marin kept winning as a pro player, as his teams reached the NBA playoffs in seven of his eleven-year career. Marin led the NBA in free throw percentage in 1972, and scored 12,541 career points.

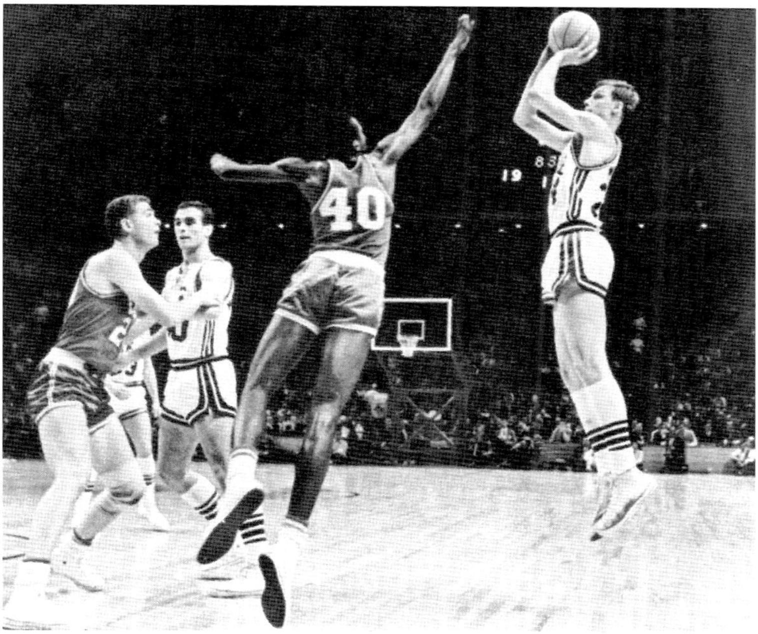

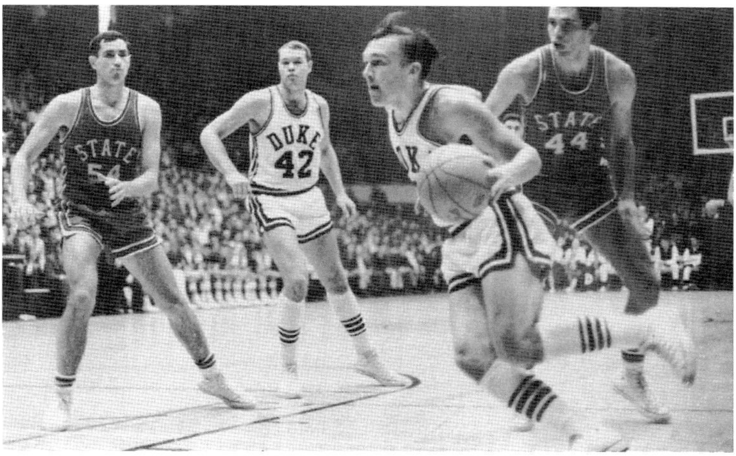

Bob Verga could score like few players in Duke history could. In 1964, playing on the freshman team, he set the record for most points ever in Cameron Indoor Stadium history, scoring 51 points. He just kept on scoring in his varsity years, averaging 22 for his career, with a high of 26.1 in his senior year of 1966–67. Verga was a two-time All-American selection, and his 22-point career average is the third highest in Duke history, trailing only Art Heyman's 25.1 and Dick Groat's 23. Verga kept right on scoring in the pros, averaging 21.2 points a game in five seasons in the American Basketball Association, and earning all-pro with the Carolina Cougars.

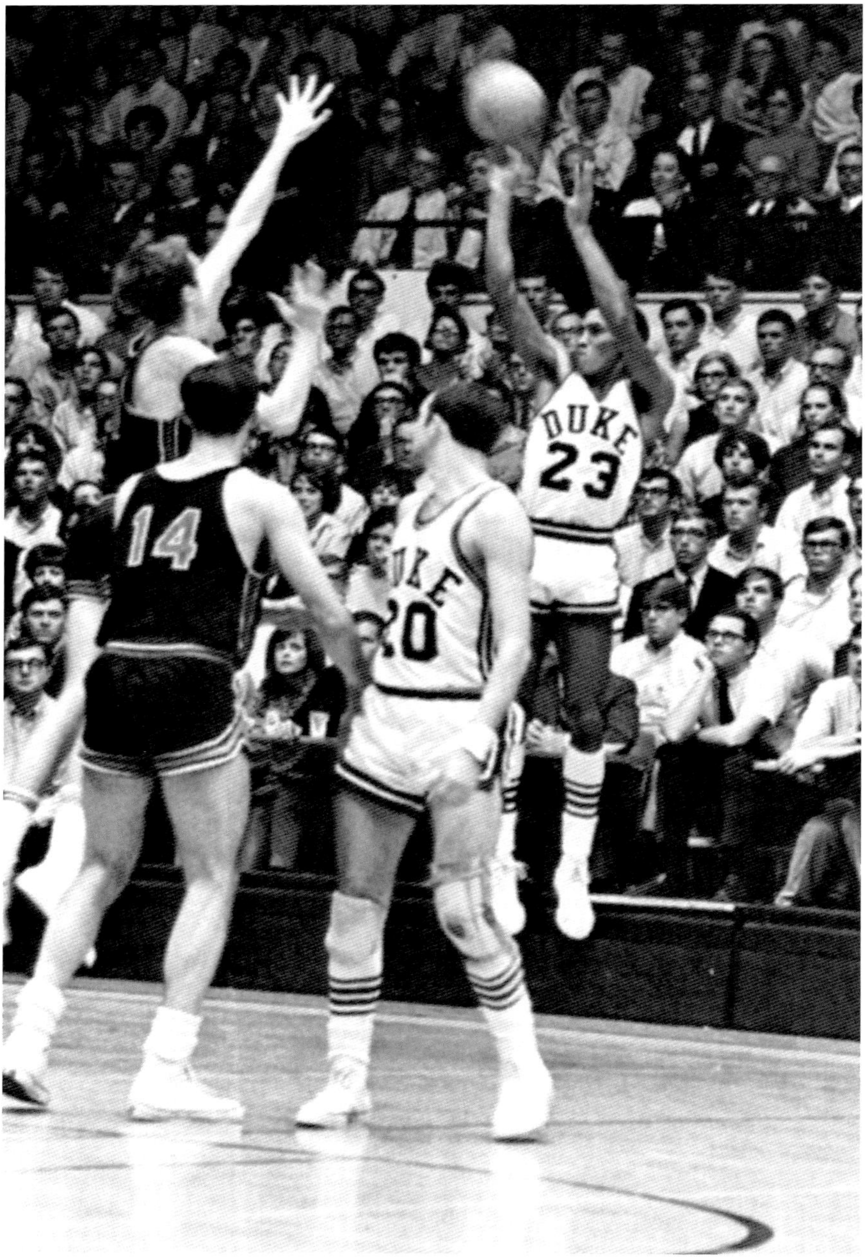

C.B. Claiborne was the first black athlete in Duke history, playing basketball from 1965 to 1969, and appearing in 53 varsity games. Claiborne scored a career high 15 points against Clemson. After graduating in 1969, Claiborne eventually earned a PhD and became a college professor.

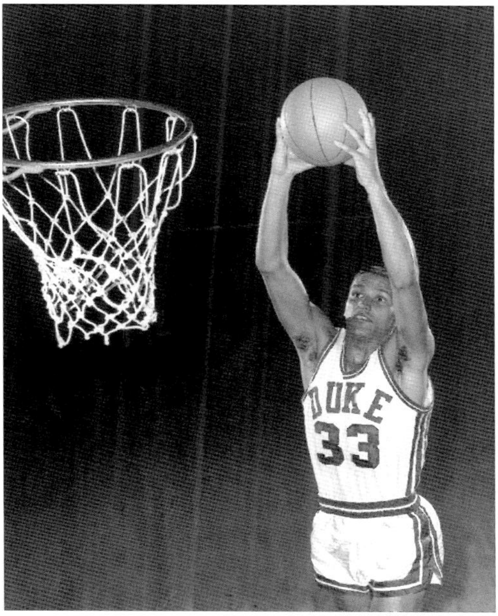

Steve Vacendak was ACC player of the year in 1966, as Duke went 26 and 4, won the ACC Tournament and reached the Final Four, where it lost to Kentucky 83 to 79. Duke had a 72–14 overall record during Vacendak's three years, including two Final Four trips. After college, Vacendak played in the ABA. He later became an assistant athletic director at Duke. *Courtesy of Duke Sports Information.*

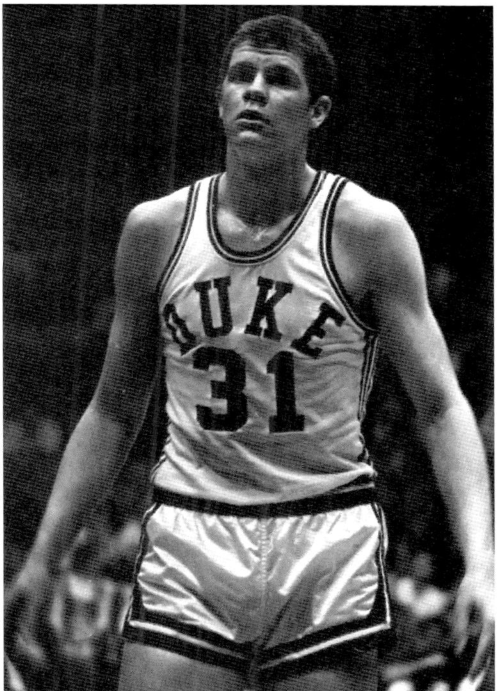

Randy Denton averaged 12.7 rebounds over his three-year varsity career from 1968 to 1971, and also averaged 19.7 points a game. His 25 rebounds against Northwestern in 1971 are the second highest single game total in Duke history, behind Bernie Janicki's 31 in 1952. In Denton's senior year, he averaged 20.4 points and 12.8 rebounds per game, as Duke won 20 games, lost 10 and played in the NIT under head coach Bucky Waters.

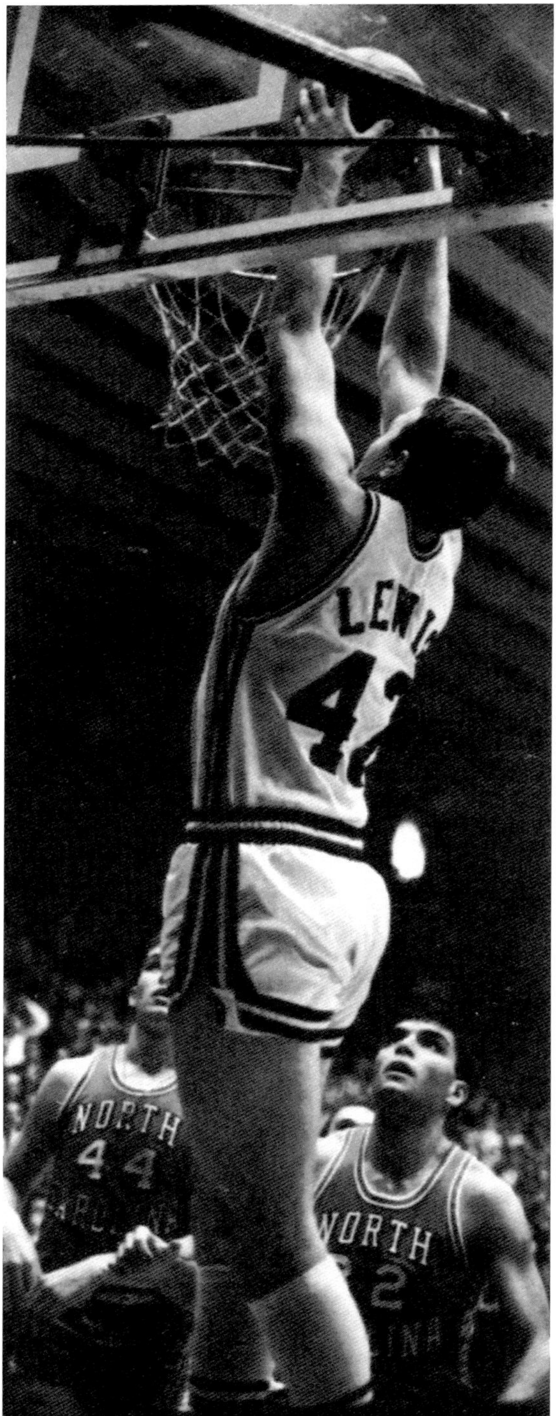

Mike Lewis, from Missoula, Montana, was often referred to as the Missoula Mountain. Big and strong, Lewis averaged 12.5 rebounds per game for his career. Only Randy Denton's career average of 12.7 was better at Duke. In his senior year of 1967–68, Lewis averaged 21.7 points and 14.4 rebounds a game, earning him status as an All-American. He had 34 points and 22 rebounds against North Carolina State in his senior year. Duke, under Coach Vic Bubas, won 66 games with 19 losses in Lewis's three varsity seasons, reaching the Final Four in 1965–66 and finishing number two in the nation in the final AP poll. Lewis went on to play 6 seasons in the American Basketball Association.

Jeff Dawson only played one varsity season at Duke, which was during the basketball season of 1970–71. But during that one season, Dawson showed why he was heavily recruited, scoring 22 points in a game against UNC and 20 in a game versus NC State. Despite his fine year, Jeff decided to transfer to Illinois, where his brother Jim also played.

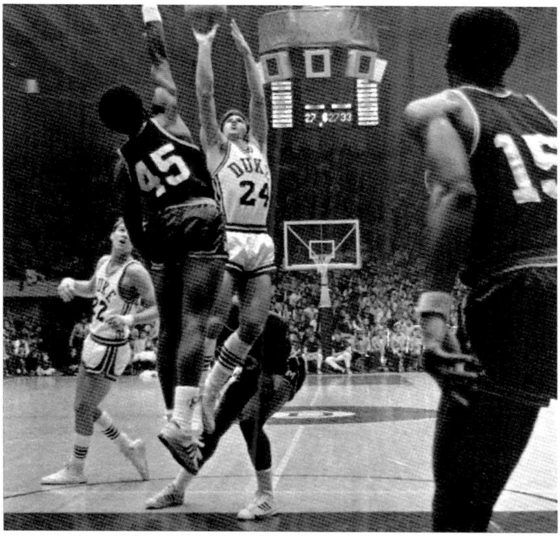

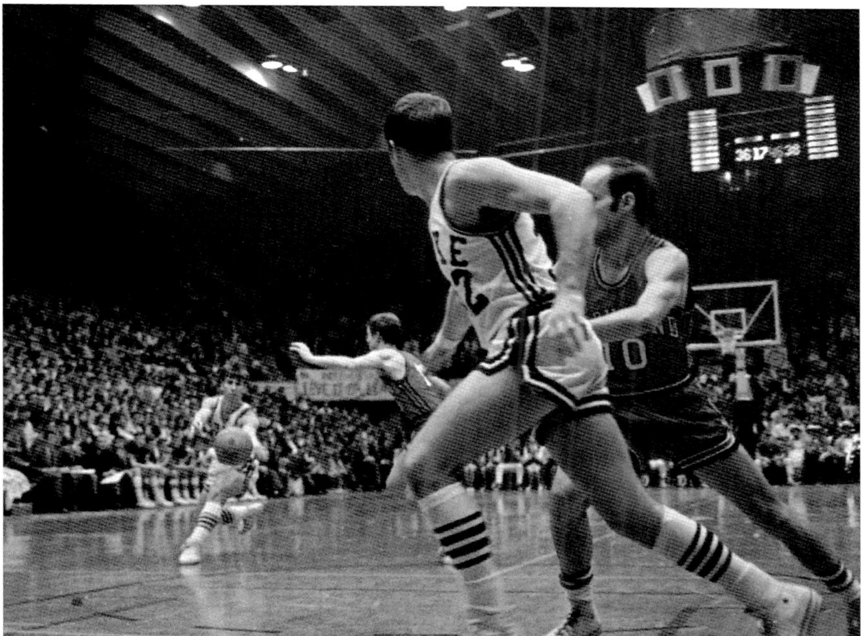

Dick DeVenzio is shown bouncing a pass to Brad Evans in 1970. Evans played basketball and football at Duke. He scored a career high 26 points against Penn State. DeVenzio played point guard during his career from 1968 to 1971. He once had 12 assists in a game against NC State, and was Duke's career assists leader with 388 when he graduated, a record now held by Bobby Hurley.

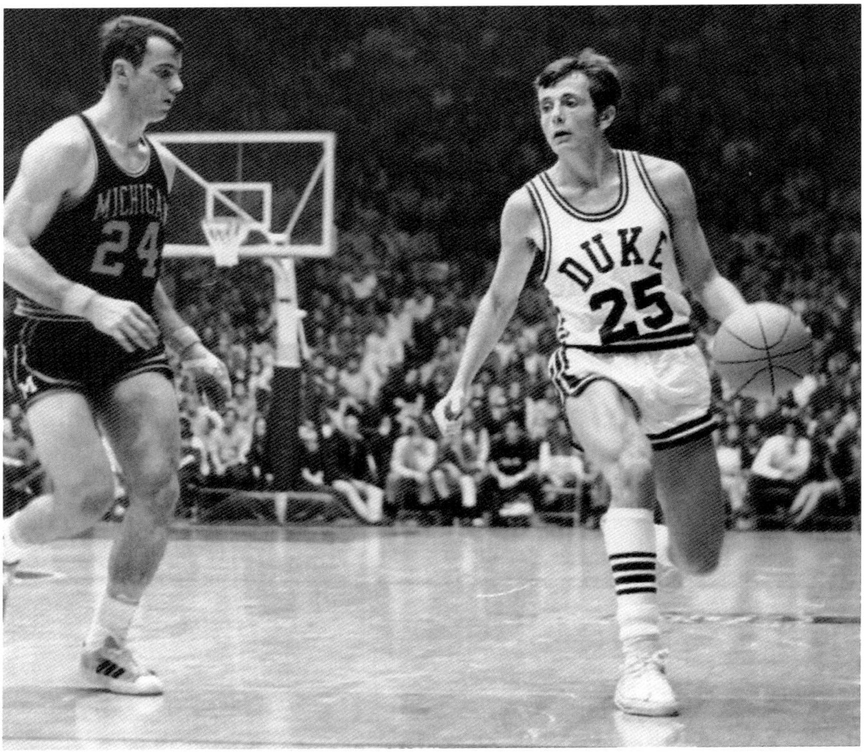

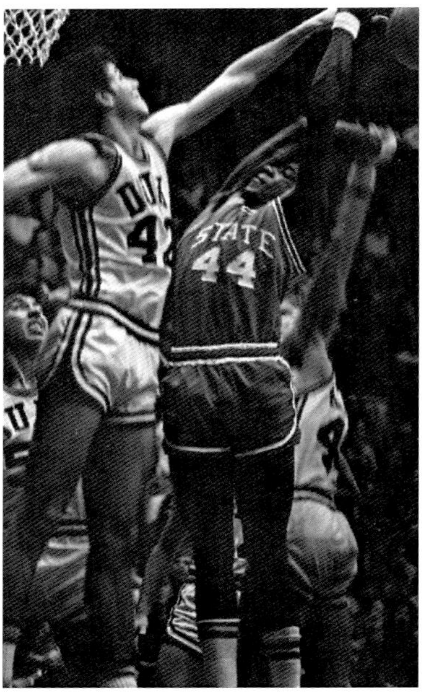

Above: Gary Melchioni played from 1971–73 on the varsity team, and was chosen as Duke's MVP in 1973. That year, Melchioni scored 39 points in an upset win over the third-ranked Maryland Terrapins. Drafted in the second round of the NBA draft, Melchioni played two years and averaged 8 points a game in 137 games played. Gary's son, Lee, played for Duke from 2002 to 2006.

Left: Bob Fleischer of Duke blocks a shot by the great David Thompson of NC State during a game in 1974. Fleischer, a six-foot, eight-inch player from Youngstown, Ohio, averaged 15.7 points and 12.4 rebounds a game during the 1973–74 season, and 17.2 points and 10.5 rebounds a game during 1974–75. Thompson is considered by many to be the ACC's greatest player ever, leading NC State to a national title in 1974. Thompson once scored 40 points and had 14 rebounds in a game against Duke at Reynolds Coliseum, the home court of the Wolfpack during his playing days.

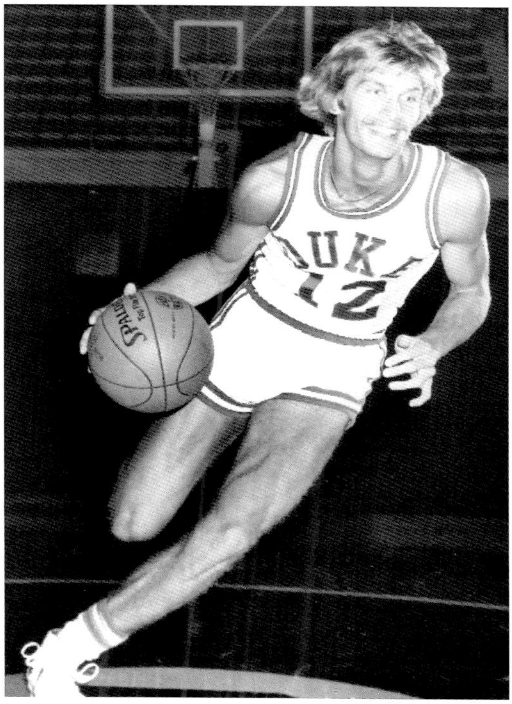

Tate Armstrong was noted for his scoring ability, as he averaged 24.7 points a game as a junior and 22.7 as a senior. In the fifth highest single game point total in Duke history, Armstrong scored 42 points versus Clemson in 1976. Also in 1976, Armstrong was selected for the U.S. Olympic team that won a gold medal and was coached by Dean Smith. After being a first-round NBA draft pick, Armstrong played two seasons.

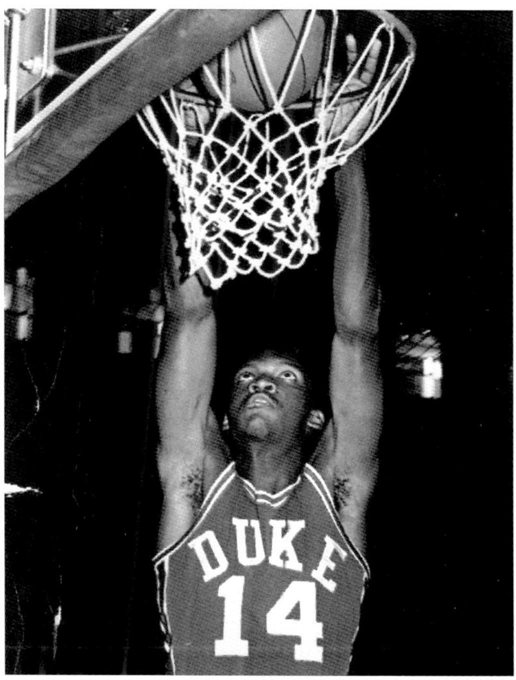

Willie Hodge scored 1,117 points and pulled down 605 rebounds in his Duke career from 1972 to 1976. As a senior, Hodge averaged 16.9 points and 7.8 rebounds a game. Against East Carolina in his senior year, Hodge had 35 points and 16 rebounds.

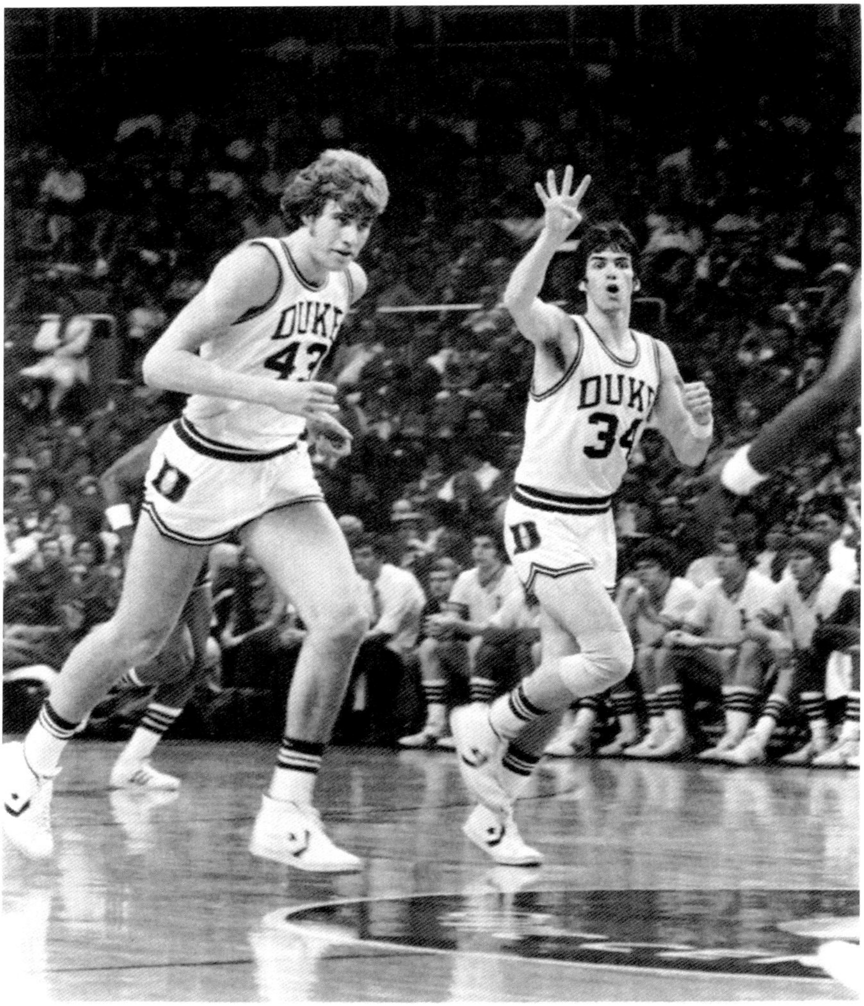

Mike Gminski, on the left, and Jim Spanarkel, on the right, both were named All-Americans during the 1977–78 and 1978–79 seasons. Gminski, a six-foot, eleven-inch player from Monroe, Connecticut, averaged 20 points and 10 rebounds a game in 1977–78 and 18.8 points and 9.2 rebounds in 1978–79. Spanarkel averaged 20.8 points in 1977–78 and 15.9 in 1978–79. Bill Foster was the coach of both teams.

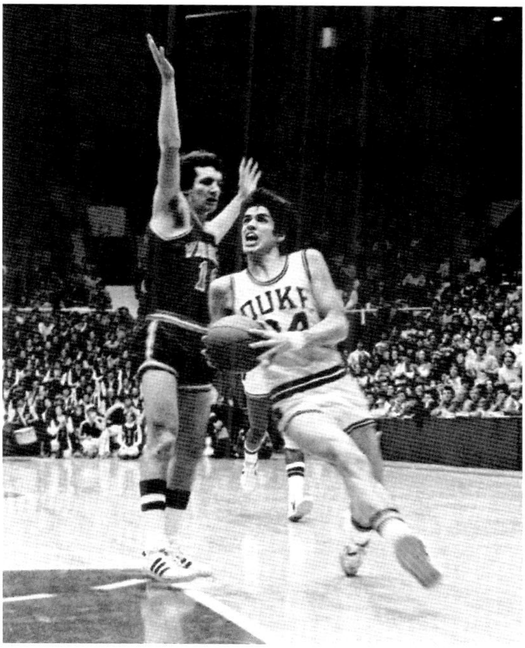

Jim Spanarkel had a great career at Duke from 1975 to 1979. But probably his best year was 1977–78, when he led Duke to a 27 and 7 record and helped them to the NCAA championship game, where Duke lost to Kentucky 94 to 88. Spanarkel delivered when it counted most during this season, as he was MVP at the ACC Tournament, most outstanding player in the East Regional and was named to the All-Final Four team.

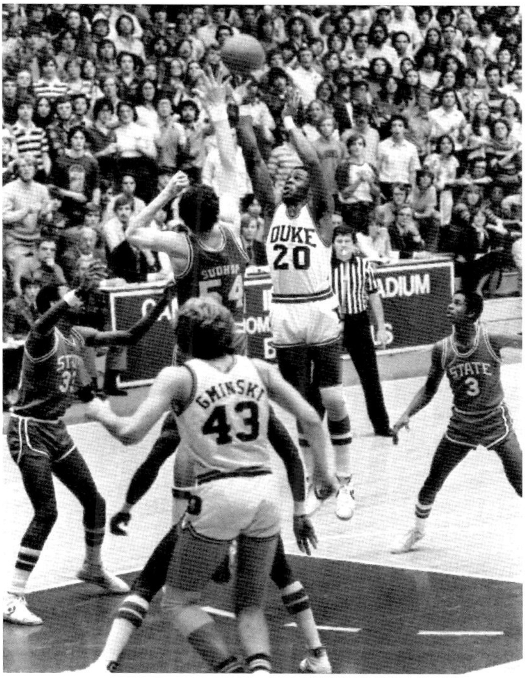

Gene Banks averaged 17.1 points and 8.6 rebounds a game as a freshman in 1977–78. Over his final three seasons, he averaged 14.3 points and 8.5 rebounds, 17.3 points and 7.7 rebounds and 18.5 points and 6.8 rebounds. His most memorable game was probably his last home game in 1981, as he threw roses to the crowd before the game against North Carolina. He then hit a shot at the buzzer to tie the game in regulation, and scored the winning basket in overtime as Duke won 66 to 65.

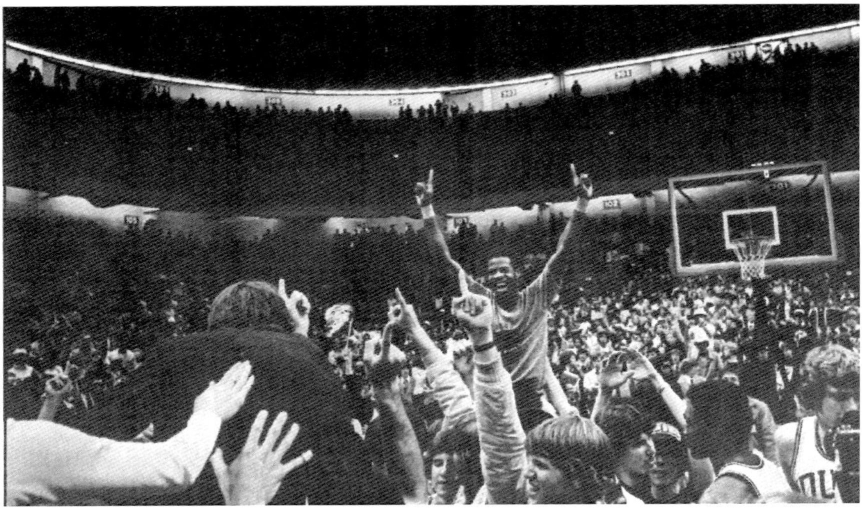

Duke has just beaten Wake Forest 85 to 77 in 1978 for the ACC Tournament Championship. Gene Banks celebrates with the number one sign. Mike Gminski scored 25 points, blocked 3 shots, had 16 rebounds and 4 assists in this game. Gminski and Jim Spanarkel made All-America for the 1977–78 year, while Banks was ACC Rookie of the Year.

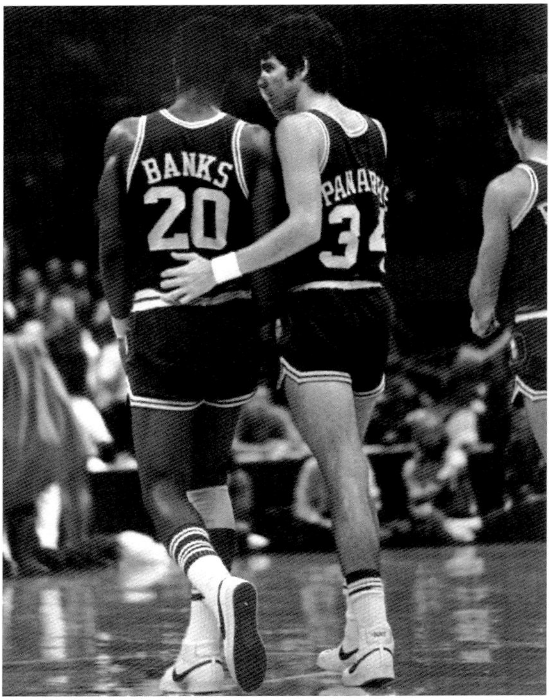

Jim Spanarkel, on the right, and Gene Banks talk strategy. Here are impressive numbers, registered over the course of a 114-game career at Duke. Jim Spanarkel averaged almost 18 points, 4 rebounds, 4 assists and 2 steals a game. Spanarkel became the first 2,000-point scorer in Duke history, and still ranks ninth on the career scoring list. After being drafted in the first round, Spanarkel went on to play five seasons in the NBA, averaging 10 points a game.

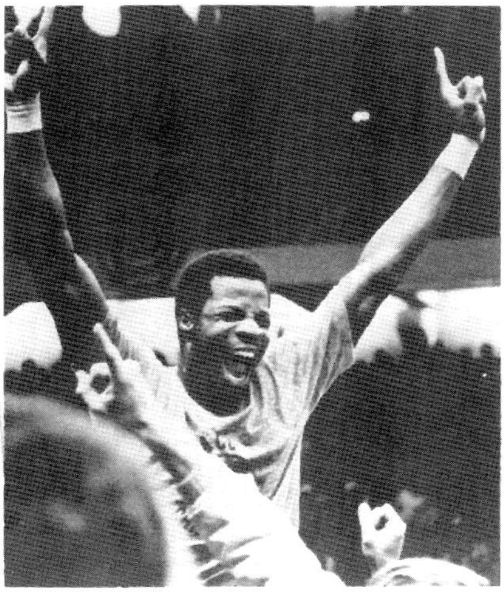

The ACC rookie of the year tells it like it is...

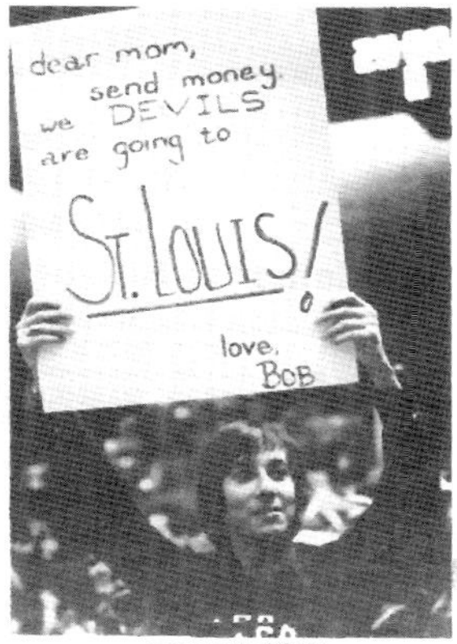

...and on to the NCAAs.

Above: Gene Banks, in 1977–78, perhaps had the best freshman season in Duke basketball history. He scored 17 points a game, pulled down nearly 9 rebounds a game, passed for almost 4 assists a game and helped lead Duke to the national championship game. In a game against Lehigh in his freshman year, Banks had a triple-double, with 13 points, 12 rebounds and 11 assists. Banks teamed with Mike Gminski and Kenny Dennard to form what became known as the Duke Power Company. For his career, Banks scored 2,079 points, good for eighth place on Duke's career list. Banks went on to play six seasons in the NBA.

Right: Vince Taylor played for two years under Bill Foster and two under Mike Krzyzewski in his career at Duke from 1978 to 1982. Named Duke's MVP in 1982, Taylor led the ACC in scoring with a 20.3 average. He scored 35 points for a career best effort against Clemson in his senior year. Chosen in the second round of the NBA draft, Taylor played one season with the New York Knicks before a professional playing career overseas.

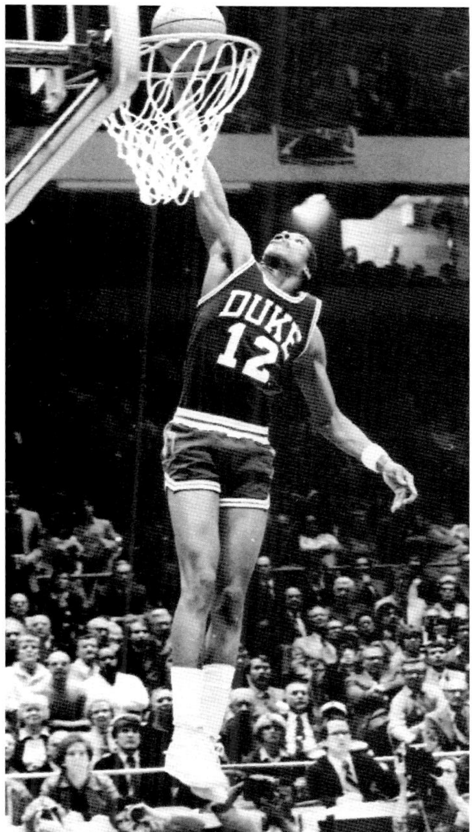

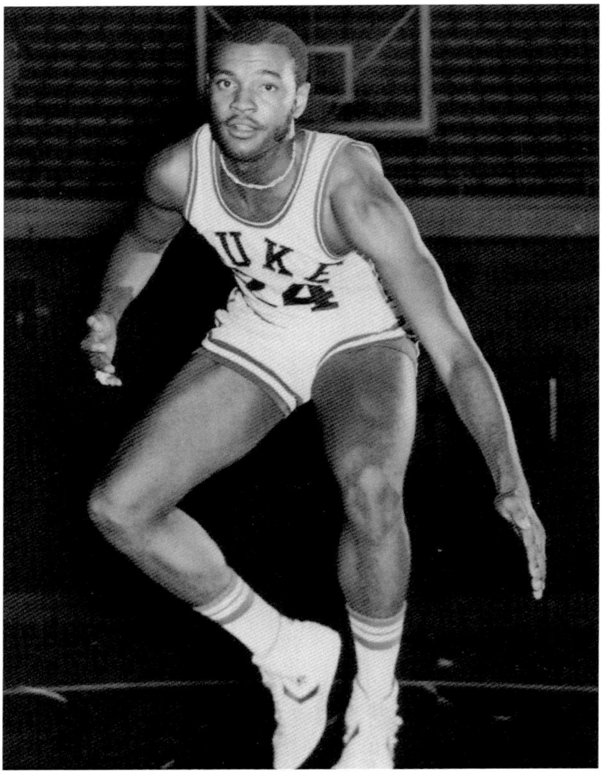

From West Orange, New Jersey, Harold Morrison was a member of Bill Foster's 1978 team that lost to Kentucky in the national championship game. Morrison started at power forward for most of the 1976–77 team, and averaged 5.5 points and 4.3 rebounds a game.

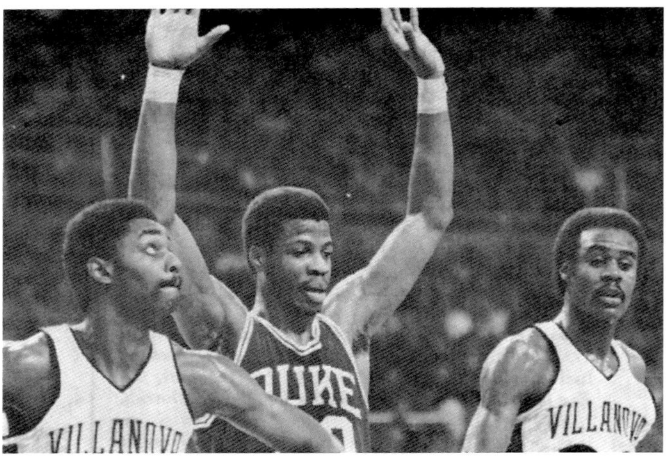

Gene Banks awaits a free throw on March 19, 1978, in a game against Villanova for the NCAA Tournament Regional Final. Duke won 90 to 72 at the Providence Civic Center to earn a trip to the Final Four. Banks scored 17 points, dished out 9 assists and had 10 rebounds in this game. Jim Spanarkel scored 22, Mike Gminski had 21 and Kenny Dennard scored 16.

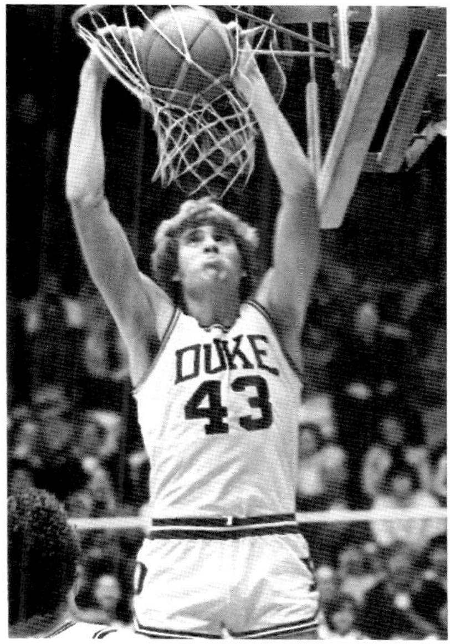

At the end of his playing career in 1980, Mike Gminski was Duke's all-time leader in points, rebounds and blocked shots. He made All-America three times and Academic All-America three times. He is the only four-year player at Duke to average double figures in points (19) and rebounds (10.2) for a career. After a very successful fourteen-year career in the NBA, in which he scored over 10,000 points, the G-man is now a college basketball television analyst.

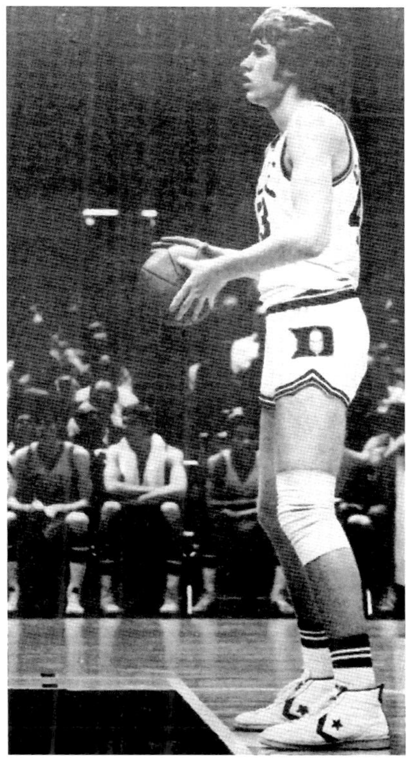

Mike Gminski could do it all on a basketball court: score, rebound, block shots and shoot free throws, among other talents. Gminski, at six feet, eleven inches, shot 84 percent from the charity stripe in 1977–78 and 1979–80, and averaged 79.2 percent for his career at Duke.

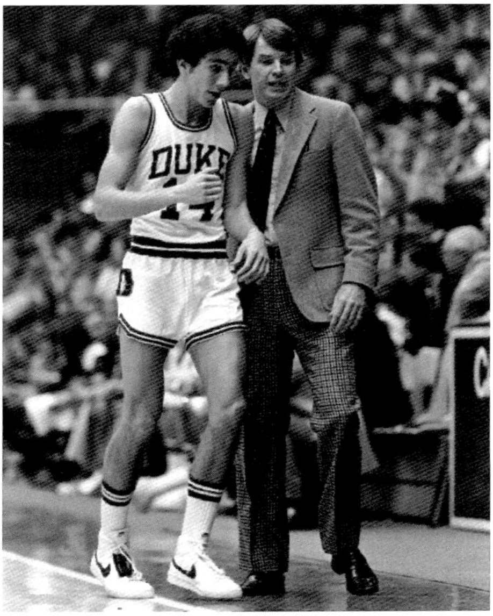

Arthur Edward "Chip" Engelland was better known for his shooting ability while playing for Duke from 1979 to 1983. Engelland's best year was probably 1982, when he averaged 15.2 points a game and led the ACC in free throw shooting with an 87.5 percentage. Engelland is shown with Bill Foster, head coach at Duke from 1974 to 1980, who took Duke to the national championship game in 1978, where Duke lost to Kentucky 94 to 88.

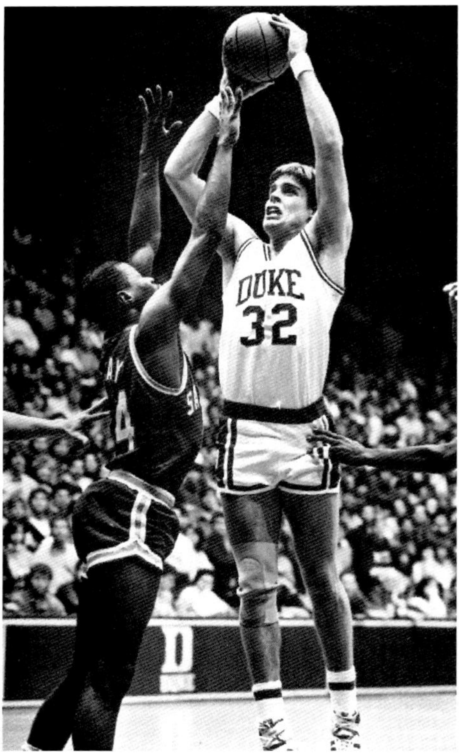

With 2,136 points for his career, Mark Alarie stands number six on Duke's all-time scoring list. From 1982 to 1986, Alarie averaged 16.1 points per game in 133 games. Alarie also grabbed 833 rebounds in his career. After being drafted in the first round, Alarie spent five seasons in the NBA.

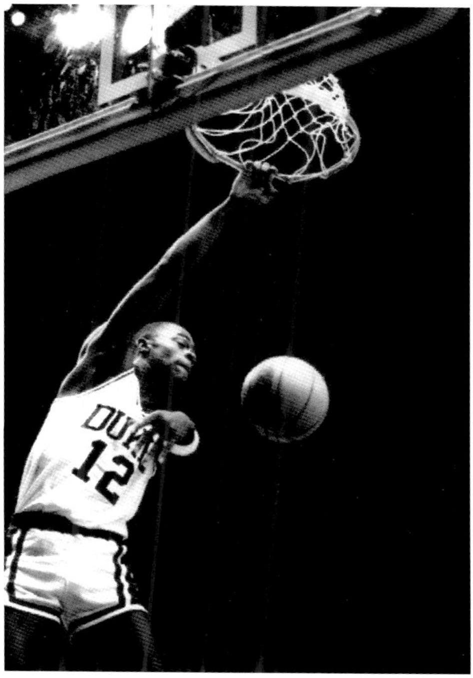

From 1982 to 1986, David Henderson scored 1,570 points and averaged a career best 14.2 points a game as a senior. In 1985, Henderson was Duke's leading scorer in an NCAA tournament game against Pepperdine, scoring 22 points. This was Coach Mike Krzyzewski's first NCAA victory; he is now the all-time leader in NCAA Tournament game victories. Henderson played one year in the NBA, and also served as an assistant coach at Duke for three seasons before being named head coach at Delaware.

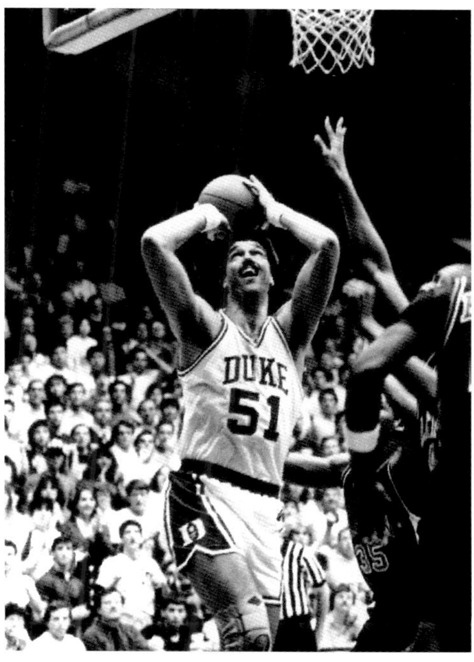

Martin Nessley played at Duke from 1983 to 1987, and still holds the distinction of being the tallest player in Duke basketball history, at seven feet, two inches. Nessley had his career game against Harvard, when he scored 25 points and had 8 rebounds. He played one year in the NBA after being drafted in the sixth round by the Los Angeles Clippers in 1987.

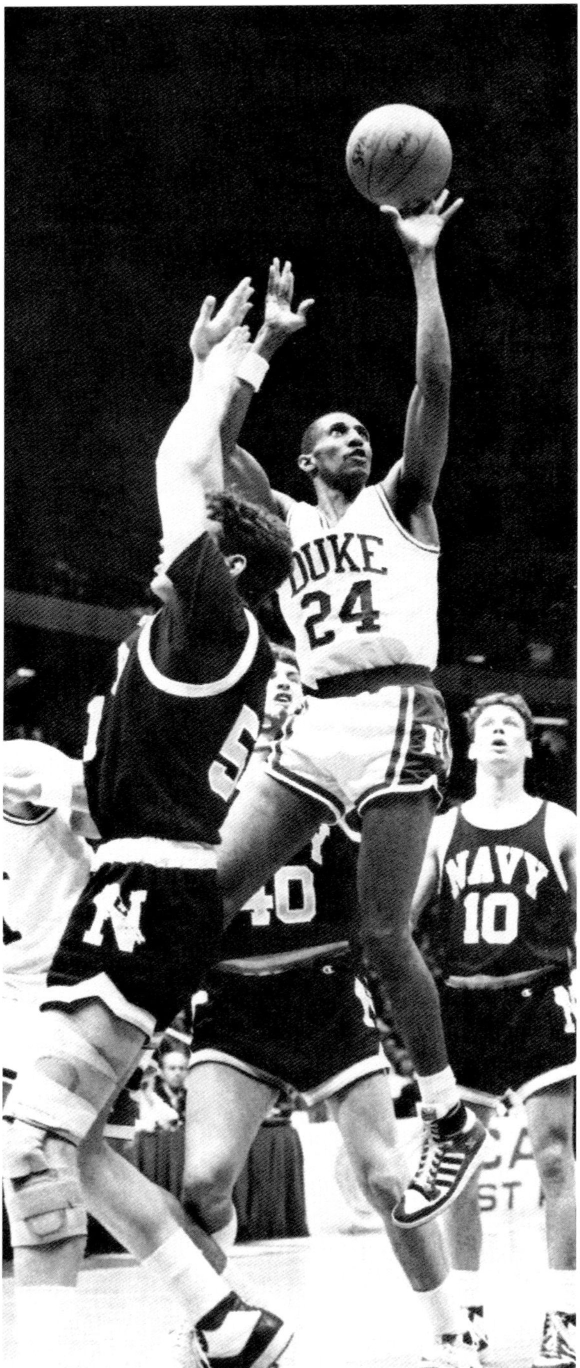

As a player at Duke, Johnny Dawkins was one of the best to ever wear the uniform. He is the only player to lead Duke in scoring each of his four years—with averages of 18.1, 19.4, 18.8 and 20.2—and is now the second highest scorer in Duke history, with 2,556 points, surpassed only by J.J. Redick with 2,769. Dawkins started all 133 games in his career, and averaged over 19 points, 4 rebounds and 4 assists in those games. In Dawkins's senior year, he led Duke to a 37–3 record and the national championship game, and he was named national player of the year. Dawkins went on to play nine seasons in the NBA before coming back to Duke, where he is now associate head coach.

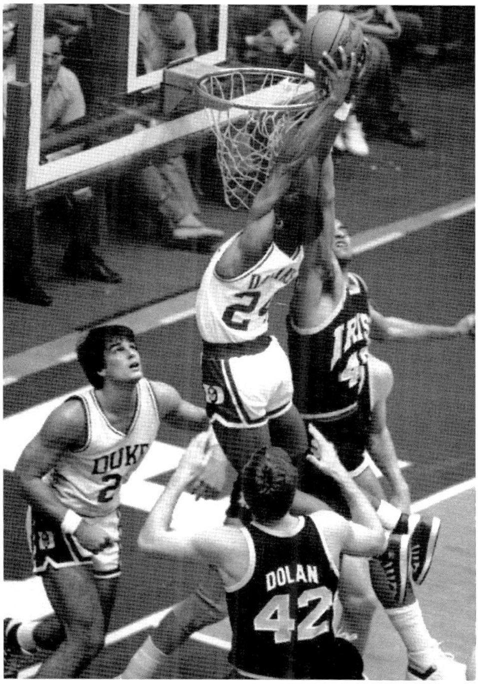

Johnny Dawkins was a great player at Duke, serving as a key figure in the early 1980s as Duke reestablished itself as one of the nation's top programs, just as it had been in the 1960s under Vic Bubas. In 1985–86, Dawkins was national player of the year as Duke went 37 and 3 and played in the national championship game, where it lost to Louisville 72 to 69. In those 6 NCAA Tournament games of 1985–86, Dawkins scored 27, 25, 25, 28, 24 and 24 points in successive games.

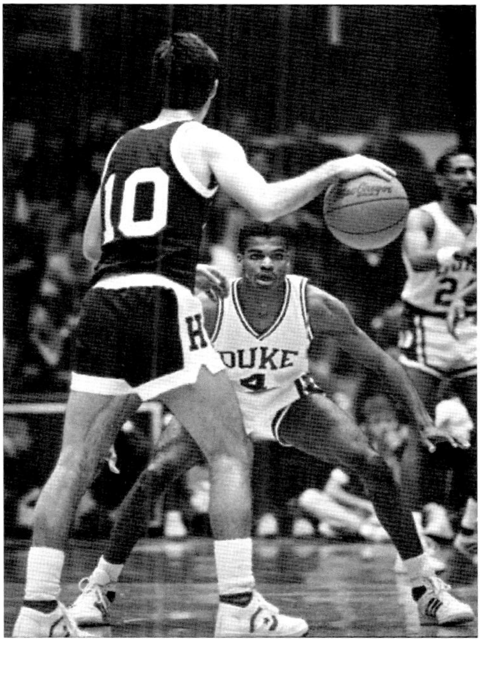

Tommy Amaker has his eyes on the ball. Amaker played at Duke from 1983 to 1987, and is considered one of the best point guards in Duke history. A complete player, Amaker was the first player to be named national defensive player of the year, winning the award in 1987. Amaker was a key reason that Coach Mike Krzyzewski was able to establish a winning tradition back at Duke, as he was a member of the 1983–84 team that was Coach K's first 20-win team, going 24 and 10 and reaching the NCAA Tournament for the first of many times for Coach K. Amaker is now head basketball coach at Harvard.

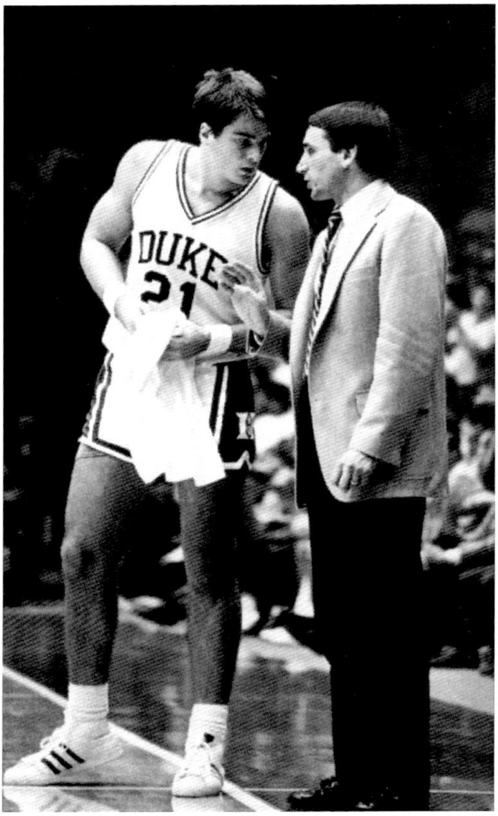

Left: Jay Bilas is now famous as a college basketball game analyst for ESPN, and is still remembered for his valuable contributions as a Duke player. During his years as a Blue Devil from 1982 to 1986, Bilas scored 1,062 points and grabbed 692 rebounds. For three of his four seasons, Bilas led the Duke team in field goal percentage.

Below, left to right: David Henderson, Jay Bilas, Johnny Dawkins, Mark Alarie and Weldon Williams, all from the 1985–86 team. This team finished 37 and 3 and lost to Louisville in the national championship game 72 to 69 in Dallas. This was Coach Mike Krzyzewski's first of ten Final Fours at Duke.

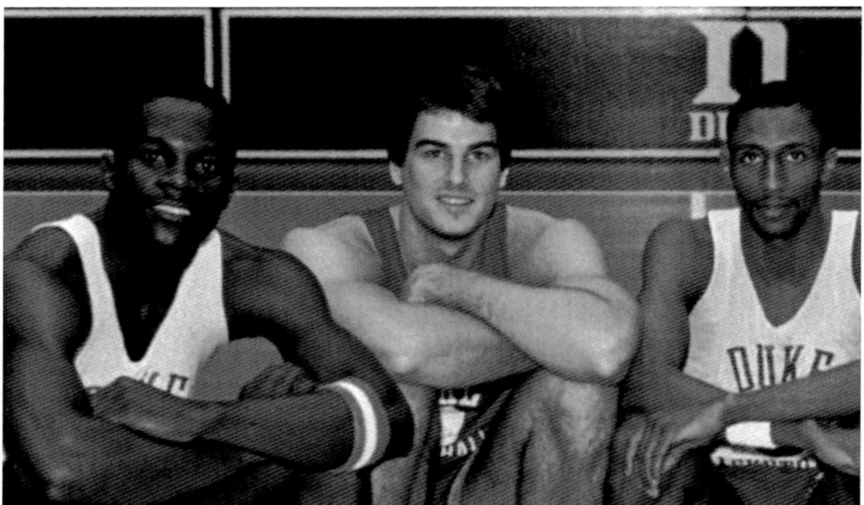

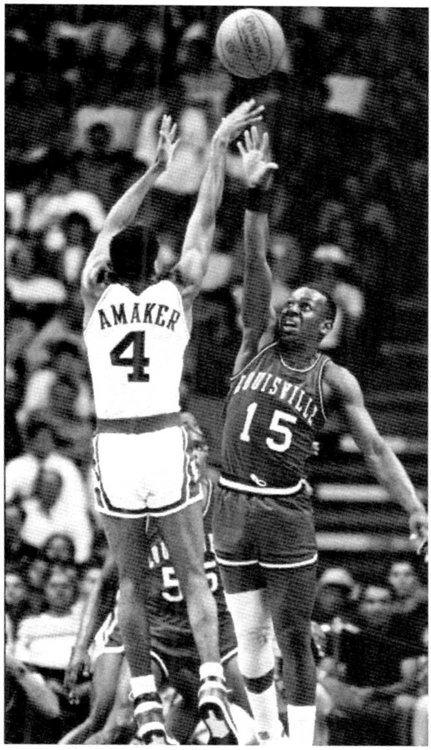

Tommy Amaker was one of the best point guards in Duke history in his career from 1983 to 1987. Amaker could do most everything on a basketball court, as evidenced by his 1,168 points, 708 assists, 308 rebounds, 195 steals and earning national defensive player of the year honors. After being an assistant coach at Duke under Coach K, Amaker went on to successful years as head coach at Seton Hall and Michigan, and is now at Harvard.

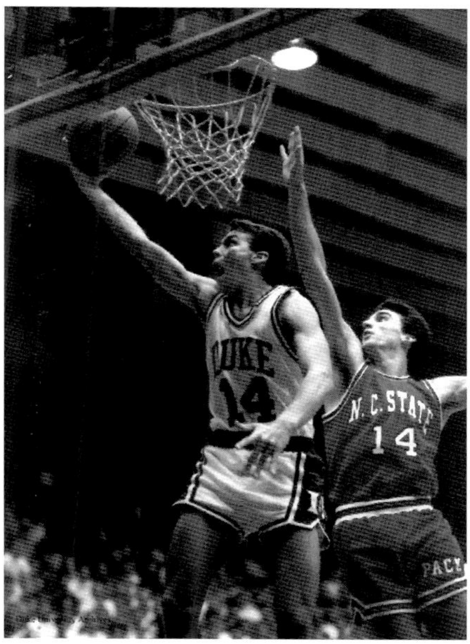

During his career at Duke from 1985 to 1989, Quin Snyder dished out 575 assists, which is the fifth most in Blue Devil history. He had perhaps his best game in 1988, in a win over UNC, scoring 21 points and dishing out 11 assists. Duke won 117 games against only 27 losses during Snyder's four years, while playing in three Final Fours, including a loss to Louisville in 1986 in the national championship game.

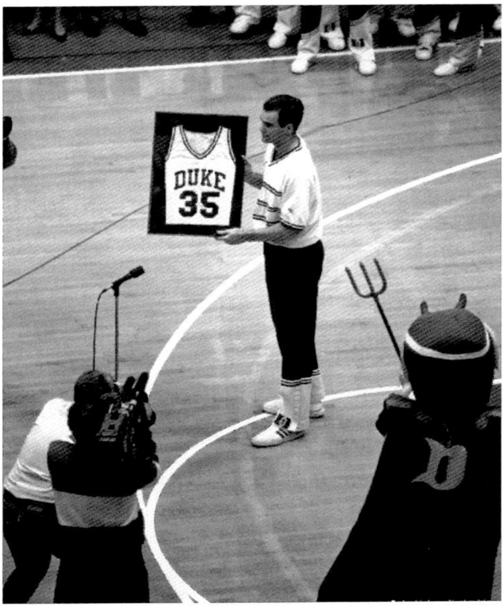

Danny Ferry is shown here during ceremonies to retire his jersey number. Ferry's versatility may have best been exemplified in his sophomore year in a game against Maryland, when he scored 20 points, grabbed 19 rebounds, had 7 assists and blocked 3 shots. His best scoring night came against Miami in his senior year, when he made 23 of 26 free throws for a school record 58 points. During his career at Duke from 1985 to 1989, Ferry won national player of the year, ACC player of the year twice, ACC athlete of the year twice and led Duke to three Final Fours in his four seasons. He was the number two choice in the 1989 NBA draft and was a member of the San Antonio Spurs title team in 2003. Ferry is now the general manager of the Cleveland Cavaliers of the NBA.

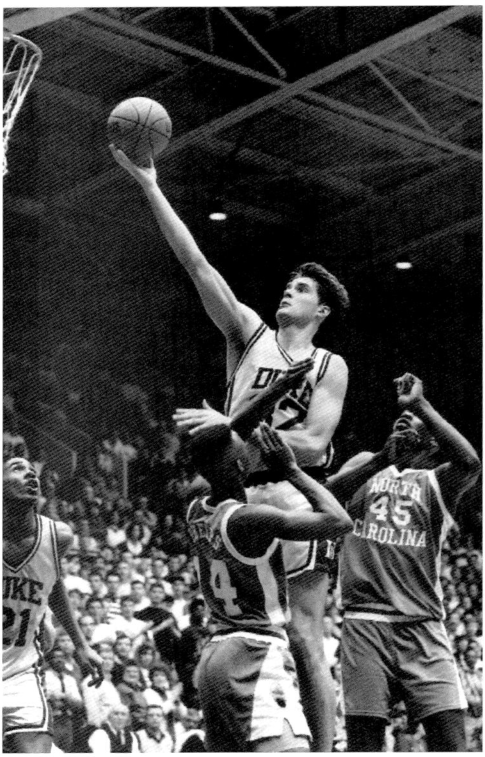

The following just about sums up the success of Christian Laettner's Duke career from 1988 to 1992: he is the only person to ever start for four Final Four teams. Duke won two national titles during his years, and played for the title another year. He could score, as evidenced by his 16.6 career average, and rebound, as shown by his career average of 7.8. Laettner was known for his clutch play, as Duke fans will forever remember his winning shot against Kentucky in the NCAA Tournament in 1992. He played with an intensity matched by few. Upon graduation, Laettner was the third pick in the NBA draft, averaged 18.2 points and 8.7 rebounds a game in his rookie year and made the All-Star team in 1997. Still very involved at Duke and with the city of Durham, there is no question that Christian Laettner was one of the greatest college players of all time.

Right: Duke played in 3 Final Fours during Danny Ferry's career from 1985 to 1989. During his senior year, Ferry was named national player of the year as Duke went 28 and 8 and lost to Seton Hall in the Final Four, despite Ferry scoring 34. Ferry averaged 22.6 points and 7.4 rebounds a game during his senior year.

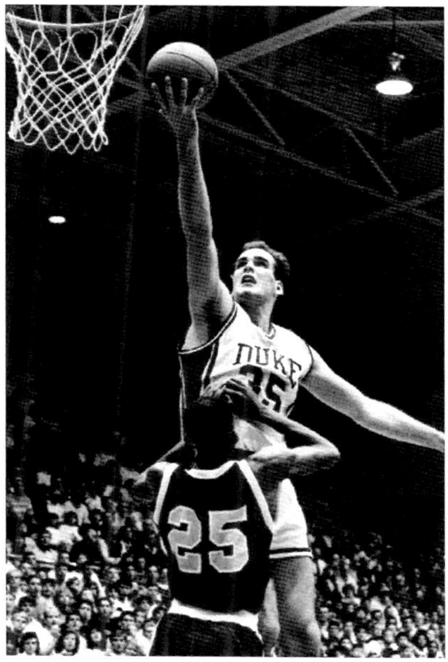

Below: While doing a graduate school internship at Duke in 1989 at Duke, I remember many workouts with Christian Laettner, and once discussing incoming freshman Bobby Hurley. When asked about Hurley's reputation, Laettner replied, "We'll see what he can do." Well, Laettner and Duke fans must have been pretty happy with what Hurley could do, as Hurley finished his Duke career as one of the best point guards in college basketball history. Duke won two national titles, played in three national championship games and Hurley set the NCAA record for career assists during his four years from 1989 to 1993.

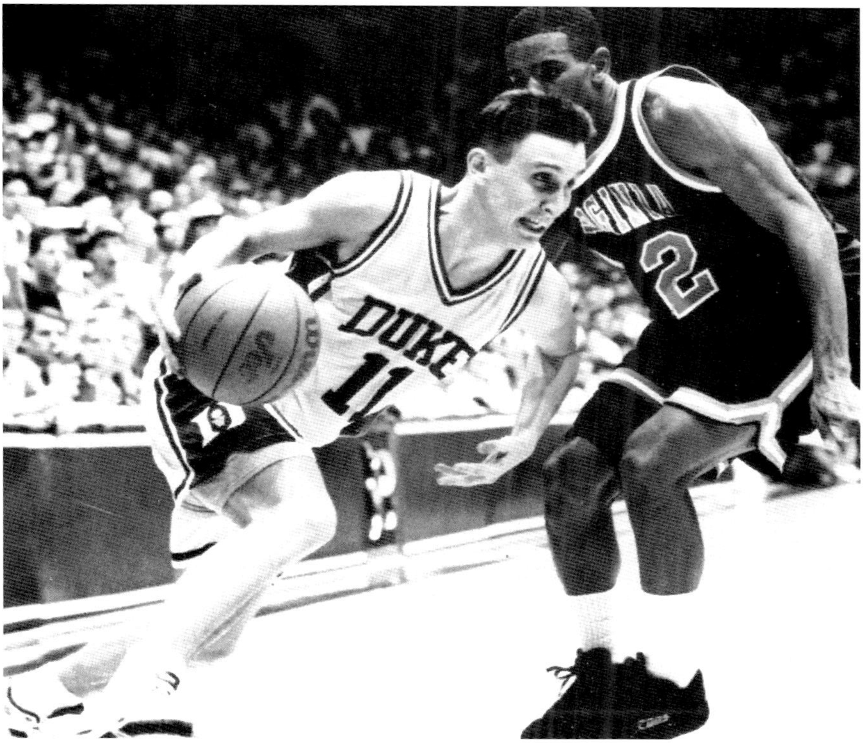

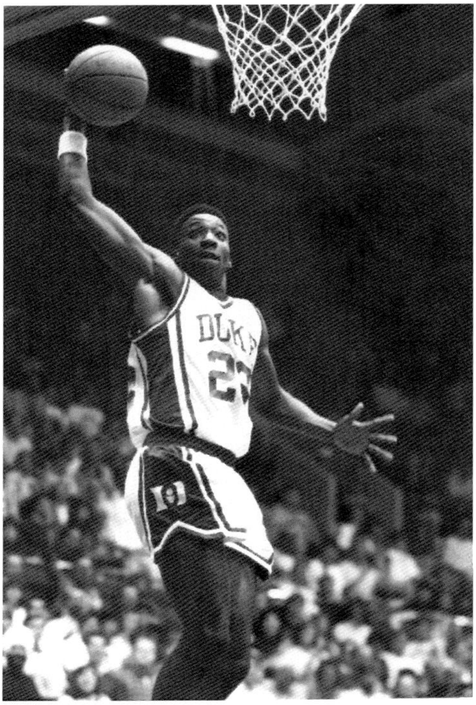

Few players in the history of college basketball played on more successful teams during their careers than Brian Davis. From 1988 to 1992, Davis's Duke teams won two national titles, went to four Final Fours and had a 21-2 record in the NCAA Tournament. A big part of that success belongs to the leadership of Davis. Davis scored 30 points during his senior year in a game against Clemson, finishing with an average of 11.2 a game. Now involved with Christian Laettner in a commercial development company called Blue Devil Ventures, Davis played one season in the NBA. *Courtesy of Duke Sports Information.*

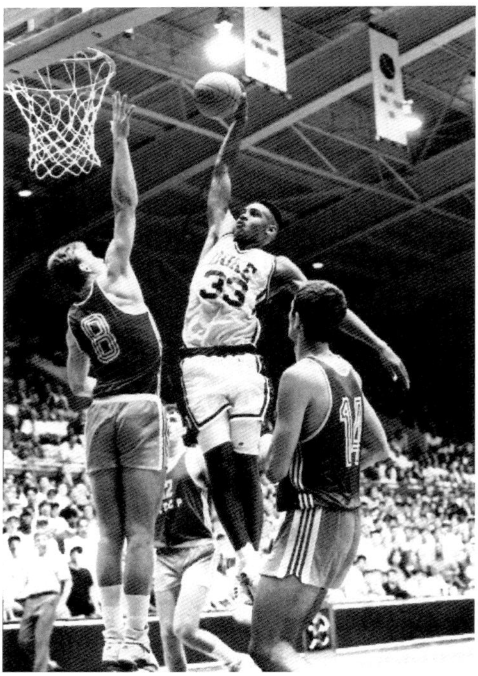

Perhaps the most athletic player in Duke history, Grant Hill could do everything on a basketball court that needed to be done. Win? There were two national championships and three Final Fours in his career from 1990 to 1994. Score? A career total of 1,924. Rebound? An average of 6 a game in his career. Pass? A career total of 461 assists. Defense? Was national defensive player of the year in 1992–93. Still playing in the NBA, Hill has made six All-Star teams.

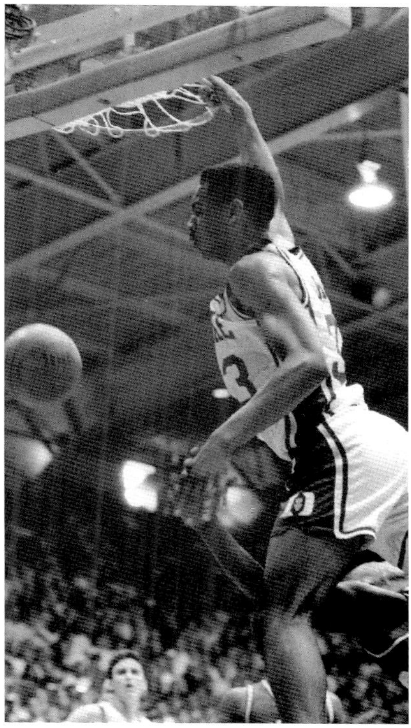

A Maryland player takes a vicious dunk from Duke's Grant Hill during this 1991 game. Hill is one of the most acclaimed players in Duke history, and Duke experienced phenomenal success during his career from 1990 to 1994. Hill was playing for the NBA's Phoenix Suns in 2008.

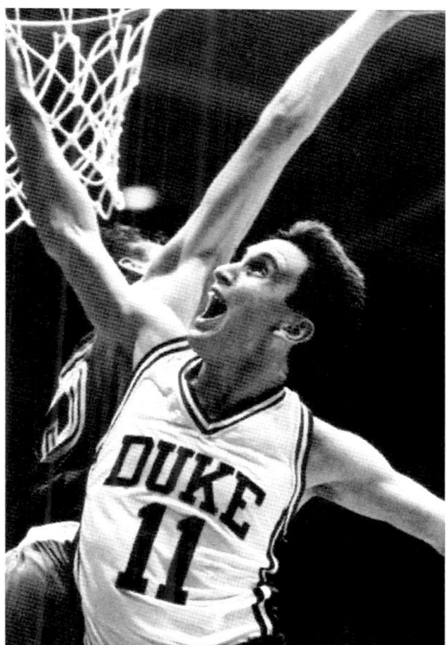

During his Duke years from 1989 to 1993, Bobby Hurley set the NCAA career assists record with 1,076. In a 1993 game against Florida State, Hurley set the Duke single game record with 16 assists. Hurley could also score, averaging 17 points a game in his senior year. In his four years, Duke won 119 games, won two national titles and played in three national championship games. After being selected as the seventh pick of the NBA draft, Hurley was involved in a traffic accident that eventually forced him to retire after five seasons.

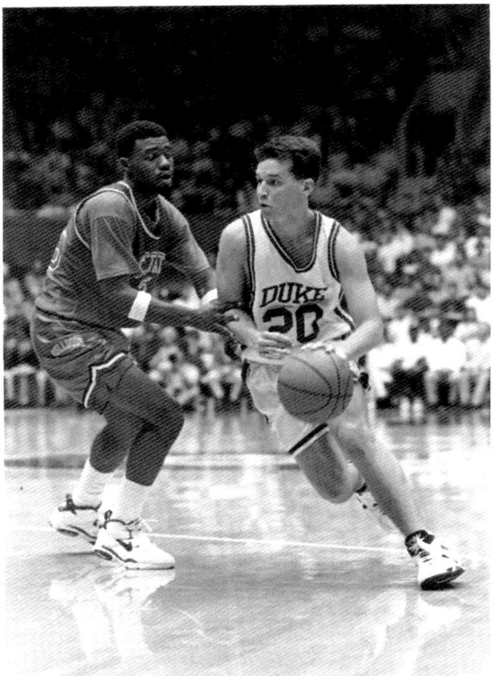

Chris Collins is now an assistant coach at Duke, but before becoming a coach, Collins had an outstanding playing career for the Blue Devils from 1992 to 1996. A valuable player for Coach Mike Krzyzewski all four of his years, Collins probably had his best season as a senior. That year, he averaged 16.3 points a game, made the All-ACC second team and scored 30 points against Iowa. Chris is the son of former NBA player and coach Doug Collins. *Courtesy of Duke Sports Information.*

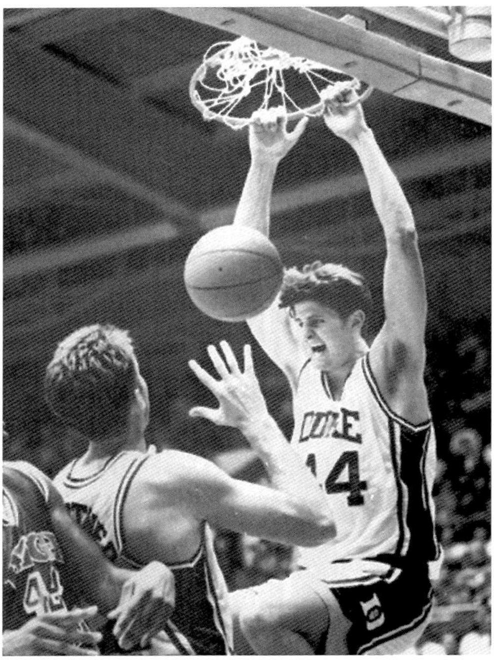

During his senior year of 1995, Cherokee Parks averaged 19 points and 9 rebounds a game. In 1994, in a game against Clemson, Parks blocked 10 shots, then a Duke record, since tied by Shelden Williams. Nicknamed "Chief," Parks went on to play nine seasons in the NBA.

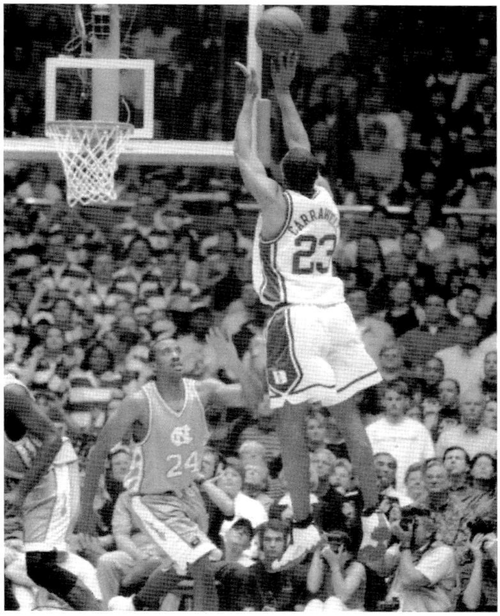

Chris Carrawell had a great career at Duke during his years of 1996 to 2000, but really blossomed during his senior year. That year he averaged 16.9 points and 6.1 rebounds, earning ACC Player of the Year and All-America. Duke won 122 games against only 20 losses in his four seasons. *Courtesy of Duke Sports Information.*

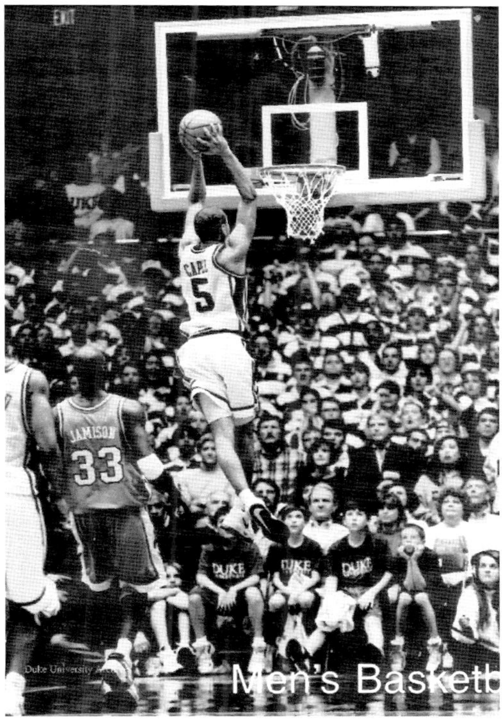

Duke fans will long remember Jeff Capel for his versatility, as he averaged 12.4 points a game for his career, while grabbing 390 rebounds and compiling 433 assists. Capel was a member of the 1993–94 team that lost to Arkansas in the national championship game. Jeff's brother, Jason, played for Duke's arch rival, the Tar Heels of the University of North Carolina. Capel is now the head coach of the Oklahoma Sooners.

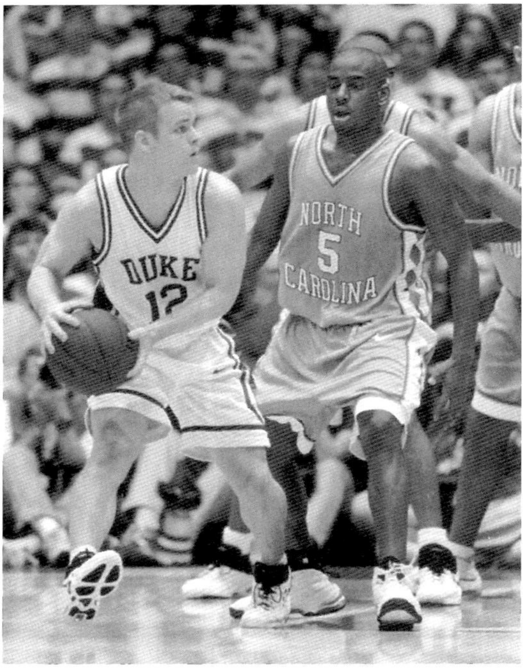

Steve Wojciechowski led the ACC in steals in 1997 and was named national defensive player of the year in 1998. Wojo, as he is affectionately known, seemed to play his best against UNC, dishing out 11 assists in a win over them in 1998, and scoring a career high 18 points in another game against the Tar Heels. Wojciechowski is now an assistant coach for the Blue Devils.

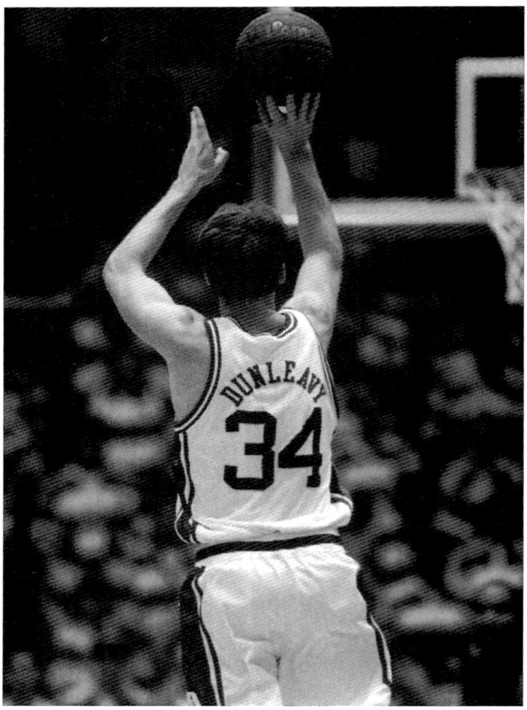

Duke won three ACC Tournament titles and a national championship in Mike Dunleavy's three years from 1999 to 2002. In his junior season, Dunleavy averaged 17.3 points and 7.2 rebounds, led Duke in blocked shots and was second on the team in steals, as he was chosen All-America. Dunleavy left early for the NBA, was selected as the third pick in the draft and is now one of the up and coming stars of the league, currently playing for the Indiana Pacers.

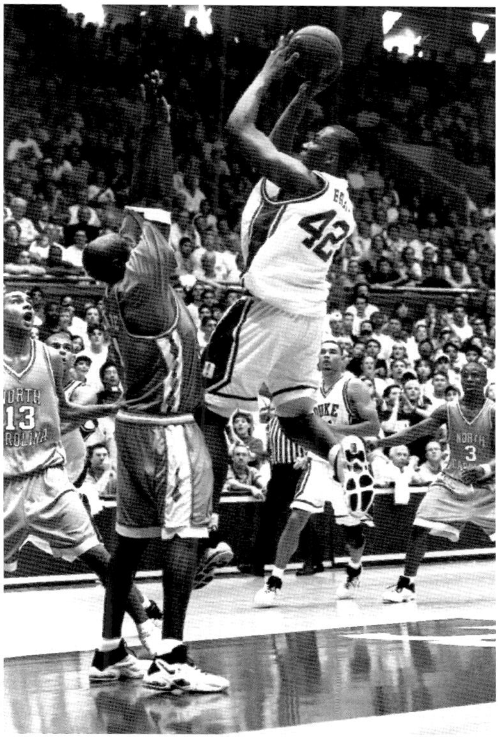

Right: Elton Brand certainly left his mark at Duke, despite his short career of two years. Brand was national player of the year in 1998–99, as he took Duke to the national title game while scoring 17.7 points and 9.8 rebounds a game. Brand had perhaps his best game against Fresno State, scoring 21 points and pulling down 21 rebounds. Chosen as one of the fifty best players in ACC history, Brand was the first pick in the 1999 NBA draft, and has since made three All-Star teams. *Courtesy of Duke Sports Information.*

Below: Despite a tragic motorcycle accident in 2003 that for the time being has ended his NBA career, Jason Williams was one of the greatest players in Duke basketball history. Duke posted 95 wins and only 13 losses in Williams's three seasons from 1999 to 2002, winning the national title in 2001 over Arizona. Williams graduated after three seasons at Duke and was the number two pick of the 2002 NBA draft.

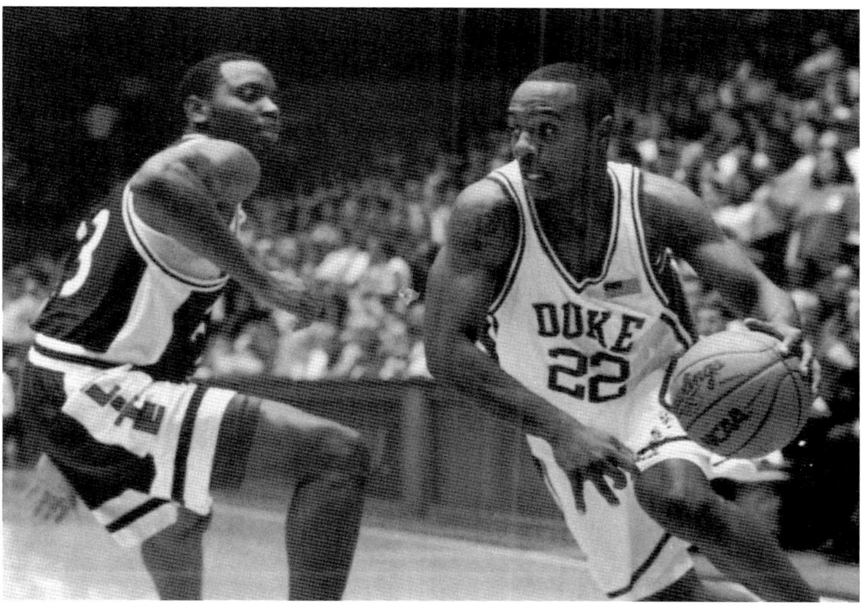

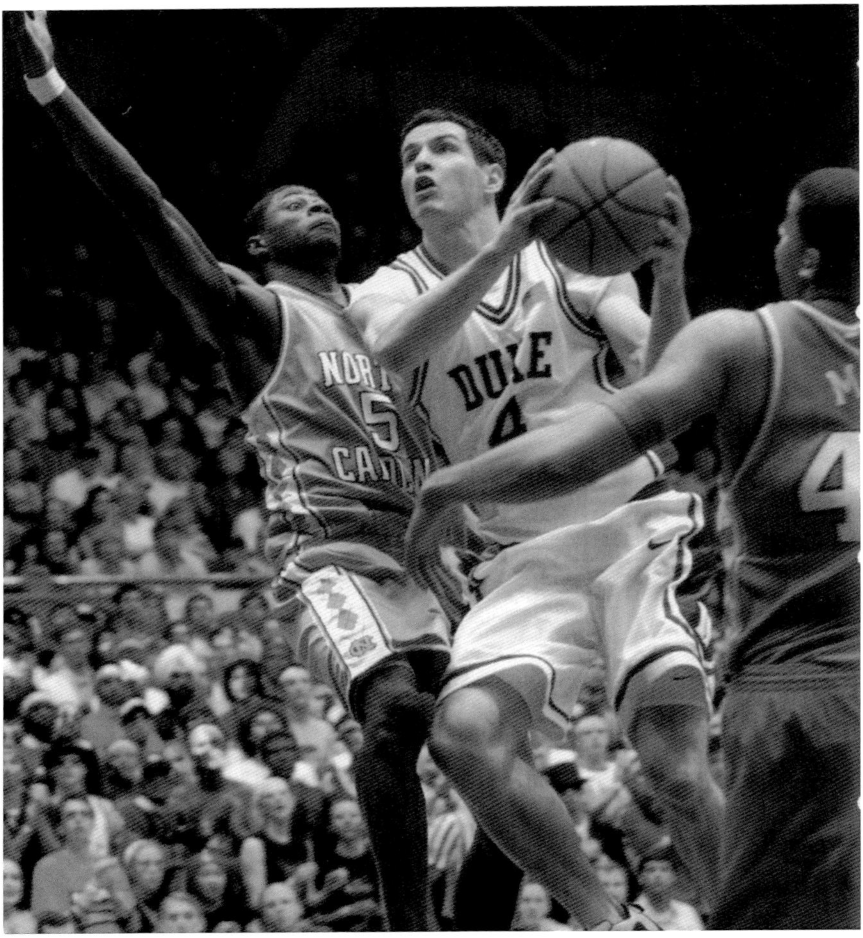

Called the best pure shooter he ever coached by Mike Krzyzewski, J.J. Redick was one of the most outstanding players to ever play in the ACC. During Redick's four seasons in Duke blue, the Blue Devils won 116 games with only 23 losses, winning 3 ACC Tournament championships and reaching 1 Final Four. Redick finished his career as the top scorer in Duke history, with 2,769 points. His 91.2 percent mark on free throws is the best in ACC history and the best in NCAA history for players making at least 600 shots. He once made 54 free throws in a row. His 26.8 points a game in his senior year of 2005–06 is the best in Duke history, topping Bob Verga's 26.1 in 1967 and Dick Groat's 26 in 1952. Redick now plays for the Orlando Magic of the NBA.

Chapter 5

TEAMS

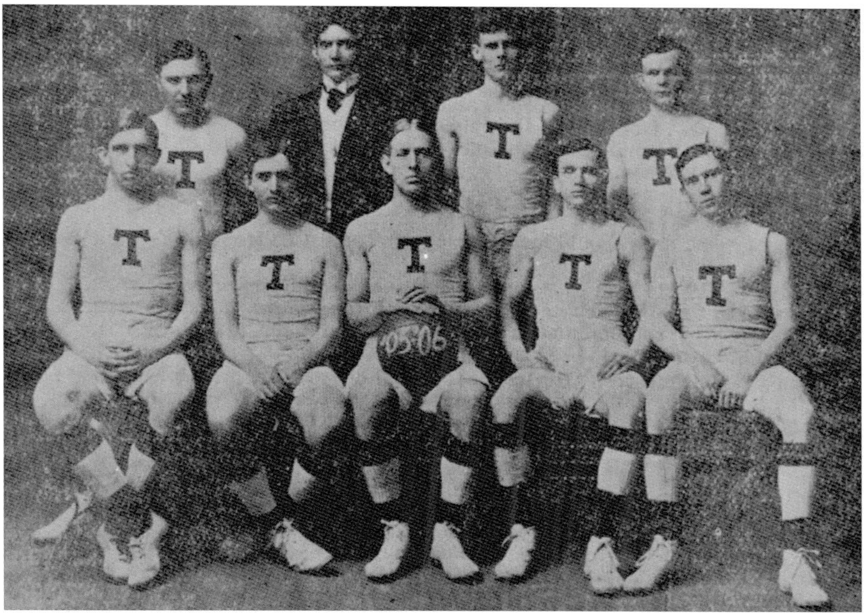

This the first team in Duke basketball history. This team won 2 and lost 3 in the 1905–06 season. Both wins came against Trinity Park, and Duke lost once to Trinity Park and twice to Wake Forest. Thad Stem Sr. from nearby Oxford, North Carolina, holding the ball in the photo, was the first captain in Duke basketball history. From this inaugural season, Duke is now one of the most successful college programs ever, having won 1,849 games with 810 losses heading into the 2008–09 season.

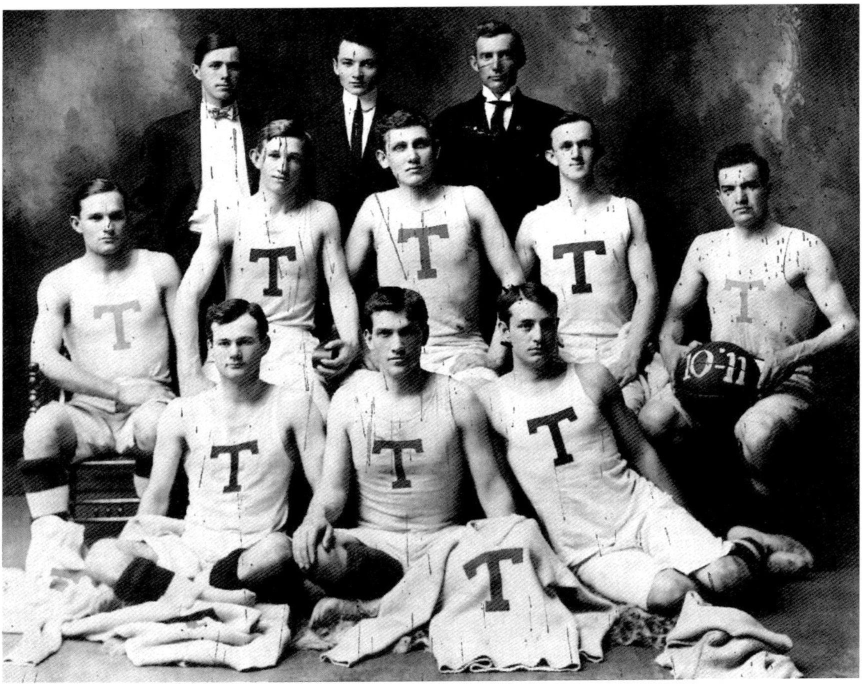

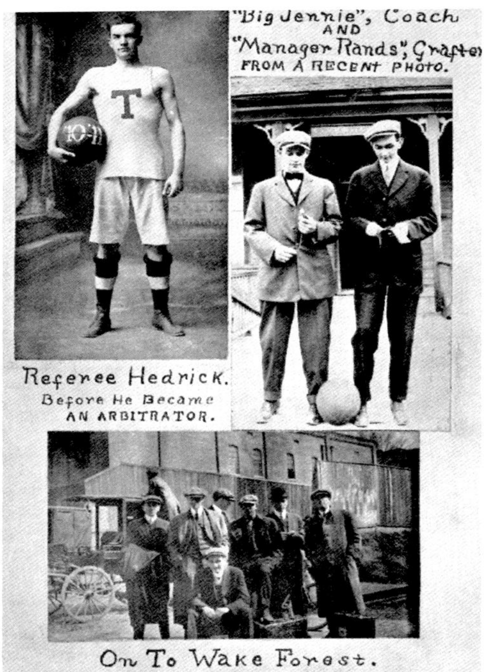

Above: Wilbur "Cap" Card led Trinity, now Duke, to 4 wins and 3 losses in the 1910–11 season. Two wins came against the Charlotte Athletic Club, along with one each against Tennessee and Virginia Military Institute. "Bull" Hedrick served as captain. Hedrick later became a law professor at Trinity.

Left: Finishing 6 and 1, the 1911–12 team helped to establish the great tradition for future Duke teams to follow. This Cap Card team beat Virginia Christian 69 to 9 and Elon 47 to 12. The captain of this team was Claude Brinn; he was the brother of Joseph Brinn, who had played for Duke on the 1909–10 and 1910–11 teams. Joseph Brinn became head coach at Duke in the 1912–13 season, winning 11 and losing 8 in his only season as coach.

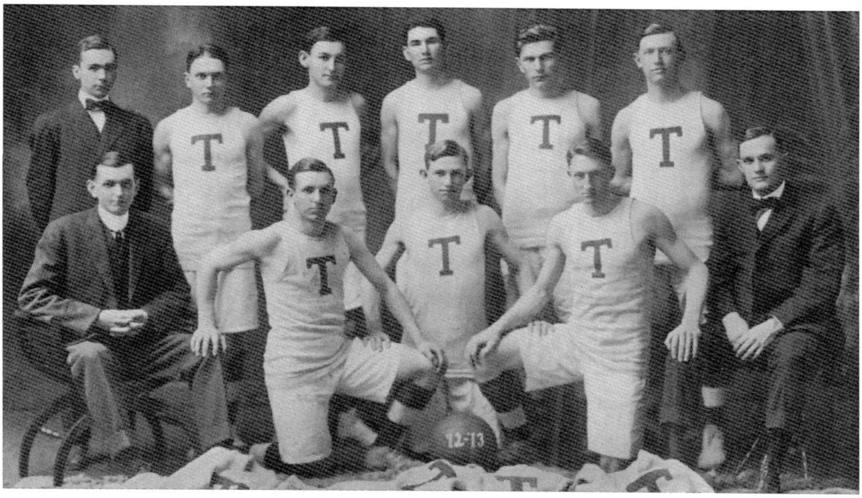

The 1912–13 team won 11 and lost 8. Joseph Brinn was the coach and his brother Claude was team captain.

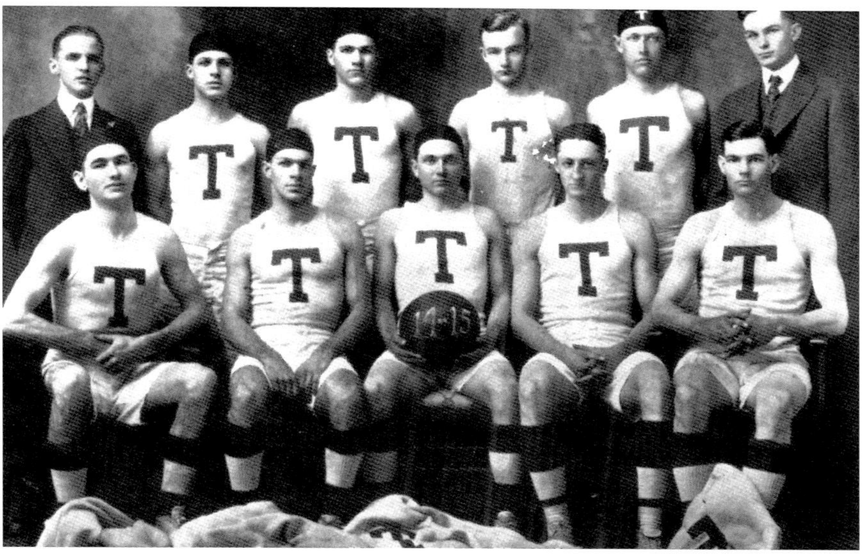

Coach Noble Clay led Trinity to a 10 and 10 record in the 1914–15 season. Clay, while coaching at Trinity in the 1913–14 and 1914–15 seasons, also served as captain and played for the Durham YMCA team. When Trinity played the YMCA, Noble actually played against the very team he coached, letting his Trinity captains do the in-game coaching. Well, Coach Clay beat Player Clay, as Trinity won both games. In another game, Trinity routed Carson-Newman 70–4!

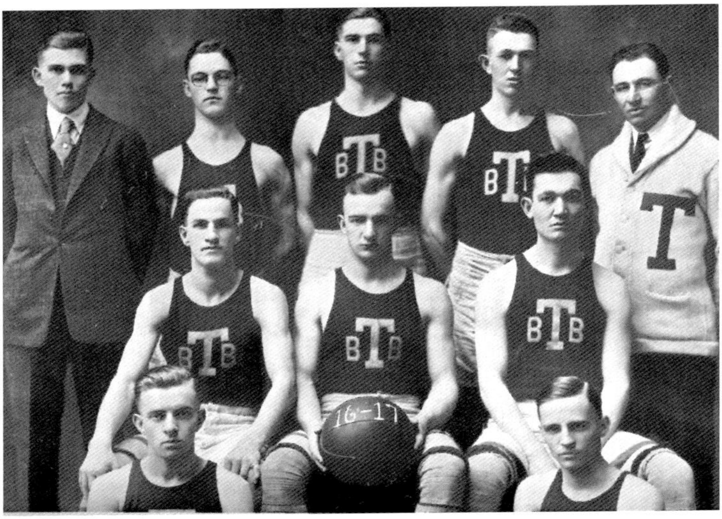

Under head coach Chick Doak, Duke won 20 and lost 4 during the 1916–17 season. Doak had previously coached at UNC, and would go on to a long coaching career at NC State, where the Wolfpack's baseball stadium, Doak Field, is named for him. Doak also coached the 1917–18 Duke team, and finished his two years at Duke with a record of 30 wins and 9 losses. His winning percentage is second only to Coach K in Duke men's basketball history.

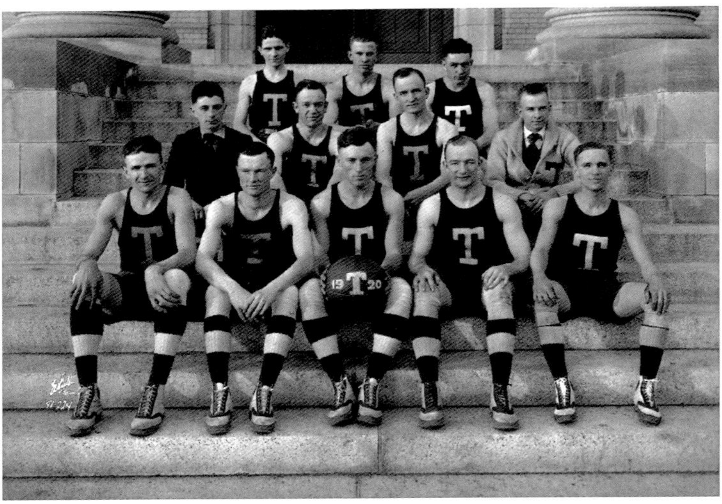

Coach Floyd Egan led the 1920–21 team to a 9 and 6 record. Egan also served as head coach of football at Duke in 1920, the first year for the sport on campus after a twenty-five-year ban. Loyd Hathaway, from Hobbsville, North Carolina, served as captain of this team.

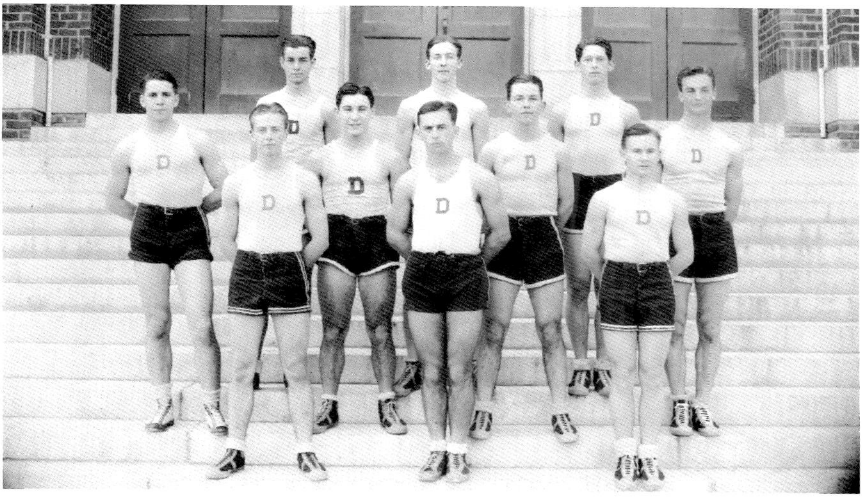

The Duke team of 1923–24 is outside Alumni Memorial Gym. The first game at Alumni was held in January of 1924, a season in which Duke finished 19 and 6 behind Coach Jesse Burbage and captain Everett Spikes. Burbage coached Duke for two seasons only, but compiled a win-loss record of 34 and 13. A native of Birmingham, Alabama, he coached a Birmingham high school team to a state title in 1919. Spikes was from Durham, North Carolina, and in addition to being captain and leading scorer on the 1924 basketball team, he also hit .532 as a senior on the baseball team. Spikes later became superintendent of city schools in Burlington, North Carolina.

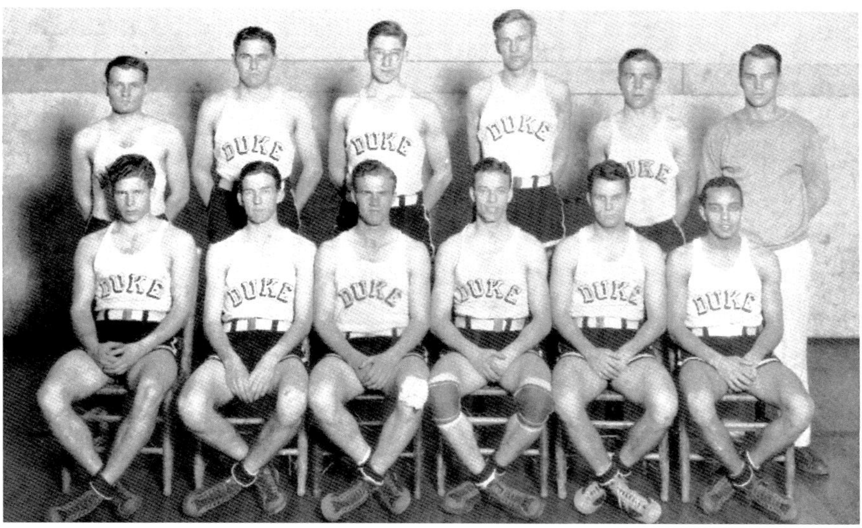

The 1928–29 team finished with a record of 12 and 8. This was Eddie Cameron's first team at Duke, and he would go on to win 226 games, holding the Duke record for most wins by a coach until Mike Krzyzewski passed him in 1990.

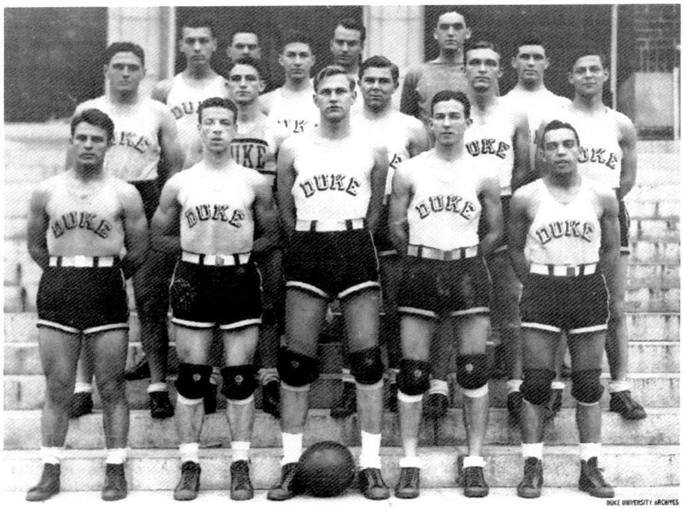

The 1929–30 team won 18 and lost only 2. Coached by Eddie Cameron, Bill Werber became Duke's first All-America basketball player in this season. Harry Councilor made All-Southern Conference, along with Werber. Joe Croson made second team All-Southern. Croson is front row, third from the left. Werber is front row, second from left.

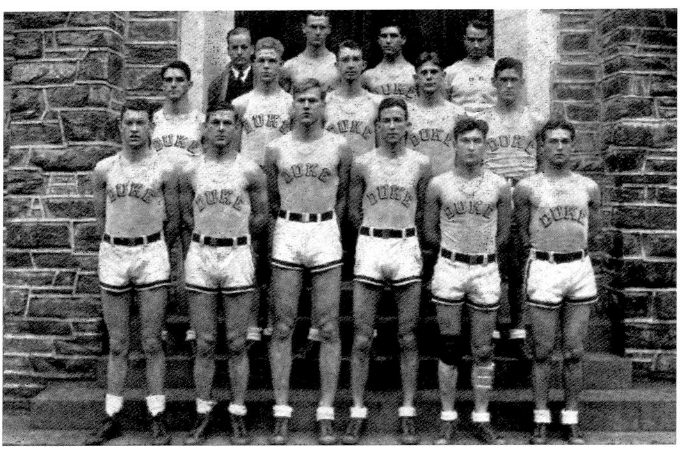

The 1930–31 team finished 14 and 7 under coach Eddie Cameron. Joe Croson is in the front row, third from the left, while George Rogers is front row, fourth from the left. Croson was six feet, four inches, and led Duke in scoring in each of his three varsity seasons. Rogers was from Asheville, North Carolina, and served as co-captain with Croson on the 1930–31 team. Rogers scored the very first basket in Card Gym when it opened in 1930 in a game against Villanova. Coach Eddie Cameron is shown in this picture on the back row, farthest to the right.

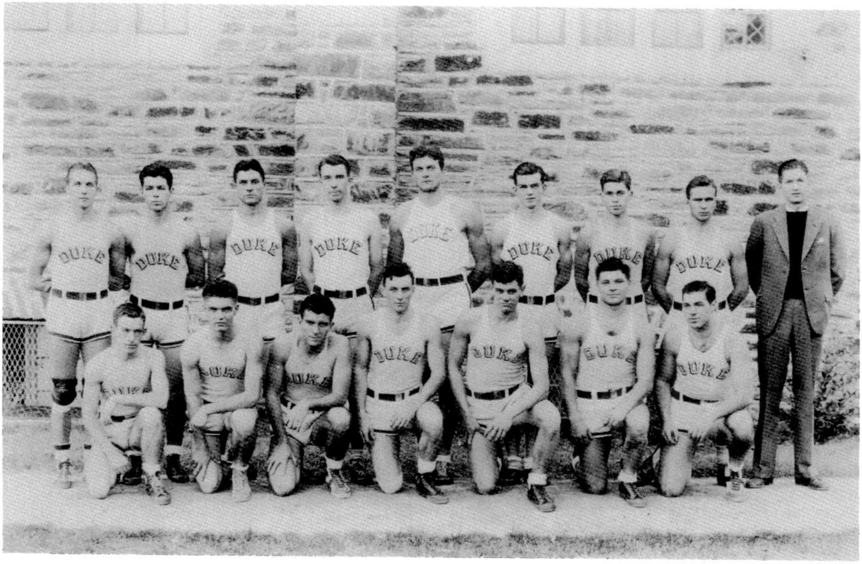

The 1932–33 team went 17 and 5 under Eddie Cameron. Jim Thompson led Duke in scoring for three straight years, from 1932 to 1934. Thompson held the career scoring record at Duke until 1945, when Gordon Carver passed him. Jim played with his brother Herb at Duke. The Thompson boys were from Washington, D.C.

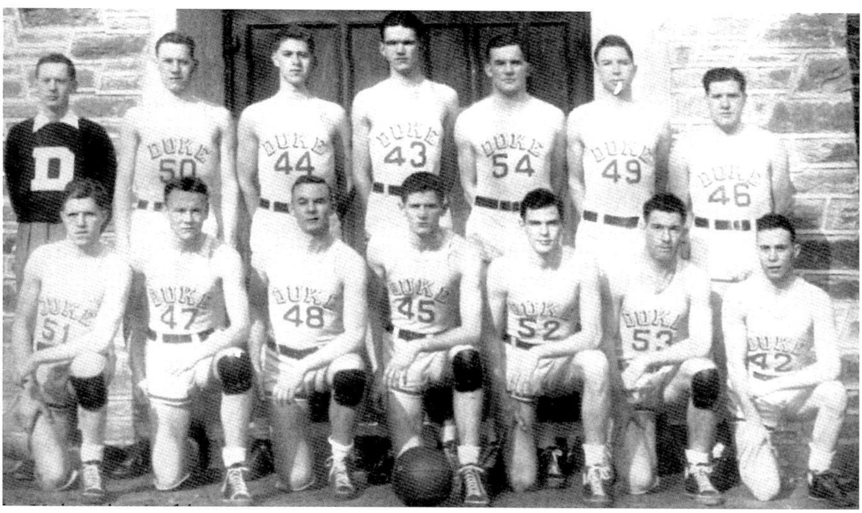

The 1935–36 team won 20 and lost only 6. The top scorer was Ken Podger, a five-foot, nine-inch guard from Kenmore, New York. Charles Kunkle served as captain.

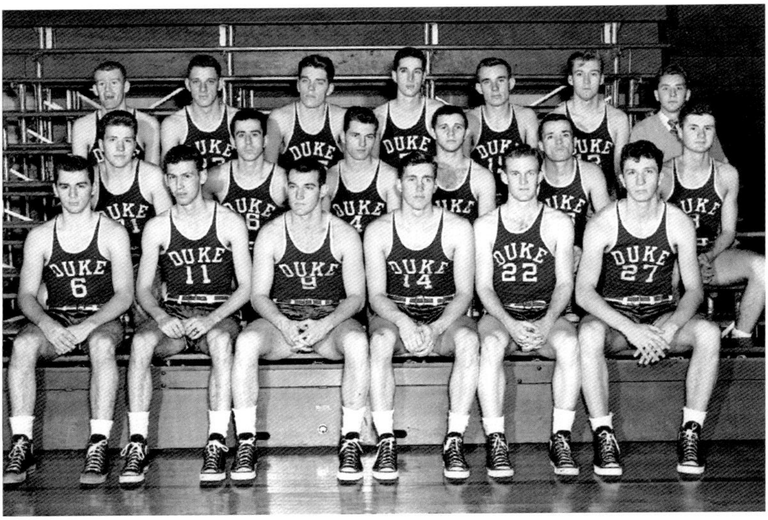

The 1948–49 team finished 13 and 9 under Gerry Gerard. Corren Youmans led Duke in scoring with 11.5 a game, followed by Ben Collins at 9.8. Youmans made first team All-Southern Conference.

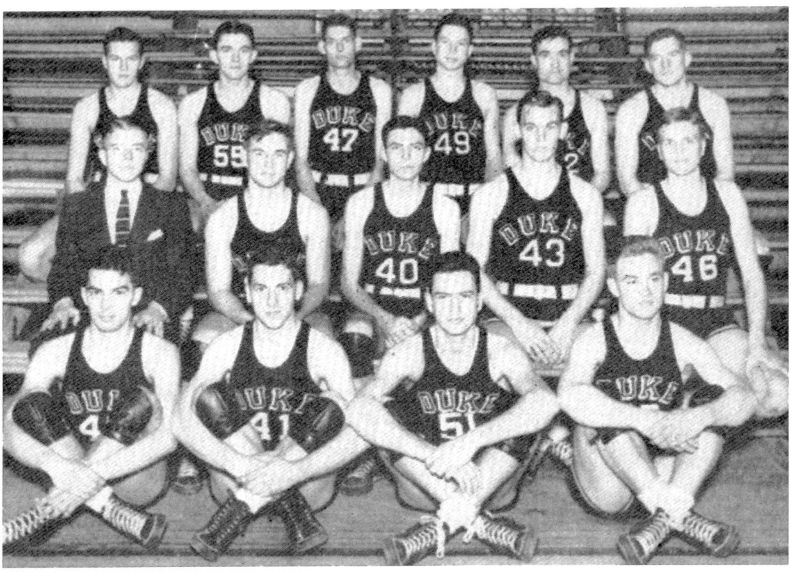

Fred Edwards served as a captain and made All-Southern conference in the 1937–38 season, as Duke went 15 and 9 and won the Southern Conference Tournament. Duke beat NC State, Maryland and then Clemson to claim its first conference tournament championship in history. Eddie Cameron coached this team. Ed Swindell, from Durham, led Duke in scoring for the year, and had a team high of 14 in the tournament championship game against Clemson.

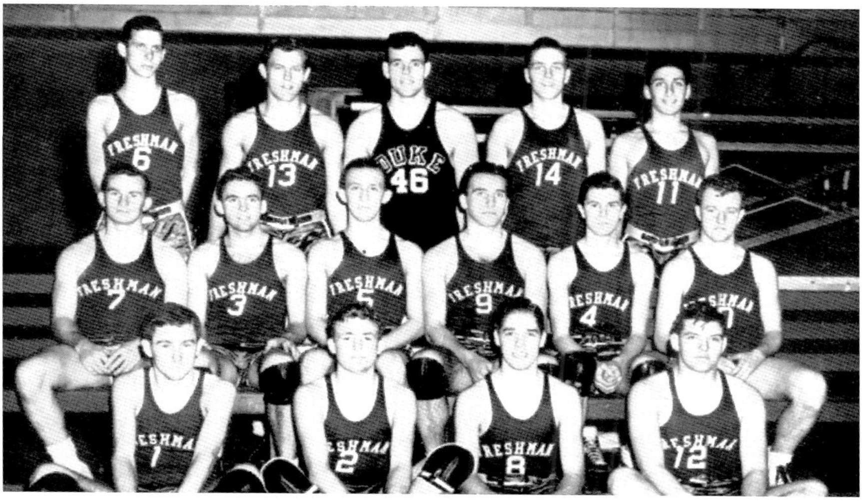

Pictured here is the 1941 freshman team.

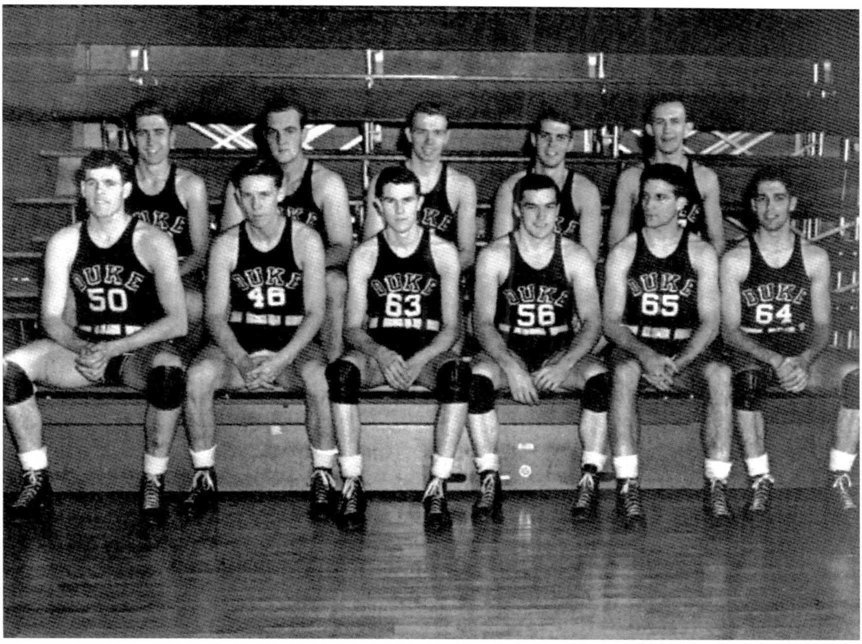

Here is the 1943 Duke basketball team.

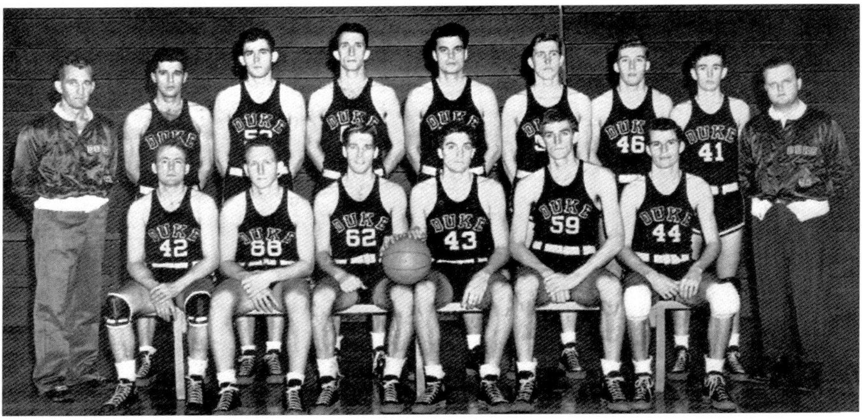

Coach Gerry Gerard led Duke to a 19 and 8 record in the 1946–47 season. Included were wins over Hanes Hosiery, Temple and the Quantico Marines. Duke lost to New York Univeristy in Madison Square Garden 64 to 61 in two overtimes in front of eighteen thousand fans. Ed Koffenberger scored 15.4 points a game while garnering All-America honors. John Seward served as a captain of this team. Seward, while serving in the army during World War II, was captured by the Germans and held in a prisoner of war camp for seventy-one days.

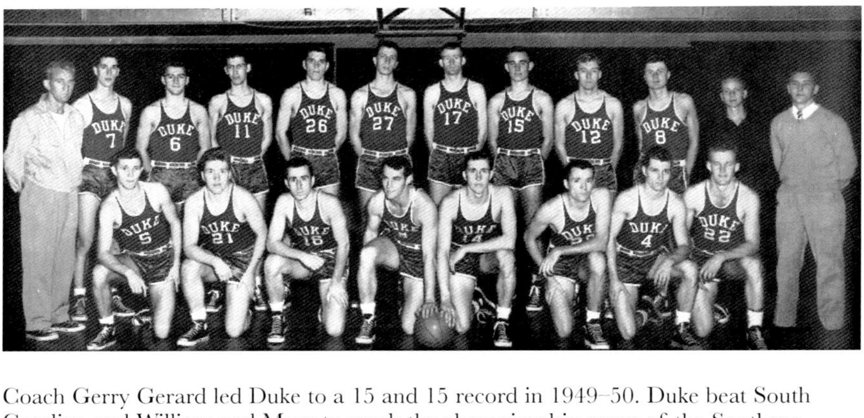

Coach Gerry Gerard led Duke to a 15 and 15 record in 1949–50. Duke beat South Carolina and William and Mary to reach the championship game of the Southern Conference Tournament, where it lost to NC State. Duke was invited to play in the NIT, where it lost to Pennsylvania at the Palestra in Philadelphia. This season was Dick Groat's first campaign at Duke, and he led the team with a 14.5 scoring average. Corren Youmans averaged 11.7 points a game.

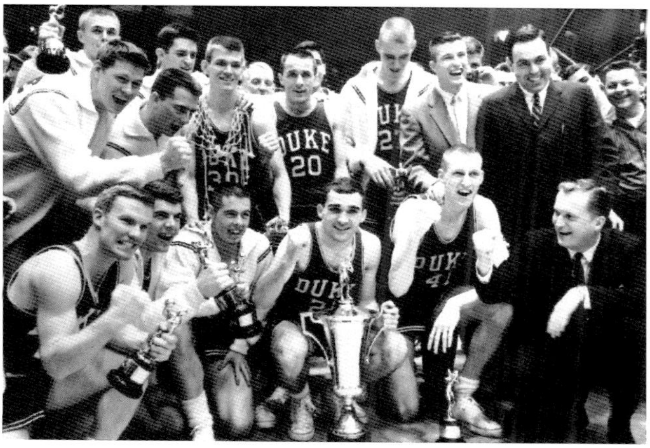

The 1959–60 season was Vic Bubas's first team at Duke, and he started his career there with a bang, winning the ACC Tournament Championship with wins over South Carolina, North Carolina and Wake Forest. In the win over North Carolina, Carroll Youngkin of Duke scored 30 points and grabbed 17 rebounds in a sparkling performance against the rival Tar Heels. Youngkin, six feet, six inches, and from Winston-Salem, North Carolina, is in the back row holding a trophy. Coach Bubas is on the far right of the front row, and Bucky Waters, an assistant coach at that time who later became Duke's head coach, is sixth from the left on the second row.

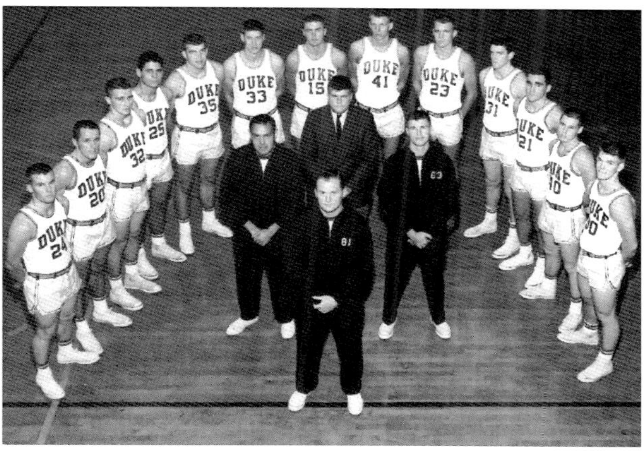

In Vic Bubas's first year as head coach, in 1959–60, Duke finished 17 and 11. Duke won the ACC Tournament Championship by defeating Wake Forest in the final, as Doug Kistler scored 22. Howard Hurt and Carroll Youngkin led this team in scoring, with both averaging 13.4 points per game. Duke, under Coach Bubas, would go on to play in three Final Fours in the six seasons following 1959–60.

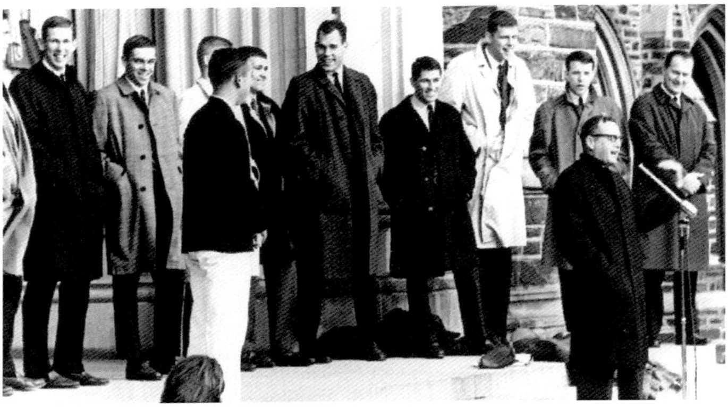

The 1963–64 team reached the NCAA championship game, losing to UCLA 98 to 83. Here they are shown getting a big send-off to the tournament. For the season, Duke finished 26 and 5 and was number three in the final AP poll. From the 1960–61 season to the 1965–66 season, Duke was one of the best programs in the nation under Vic Bubas. During those six seasons, Duke won 136 games with 28 losses, finishing in the final top ten AP poll each year and playing in 3 Final Fours.

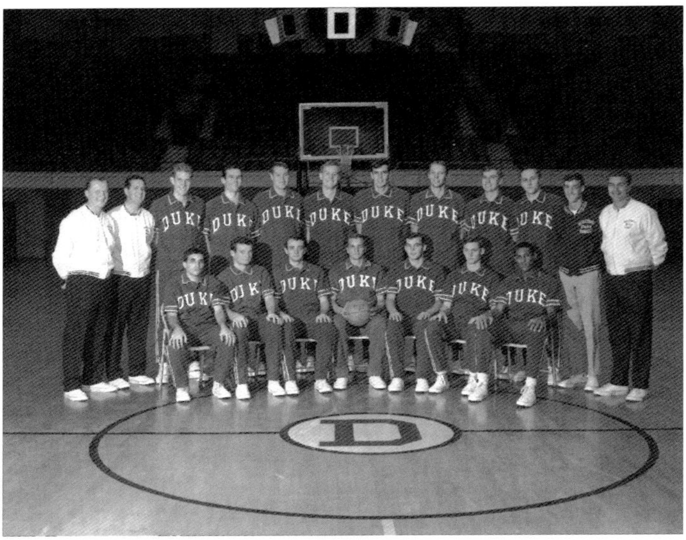

Finishing with a 22 and 6 record, the 1967–68 Blue Devils team reached the second round of the NIT. In an exciting game in Cameron Indoor Stadium, Duke beat UNC 87 to 86, as Mike Lewis scored 18 points and hauled in 18 rebounds. UNC was ranked third in the nation at that time. The six-foot, seven-inch, 225-pound Lewis, from Missoula, Montana, averaged 21.7 points and 14.4 rebounds for the season. Dave Golden averaged 13.1 points a game for this team.

1986-87 Duke Blue Devils

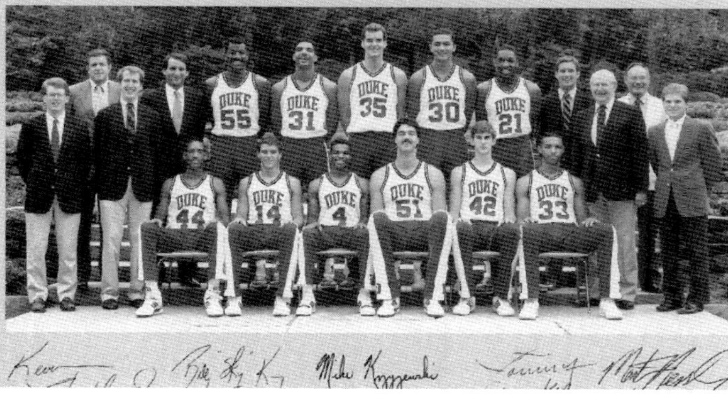

The 1986–87 team defeated Texas A&M and Xavier in the first two rounds of the NCAA Tournament, before losing to Indiana 88 to 82. Duke finished 24 and 9 for the season. Danny Ferry led the team in scoring with 14 points a game, with Tommy Amaker next at 12.3. Amaker also won the national defensive player of the year award. John Smith had a team season high of 28 points against Clemson. Ferry had 20 points and 19 rebounds in a game at Maryland.

'SPANARKS' AND OUR GANG

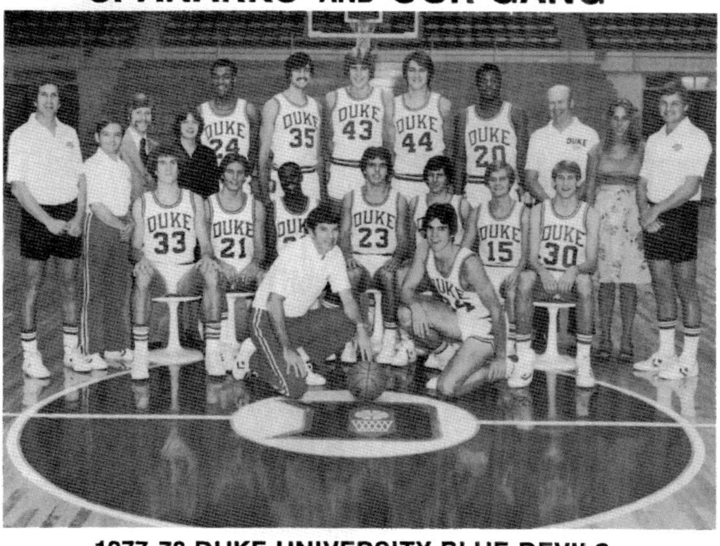

1977-78 DUKE UNIVERSITY BLUE DEVILS

Led by All-Americans Jim Spanarkel and Mike Gminski, and ACC Rookie of the Year Gene Banks, Duke won 27 and lost 7 in 1977–78. Duke, coached by Bill Foster, won the ACC Tournament. It also reached the NCAA championship game, where it lost to Kentucky 94 to 88.

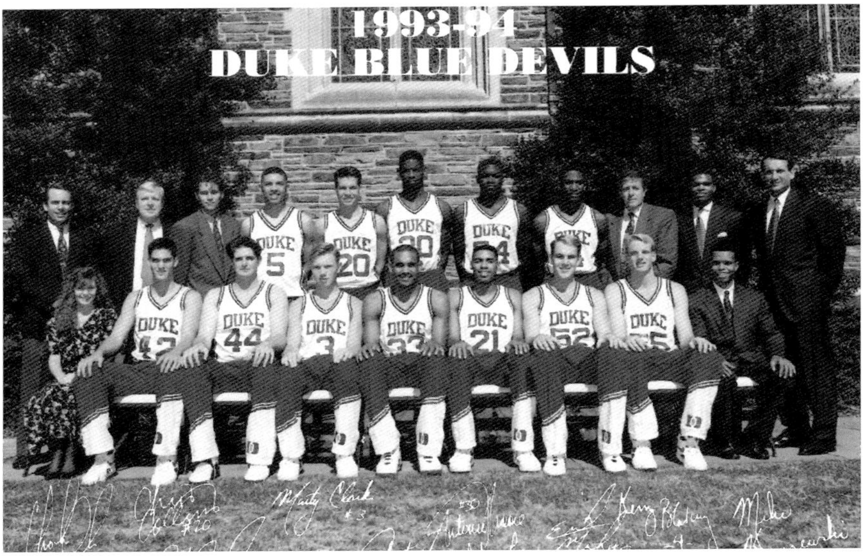

The 1993–94 team finished 28 and 6 and played in the national championship game, losing to Arkansas 76 to 72. Grant Hill led the team in scoring, with 17.4 points a game, and made first team All-America.

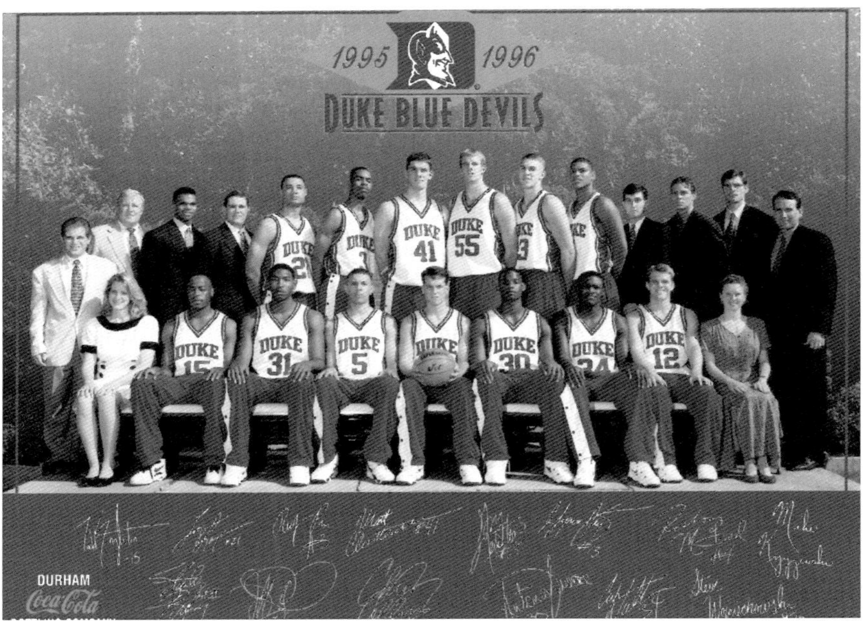

The 1995–96 team finished 18 and 13. Jeff Capel led Duke in scoring, with 16.6 points per game, while Chris Collins averaged 16.3.

Chapter 6

GAME ACTION

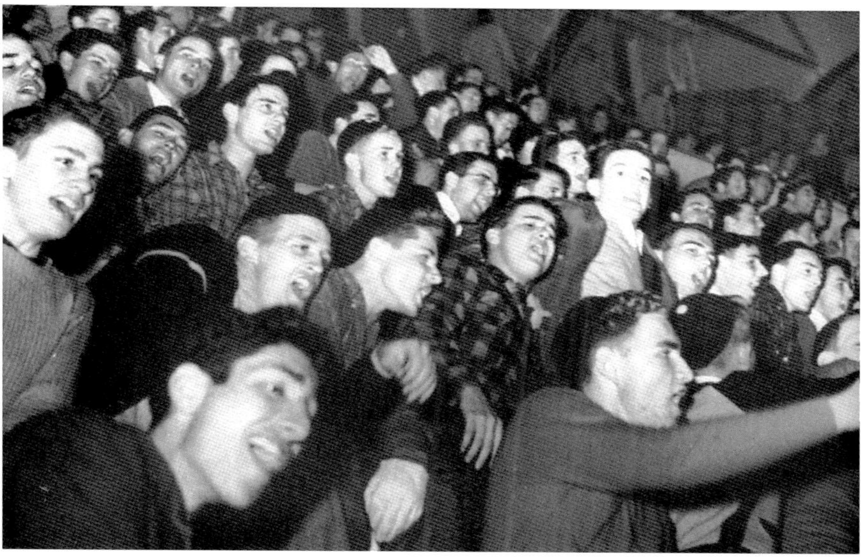

Duke basketball fans have always shown their passionate support for their Blue Devils. This photograph is from a game in Cameron Indoor Stadium in 1941.

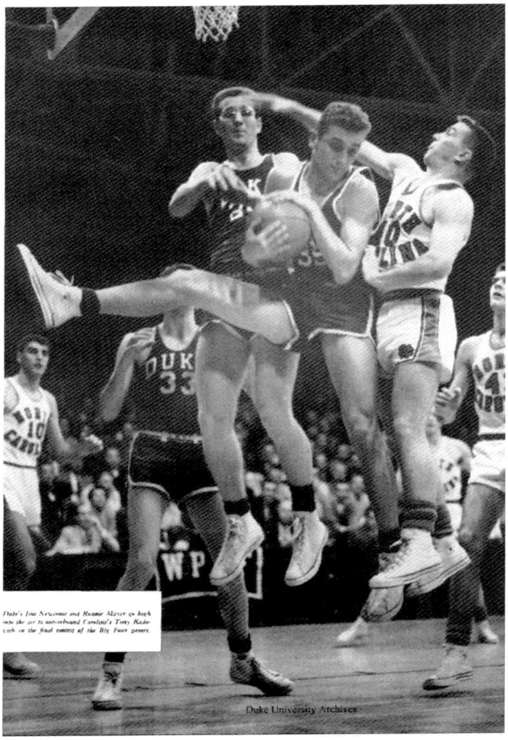

Left: Shown is game action in 1956, when Harold Bradley was coach. One member of this team was Joe Belmont, a five-foot, eleven-inch guard from Philadelphia, who made first team All-ACC as he averaged 17 points a game. Later in life, Belmont served as head coach of the Denver Rockets of the ABA, and was coach of the year in 1970.

Below: Duke students cheer their Blue Devils inside Cameron Indoor Stadium in 1943. Cameron was called Duke Indoor Stadium at that time.

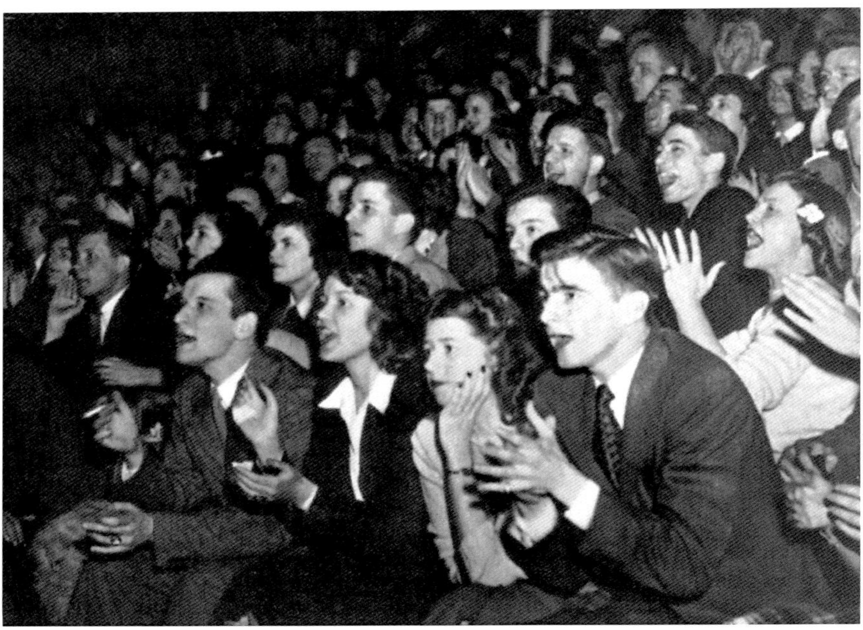

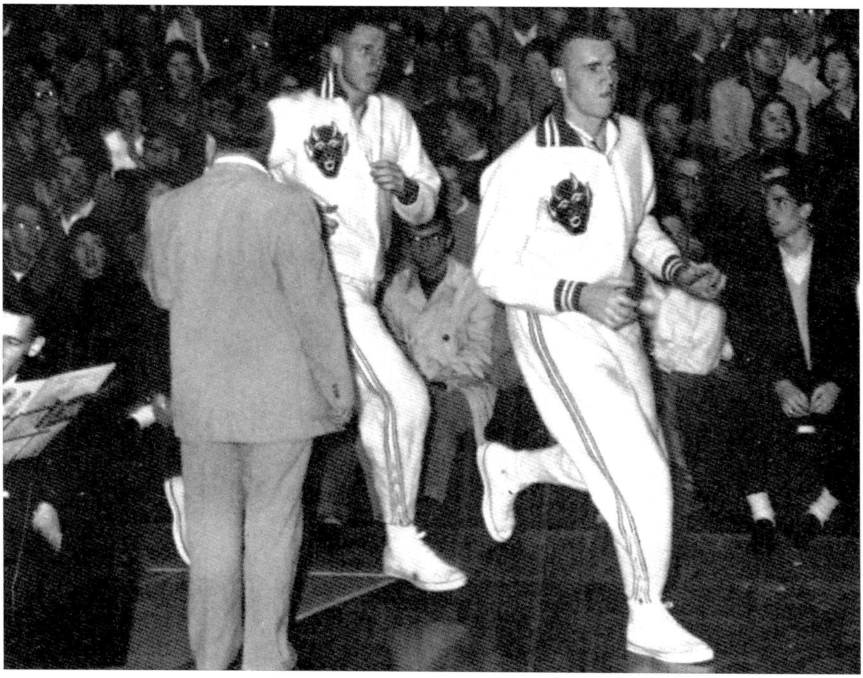

Carroll Youngkin and Doug Kistler take the court in 1959 for a game against Maryland in Duke Indoor Stadium. The 1958–59 team, coached by Harold Bradley, won 13 and lost 12. Youngkin led Duke in scoring at 15.9 points per game, while Howard Hurt averaged 15.7 per game.

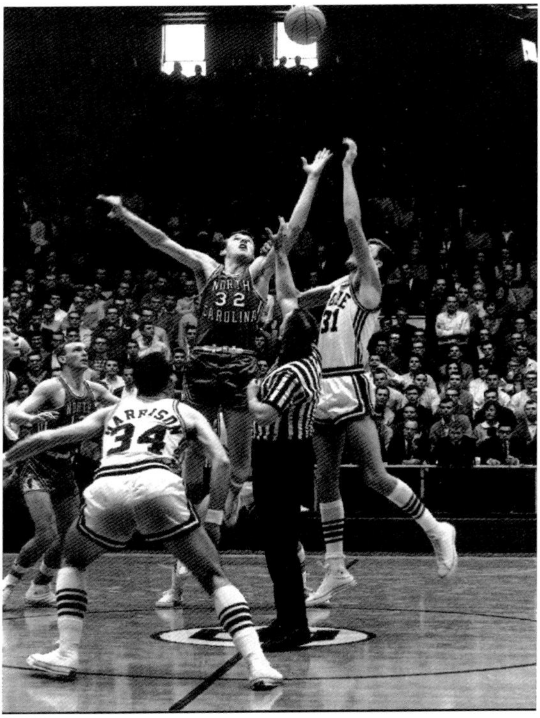

Billy Cunningham of UNC jumps for the tipoff in this game against Duke in 1963. Duke won this matchup 106 to 93 in a duel between two great All-American players, Cunningham and Duke's Art Heyman. Heyman got the best of it, scoring 40 points and grabbing 24 rebounds, while Cunningham held his own, scoring 31 and pulling down 16 rebounds. Cunningham went on to a great NBA career after averaging 24.8 points and 15.4 rebounds in his three varsity years at UNC, from 1962–63 to 1964–65.

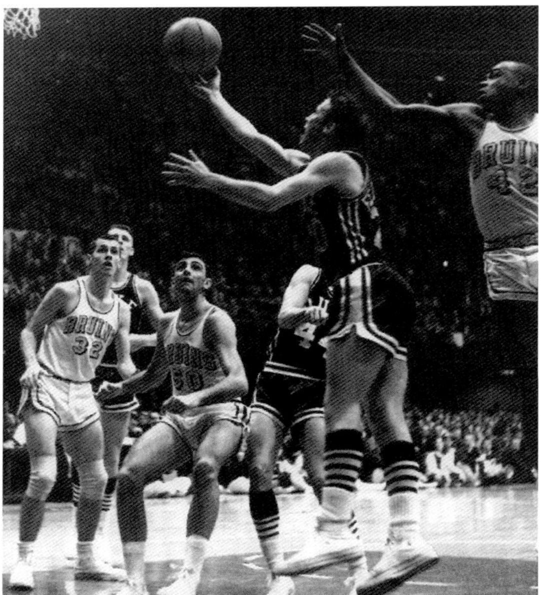

Duke University Archives

Duke played UCLA for the national championship in 1964. Duke beat Villanova, Connecticut and Michigan to reach the title game with UCLA, to whom it lost 98 to 83, despite Jeff Mullins scoring 22 points. For the season, Duke won 26 and lost 5. Mullins finished as the top scorer for Duke, with a 24.2 per game average. Mullins was ACC Player of the Year and second team All-American. Jay Buckley averaged 13.8 points and 9 rebounds a game. Buckley, a six-foot, ten-inch center from Maryland, along with being an outstanding player, also made two Academic All-America teams as well. Clay Buckley, Jay's son, was a member of Duke's 1991 national championship team.

Just like in any decade, the rivalry between Duke and UNC in the 1960s, as pictured here, was heated. Duke played in 3 Final Fours in the 1960s under Vic Bubas, while UNC under Dean Smith also participated in 3 Final Fours. Great players led UNC during the 1960s, such as Billy Cunningham, Charlie Scott and Larry Miller, while Duke was led by the likes of Art Heyman, Jeff Mullins, Bob Verga, Mike Lewis, Randy Denton and Jack Marin.

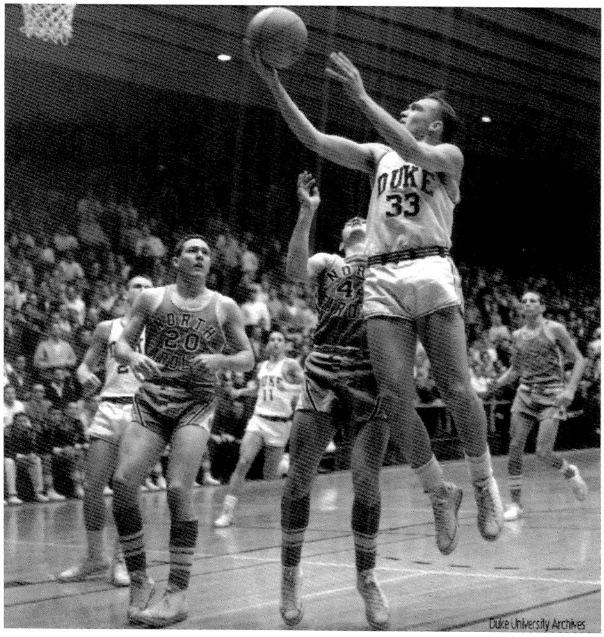
Duke University Archives

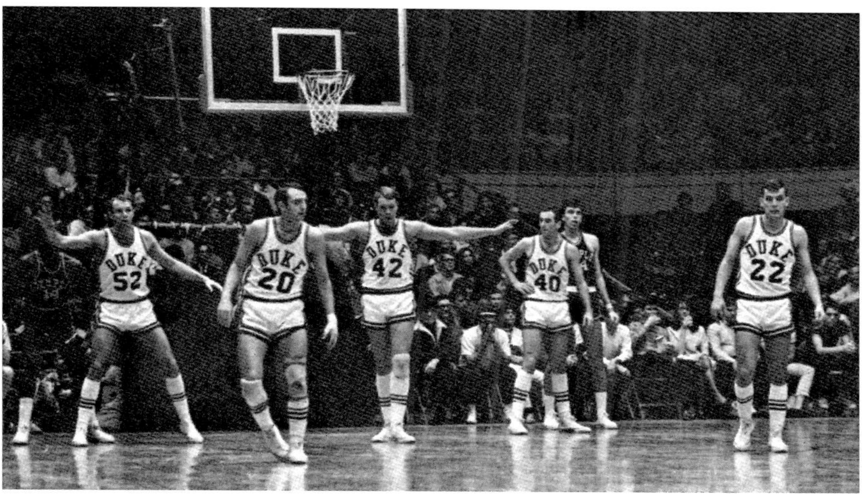

An imposing defense for Duke is ready for action against Temple in this game from 1968. Big number 42 is the "Missoula Mountain," Mike Lewis. Lewis averaged 21.7 points and 14.4 rebounds per game in the 1967–68 season. Duke won 22 and lost 6 as Lewis made All-America.

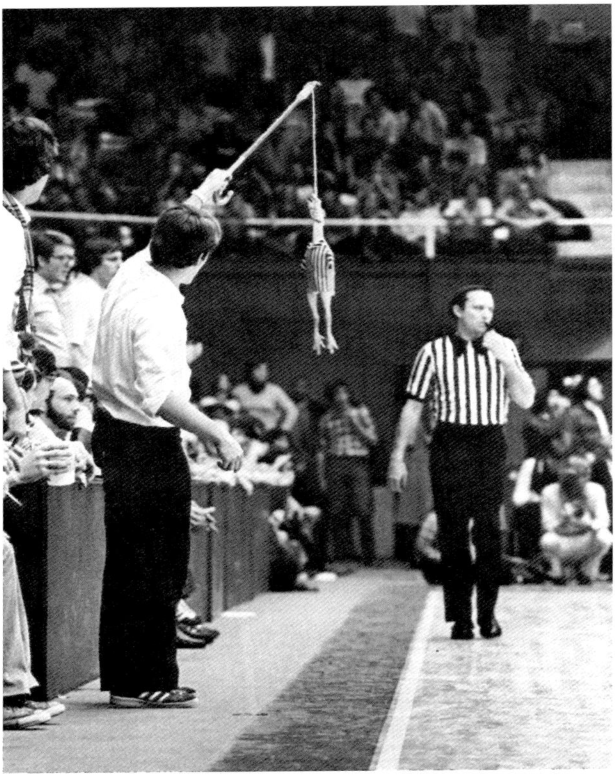

Left: A Duke fan inside Cameron Indoor Stadium in 1978 makes his feelings perfectly clear to an official.

Below: The young lady's shirt and the sign really express the passion Duke students and fans have for Blue Devil basketball. Cameron Indoor Stadium is not the largest basketball arena by any means, but there is absolutely no college basketball venue in the nation that is more alive with excitement and a sense of history on game nights.

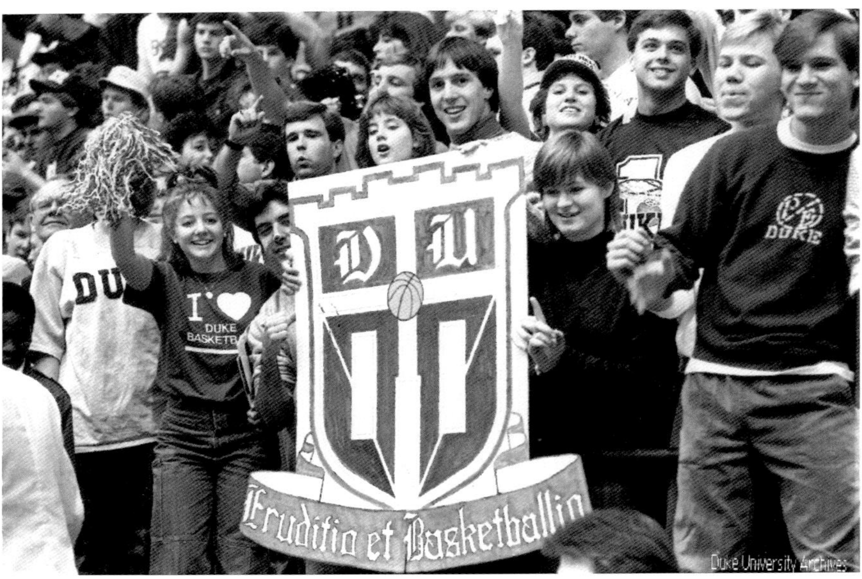

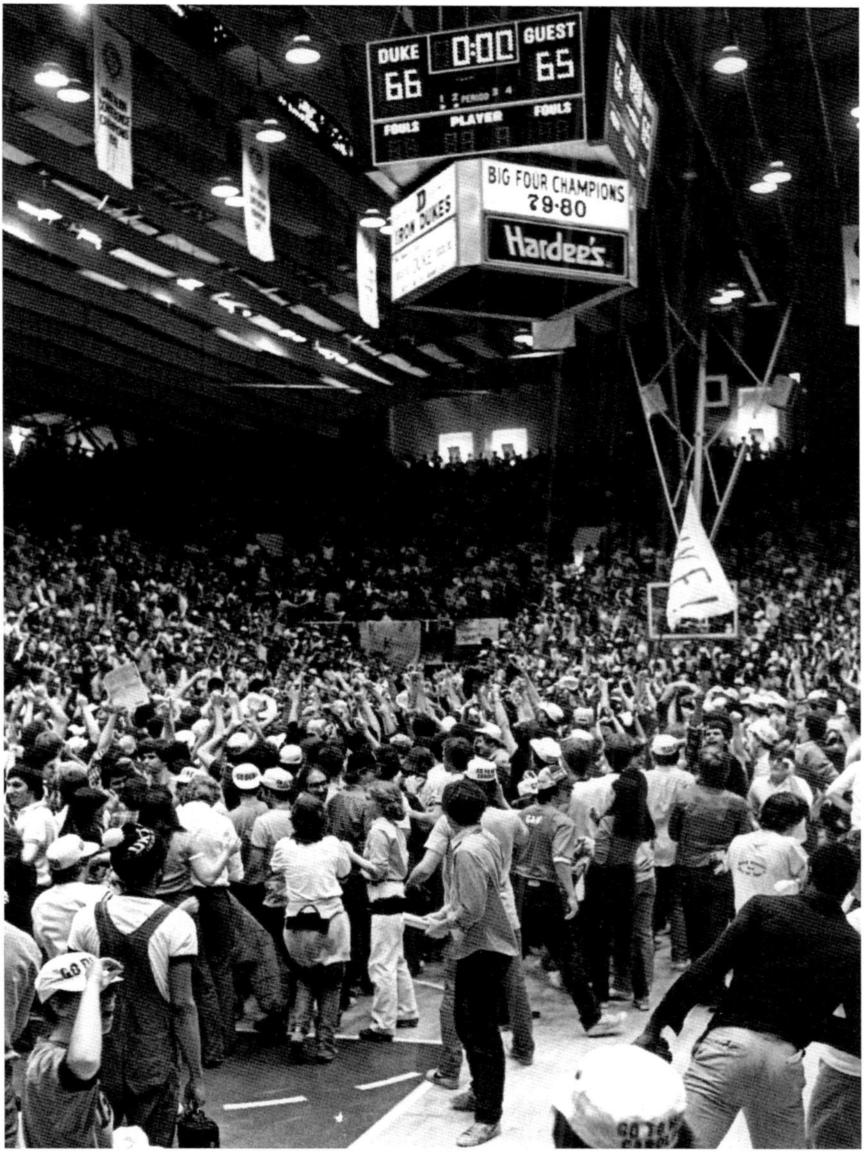

The "Guest" on the scoreboard in this game is UNC, as Duke has just defeated the Tar Heels 66 to 65 in 1981. Duke and UNC play at least twice a year, and sometimes more than that, as these two great programs usually advance far into the ACC Tournament. Gene Banks scored 25 to hand Coach K his first victory over the Tar Heels in his first season at Duke. Duke won 17 and lost 13 during Coach K's inaugural season in Durham as Banks, Vince Taylor, Kenny Dennard and Tom Emma were key players.

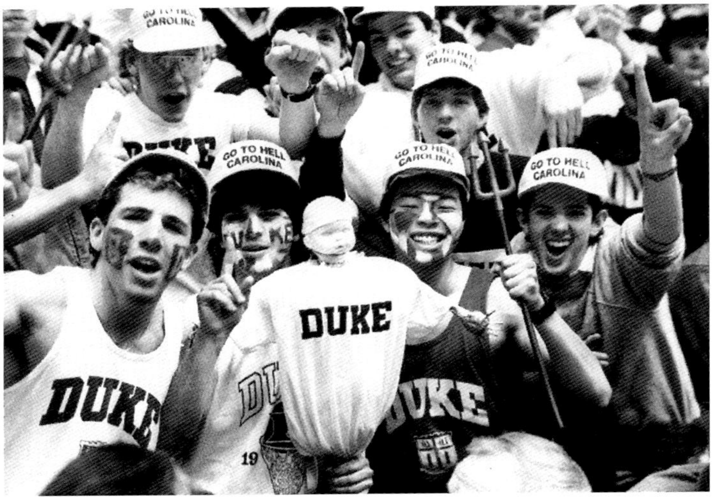

In this photograph, Duke students and fans show their feelings for the University of North Carolina Tar Heels. Located only about ten miles apart, Duke and UNC are two of the best programs in the history of college basketball, having won 7 national championships and together playing in 31 Final Fours. From Frank McGuire to Dean Smith to Roy Williams, great coaches have directed UNC, just as at Duke, from Cap Card to Eddie Cameron to Vic Bubas to Mike Krzyzewski.

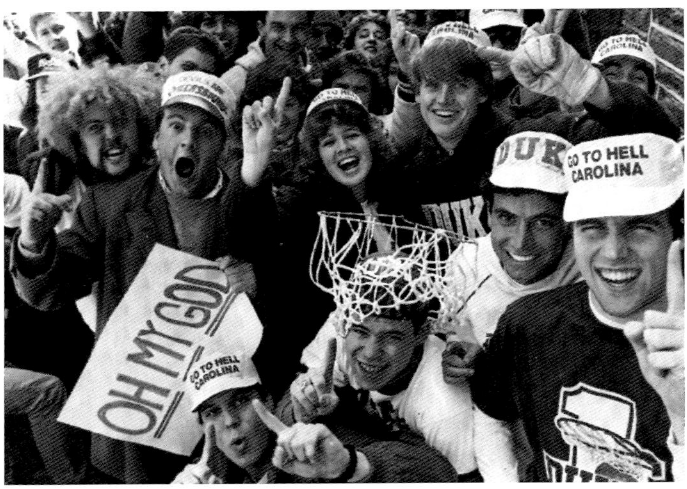

Some Duke fans show their feelings for the University of North Carolina. The rivalry between Duke and UNC is perhaps the most recognized and heated one in college basketball. The proximity of the campuses, the fact that they recruit many of the same high school players and the fact that these two programs are among the best in the nation just adds to the intensity of their annual battles.

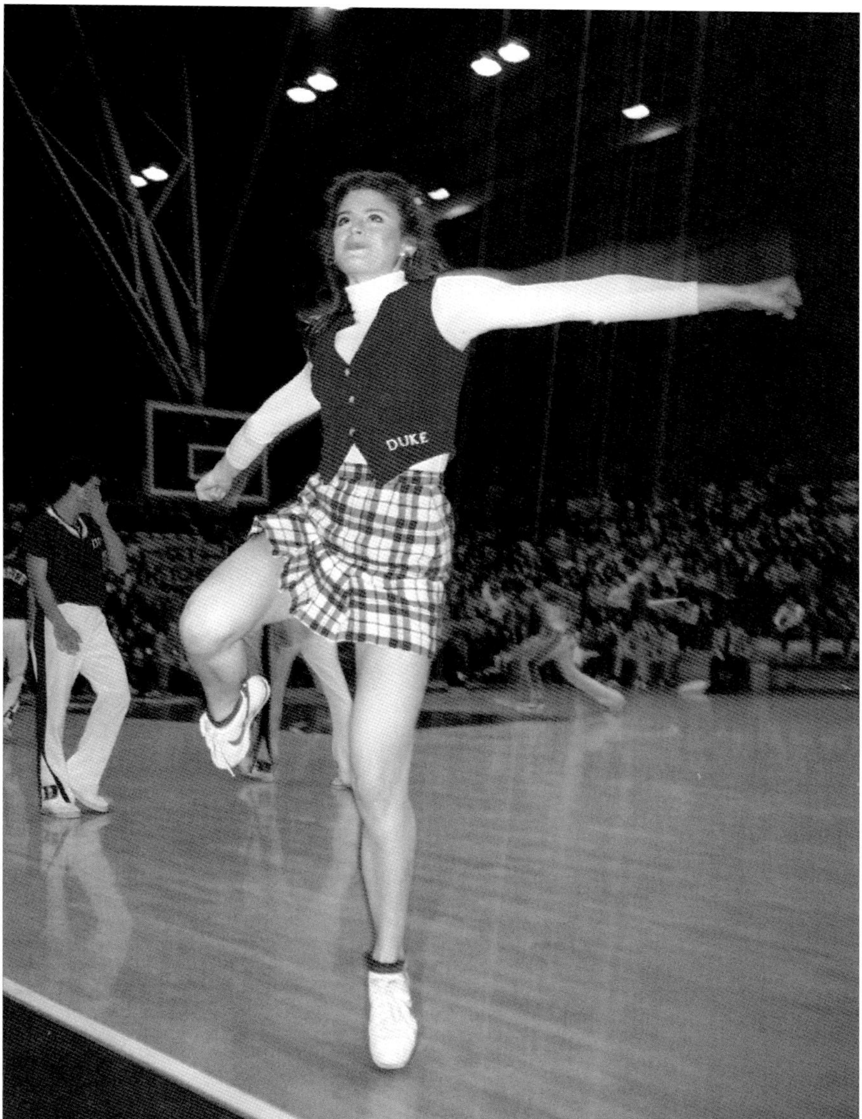

A pretty Duke cheerleader pumps up the crowd during another big game. Attending a game in Cameron Indoor Stadium is truly an experience to treasure, from great basketball to the clever antics of the Cameron Crazies to the wholesome family atmosphere in perhaps the most famous college basketball arena in the country.

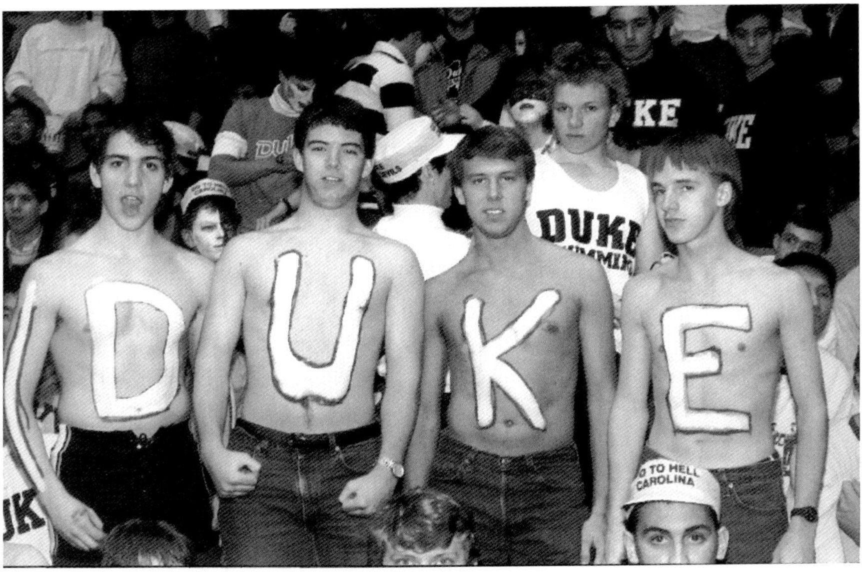

Duke students inside Cameron Indoor Stadium cheer for their Blue Devils in 1987.

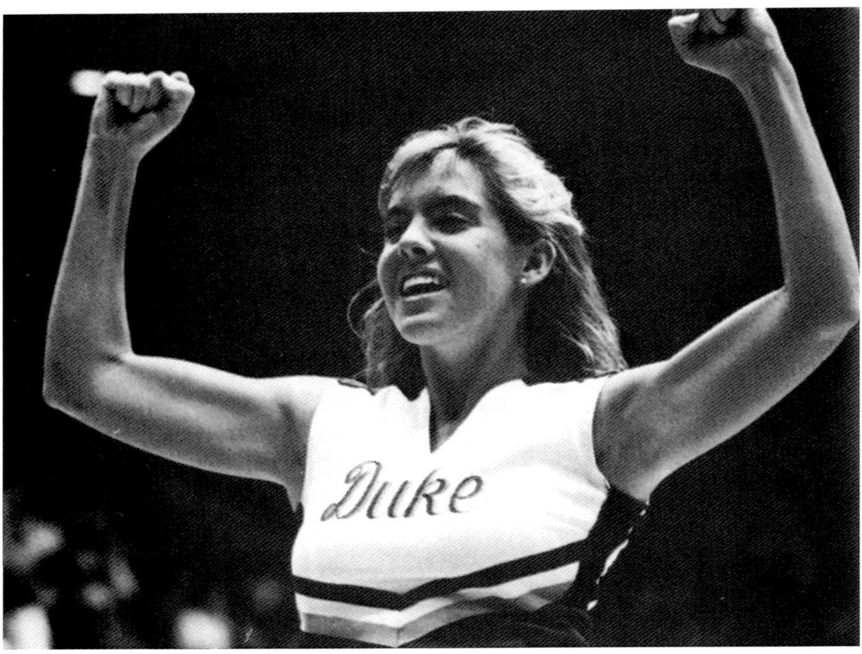

Another pretty Duke cheerleader shows her enthusiasm for the Blue Devils in 1990.

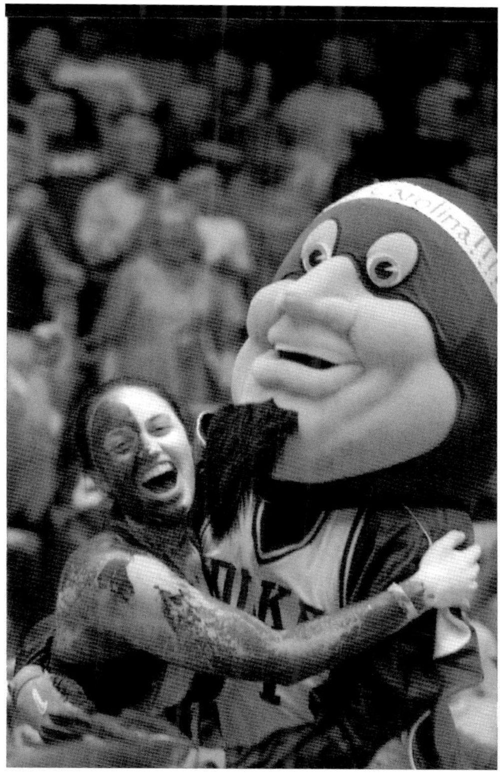

A Cameron Crazy hugs the Duke mascot during a 2005 game.

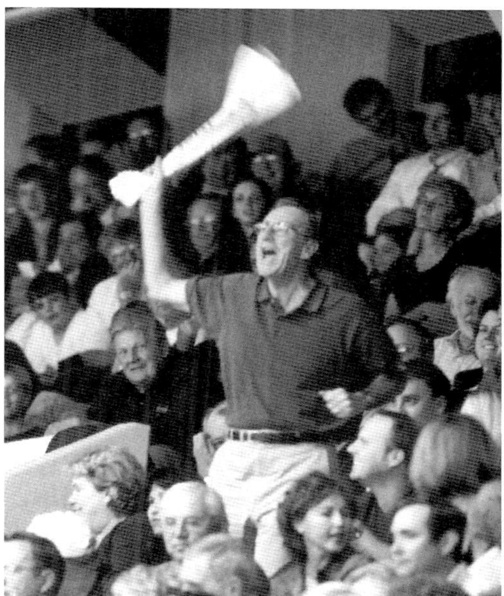

Herb Neubauer is known among Duke basketball fans as "Crazy Towel Guy." Neubauer gets the Cameron Crazies going when he stands and twirls his towel.

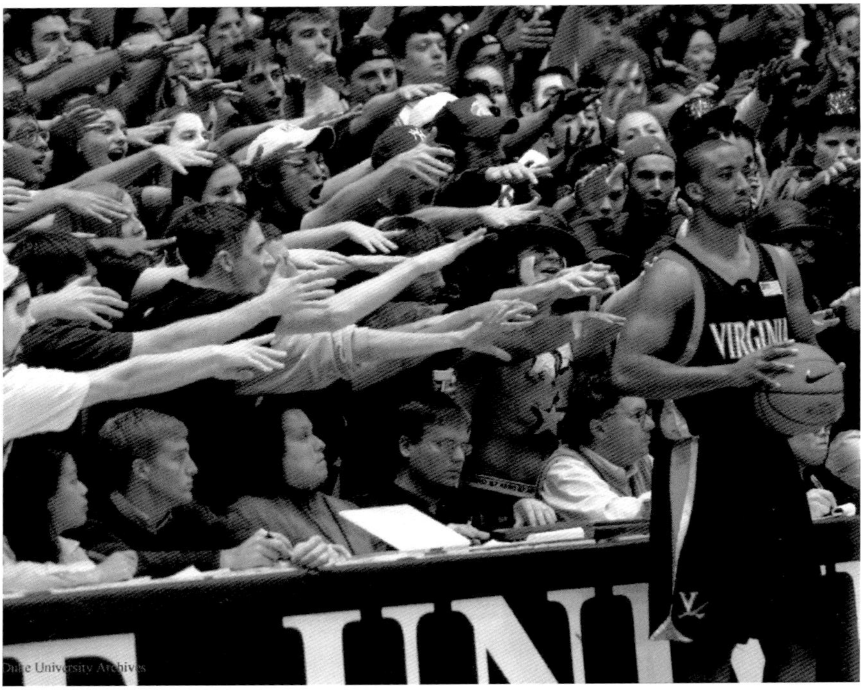

There is no doubt that the Cameron Crazies of Cameron Indoor Stadium intimidate many opposing players and teams. Here a Virginia player is the focus of Duke fans' attention.

Chapter 7

WOMEN'S BASKETBALL

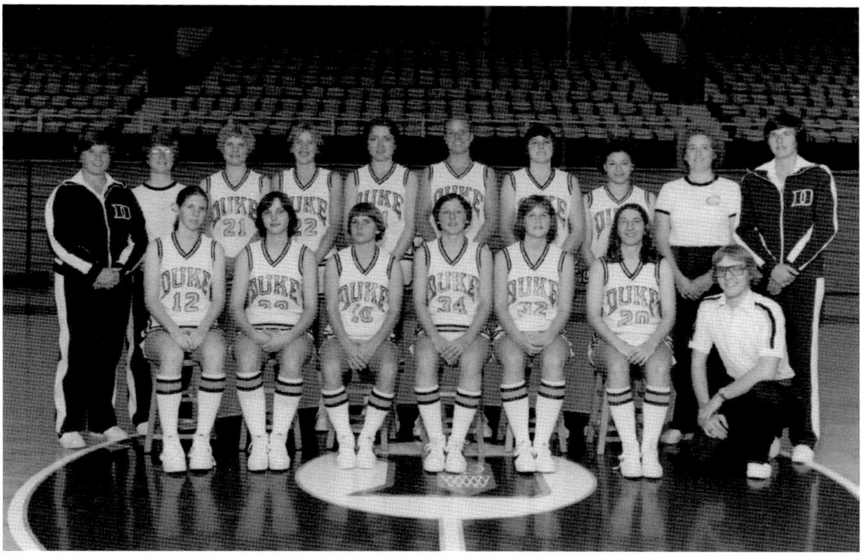

The 1978–79 women's team finished 11 and 11, and was coached by Debbie Leonard. Barb Krause was the leading scorer, at 14.5 points a game. Krause was also quite a rebounder, once pulling down 24 in a game against Catawba. *Courtesy of Duke Sports Information.*

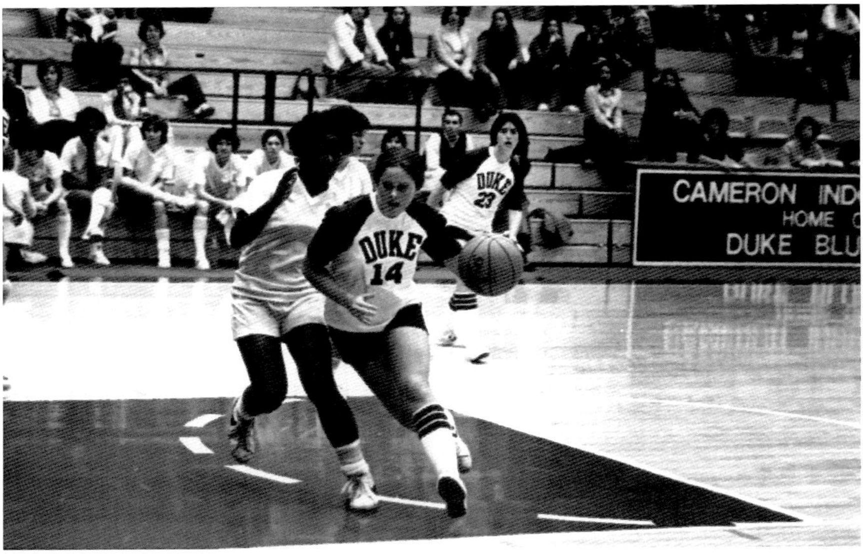

Unlike today, when Duke has one of the top women's programs in the nation, attendance at games was once sparse and wins were few. This photo shows Ruth Ellis of Duke in 1978, when Duke won only 1 game with 19 losses.

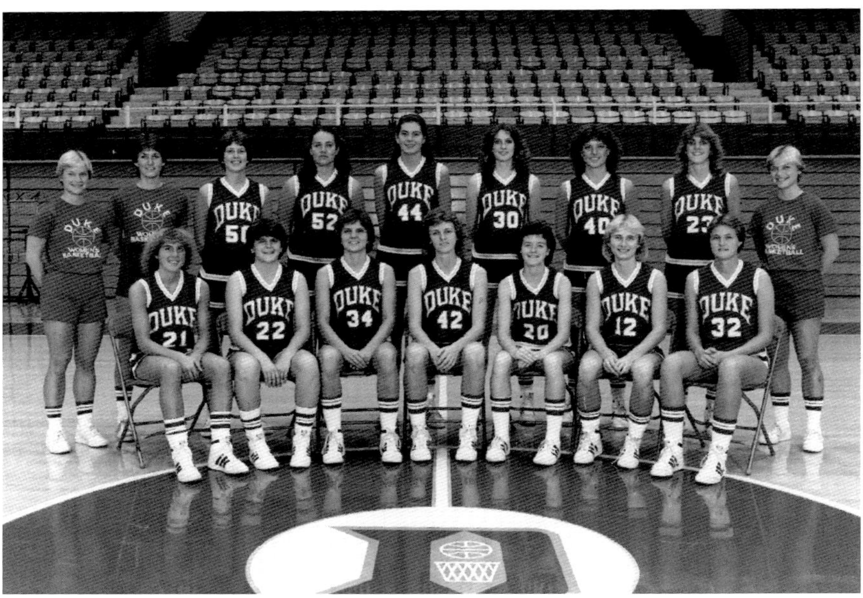

Under Debbie Leonard, the 1982–83 women's team won 15 and lost 10. Jennifer Chestnut led Duke in scoring at 14 points a game. A six-foot, one-inch forward from Houston, Chestnut led Duke in rebounding in each of her last three years.

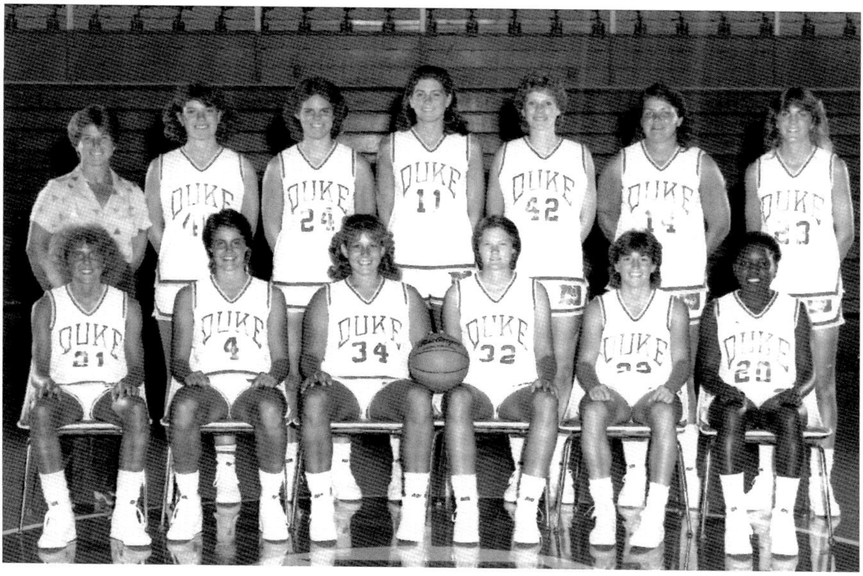

Above: Debbie Leonard's Blue Devils won 19 and lost 8 in the 1984–85 season. Chris Moreland led Duke in scoring with 17.6 points a game, and would go on to lead Duke in scoring for all of her four years.

Right: Chante Black is pictured here in game action. Black pulled down 16 rebounds in a game against Clemson in her freshman year.

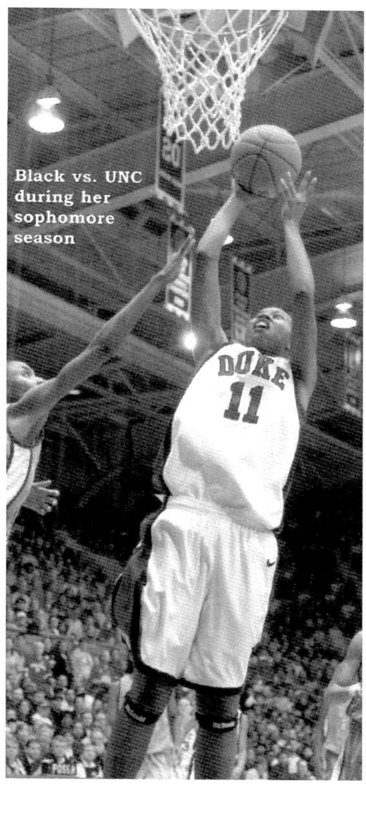

Black vs. UNC during her sophomore season

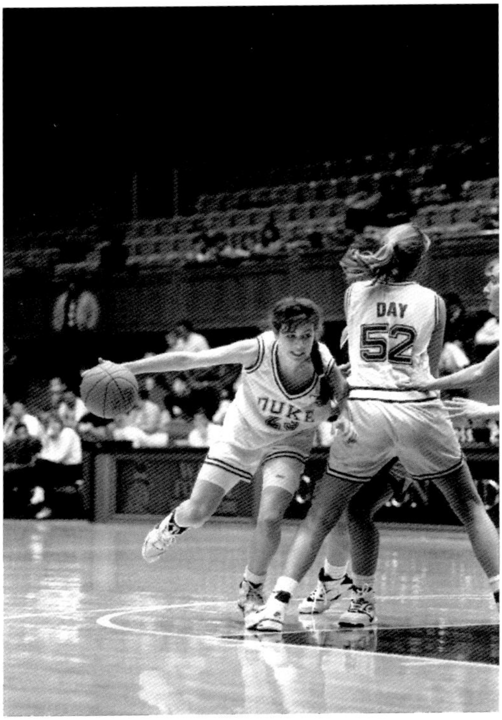

Carey Kauffman works around a screen set by teammate Alison Day. Kauffman averaged 14.1 points and 8.4 rebounds a game during the 1994–95 season. Against UNC-Asheville during that season, Kauffman scored 35 points and grabbed 19 rebounds. Kauffman came from quite a basketball family, as her father, Bob, played in the NBA and her sisters Lara and Joanna played at Georgia Tech. Day averaged 16.1 points and 6.6 rebounds a game during 1994–95, when Duke reached the NCAA Tournament for the first time under Coach Gail Goestenkors.

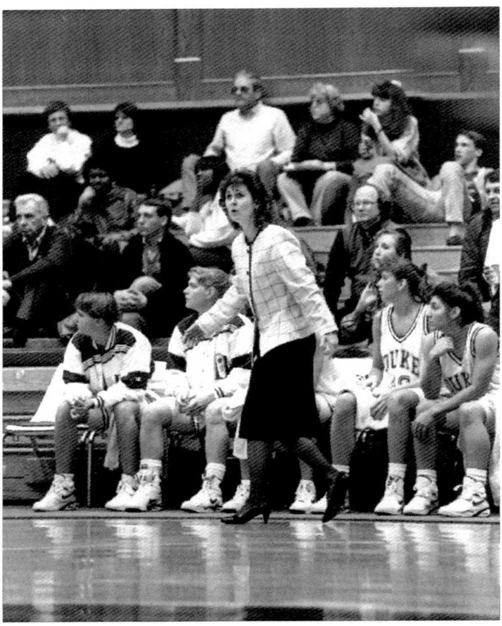

Gail Goestenkors is pictured here early in her career as Duke women's basketball coach. After posting a record of 12 wins and 15 losses in her first year at Duke in 1992–93, Coach G never had another losing record in her career, taking Duke to 4 Final Fours before resigning in 2007 to take the women's head basketball coaching position at Texas. From the 2000–01 season to her resignation after the 2006–07 season, Duke won 220 games while losing only 25.

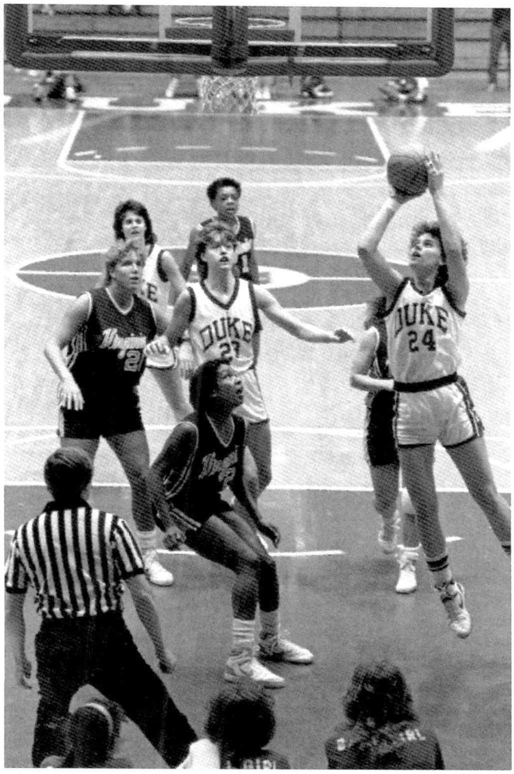

Right: Chris Moreland was the first Duke women's basketball player to make All-America, doing so in 1988. For her career, Moreland averaged 20.1 points and 11.1 rebounds per game. Duke had some very good teams while Moreland played, going 19–8, 21–9, 19–10 and 17–11 from 1984–85 to 1987–88. These teams were coached by Debbie Leonard. In the picture above, Moreland shoots the ball in a game against Virginia. *Courtesy of Duke Sports Information.*

Below: Coached by Gail Goestenkors, the Duke women won 22 and lost 9 in the 1994–95 season. This marked the first of 13 straight appearances in the NCAA Tournament for Duke under Goestenkors, who is now the head coach at the University of Texas. Alison Day led Duke in scoring with 16.1 points per game.

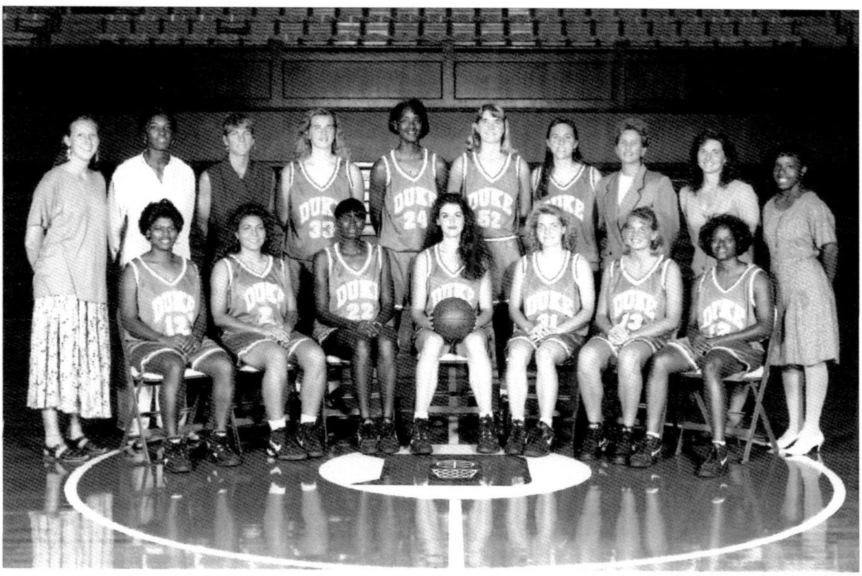

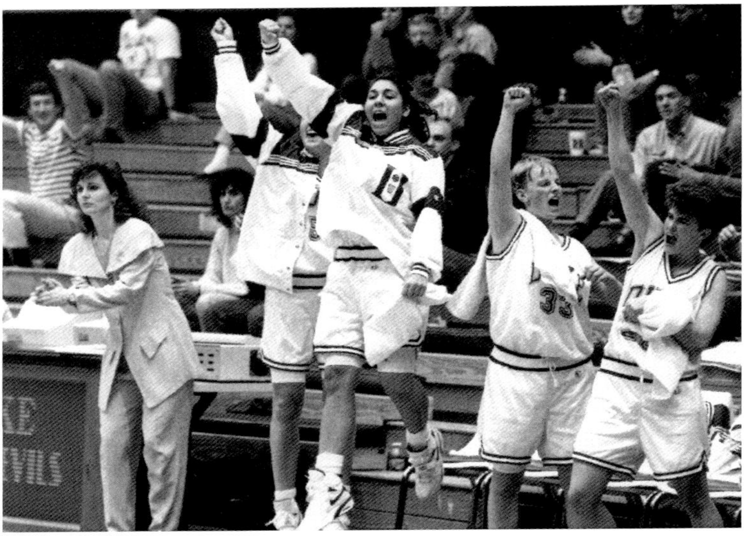

Coach Gail Goestenkors is shown during the 1997–98 season, when Duke won 24 and lost 8. The next season, 1998–99, Coach G would lead Duke to its first women's Final Four with a record of 29 and 7.

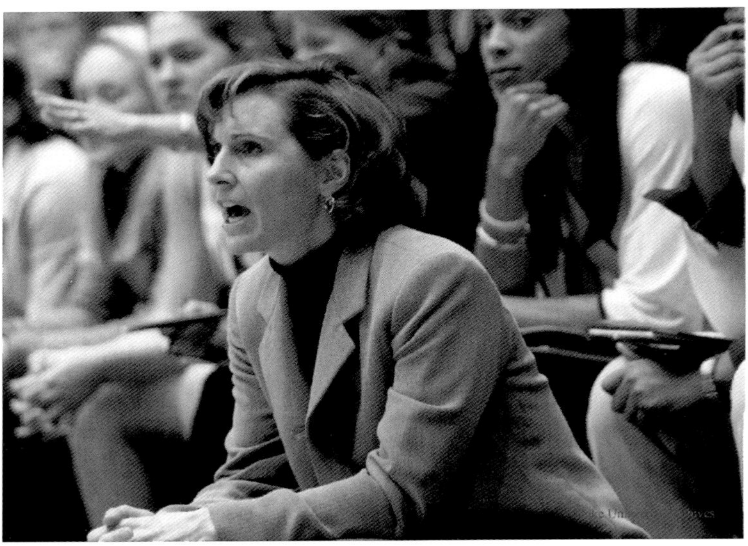

Gail Goestenkors coached women's basketball at Duke from 1992 to 2007. At Duke, her record was among the best in the nation. Duke won 8 ACC regular-season championships, 5 ACC Tournament Championships, appeared in 4 Final Fours and played in the national championship game twice. Her overall coaching record at the time of this writing was 396 wins and 99 losses, for an 80 percent winning percentage. Goestenkors played for Saginaw Valley State from 1981 to 1985.

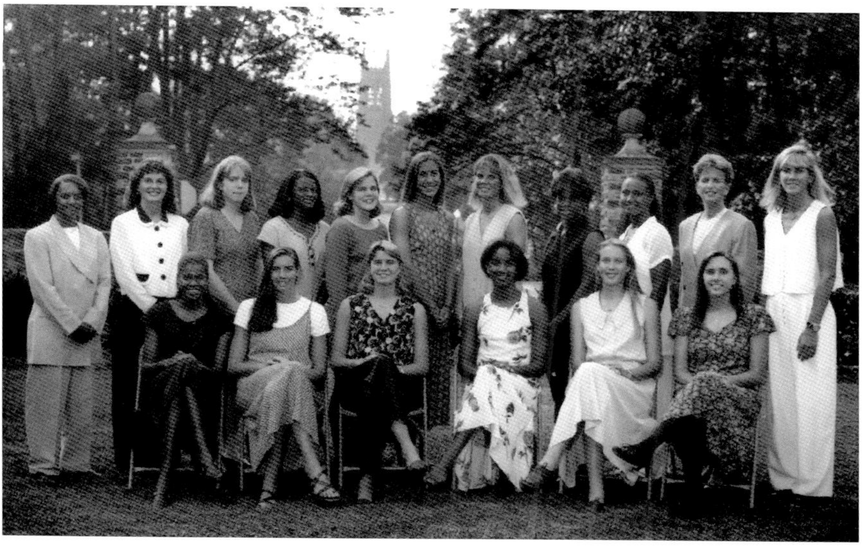

The 1997–98 women's team won 24 and lost 8, which included 3 wins in the NCAA Tournament. The leading scorer was Nicole Erickson at 12.8 points per game.

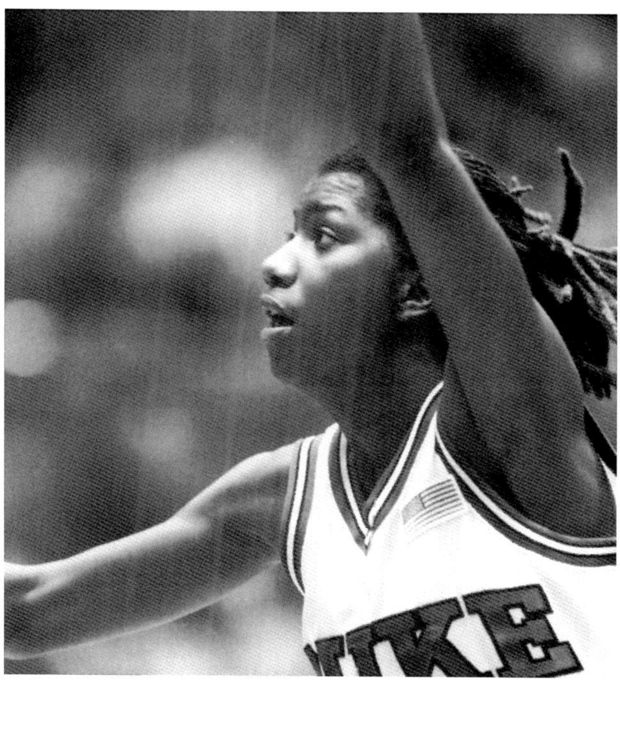

Iciss Tillis experienced nothing but success during her four seasons at Duke from 2000 to 2004: 4 ACC regular-season championships, 4 ACC Tournament titles and 2 Final Fours attest to that fact. Tillis was All-America in both 2002–03 and 2003–04. Over the 137 games played in her career, Tillis averaged 13 points and 7 rebounds.

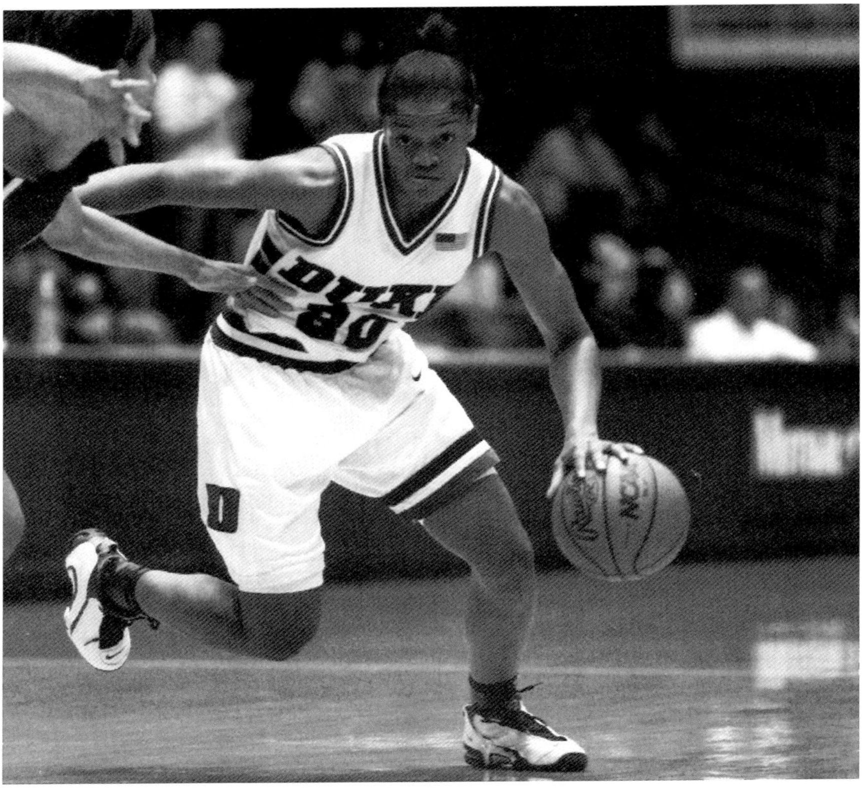

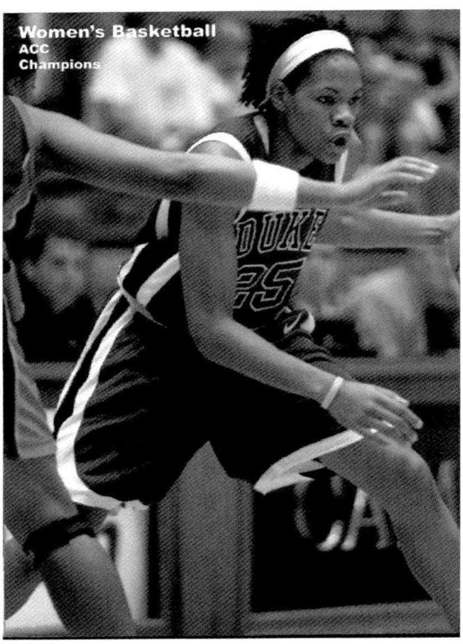

Above: The first female player to have her jersey number retired at Duke, Alana Beard is now a star in the WNBA. Beard finished her career at Duke in 2004 as the leading scorer in Blue Devil women's history, number one in career steals, number two in assists and number four in rebounds. Duke was an amazing 126 and 14 during Beard's four seasons, and played in 2 Final Fours.

Left: A total of 2,122 points, 874 rebounds and 413 assists in her career speak to the great all-around ability of Monique Currie. Currie once had a triple-double against Florida State with 21 points, 12 rebounds and 11 assists. On February 19, 2006, she set the all-time Duke women's record for most points in a game, scoring 43 against Miami. Monique also holds the record for best free throw percentage in a game, making 14 of 14 versus UNC in 2002. Currie is now a star player in the WNBA.

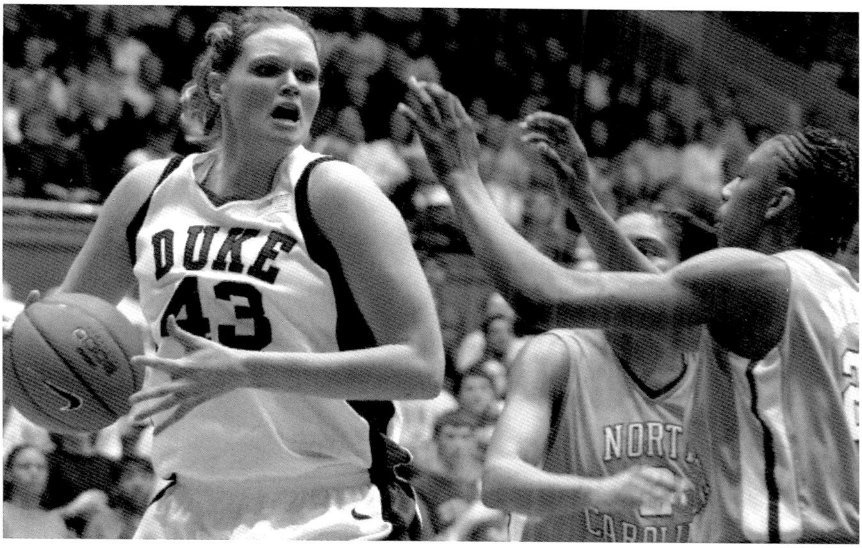

Along with experiencing great success as part of Duke teams from 2003 to 2007, Alison Bales also became the top shot blocker in Duke women's history. Good timing and anticipation, along with the fact that she is six feet, seven inches, helped Bales accomplish this record. But Bales had an all-around game, as evidenced by her 19 points and 12 rebounds against Maryland in the 2006 national championship game.

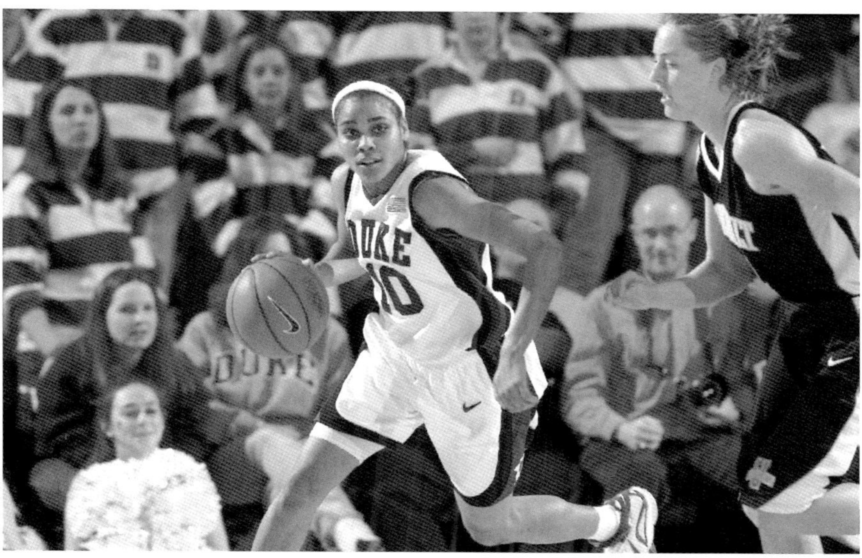

Lindsey Harding, born in Mobile, Alabama, was the national player of the year for the 2006–07 season. She was selected first in the WNBA draft in 2007. Her jersey was retired at Duke in 2008.

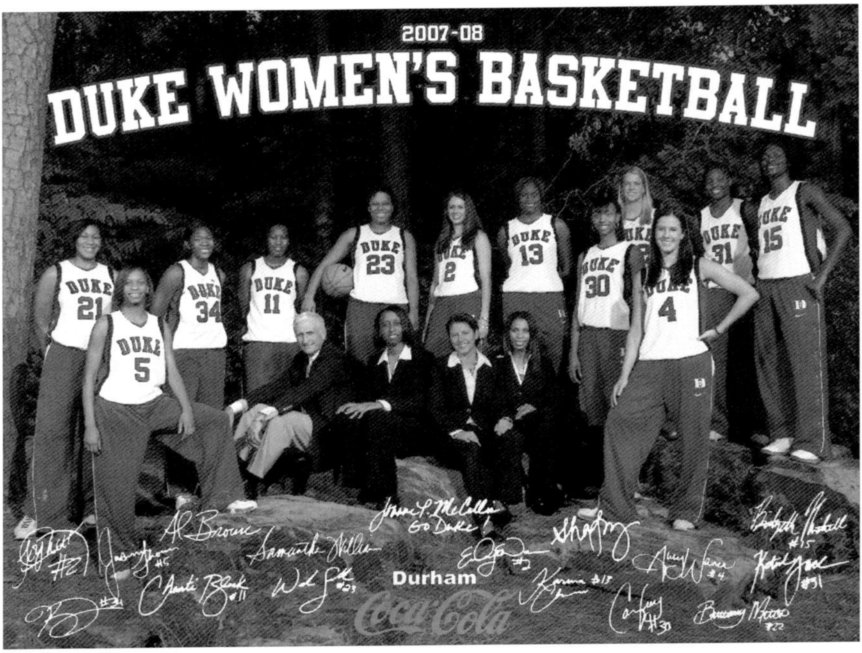

This is the 2007–08 Duke women's basketball team. Joanne P. McCallie, seated third from the left, became coach of Duke in 2007, after Gail Goestenkors left for the University of Texas. *Courtesy of the author.*

Chapter 8

OFF THE COURT

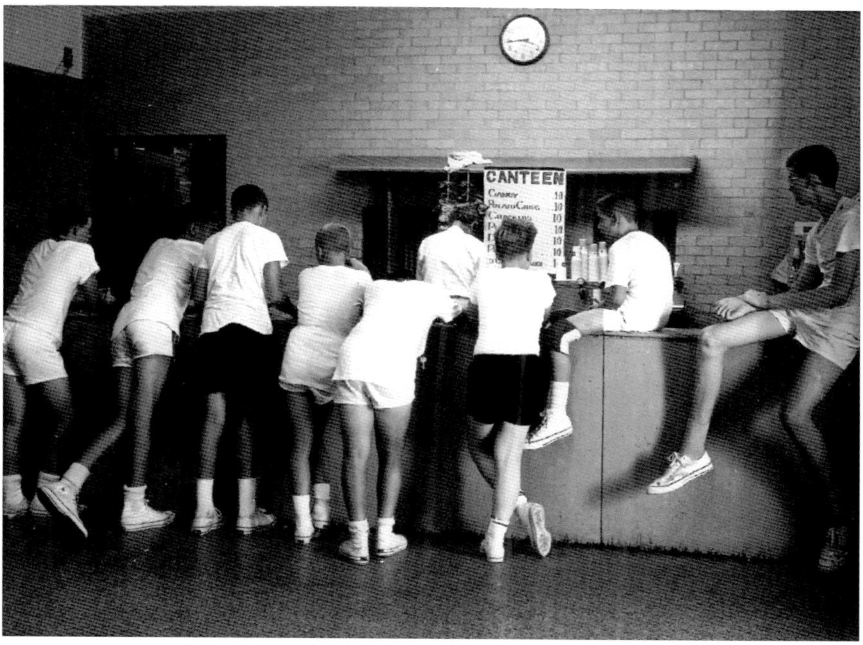

Some boys attending one of Vic Bubas's basketball clinics in the 1960s take a refreshment break.

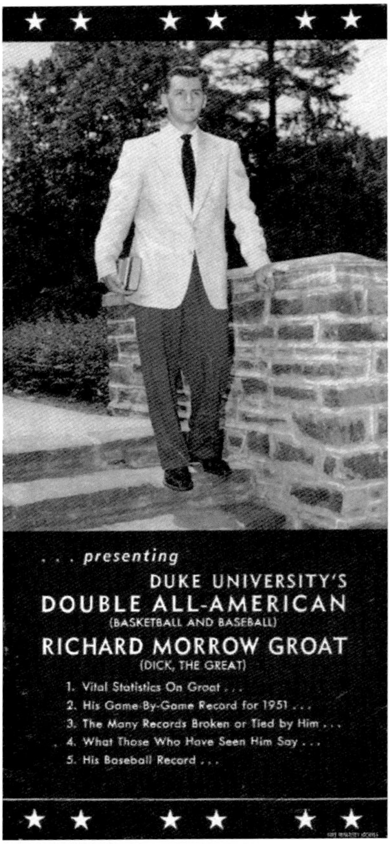

Dick Groat, a six-foot guard from Swissvale, Pennsylvania, is shown here during his days as a Duke student and athlete from 1949 to 1952. Groat was an All-American player in basketball and baseball, and was the first Duke athlete to have his jersey retired. Groat is now a radio broadcaster for the University of Pittsburgh.

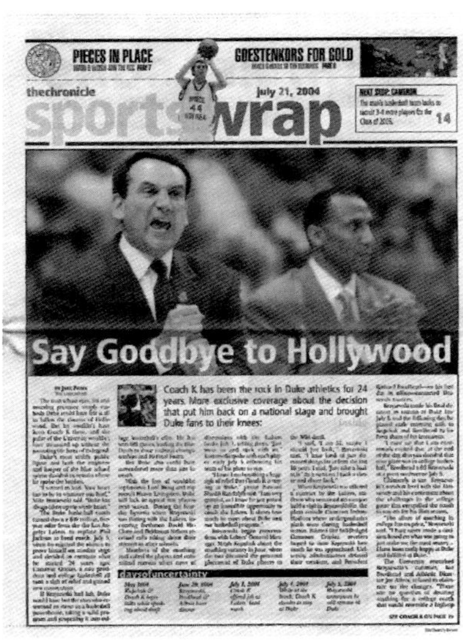

The *Chronicle*, Duke's campus newspaper, heralded the decision of Coach K to remain at Duke in 2004. Mike Krzyzewski turned down a job offer from the Los Angeles Lakers for five years at $40 million. Coach K said at the time, "I wanted to lead. Your heart has to be in whatever you lead. Duke has always taken up my whole heart." Duke fans rejoiced at the news that their beloved Coach K was staying in Durham.

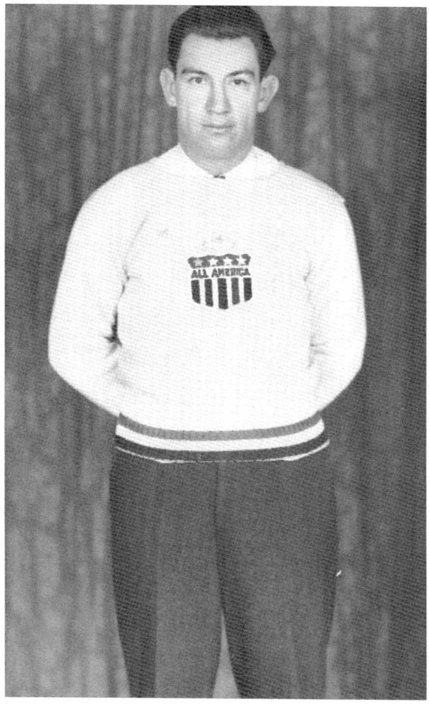

Right: Ace Parker just might be the greatest athlete who ever participated in Duke sports. Ace was an All-American in football while playing for the legendary Wallace Wade at Duke, and he also starred in baseball and played on the 1936 basketball team. Parker went on to be the NFL MVP in 1940 and is now a member of the NFL Hall of Fame. He also played Major League baseball with the Philadelphia Athletics, hitting a home run in his first big league at-bat. Ace came back to Duke in 1947 and served as an assistant football coach through 1965 and as head baseball coach from 1953 to 1966. In baseball, Parker took Duke to the College World Series in 1953 and 1961.

Below: Add Penfield, *right*, accepts an award from Carl James in Cameron Indoor Stadium in 1975. Penfield was a longtime radio play-by-play man for the Blue Devils in basketball and football. After graduating from Duke in 1940, Penfield broadcast Duke basketball and football for most of the 1950s and 1960s, and part of the 1970s. *Courtesy of Add Penfield.*

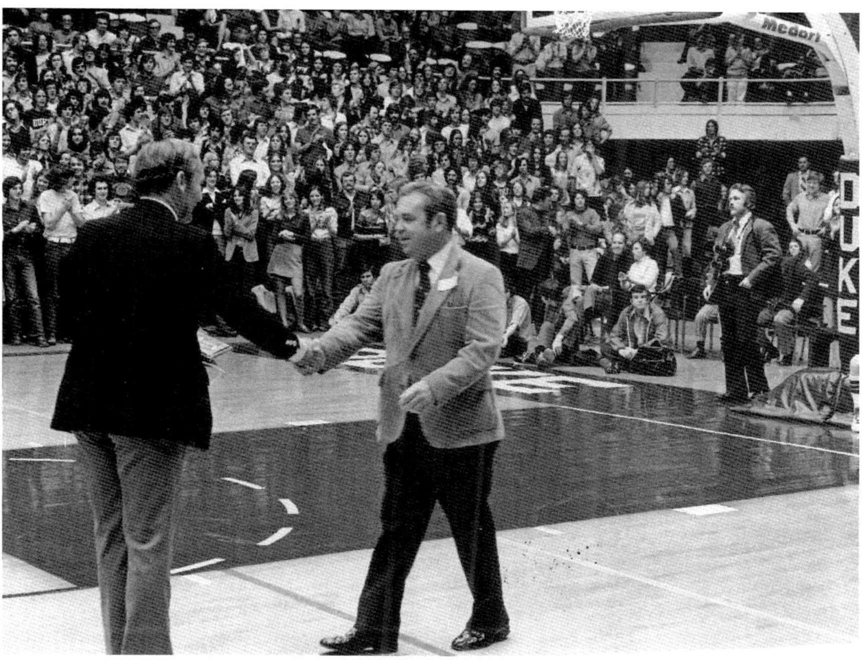

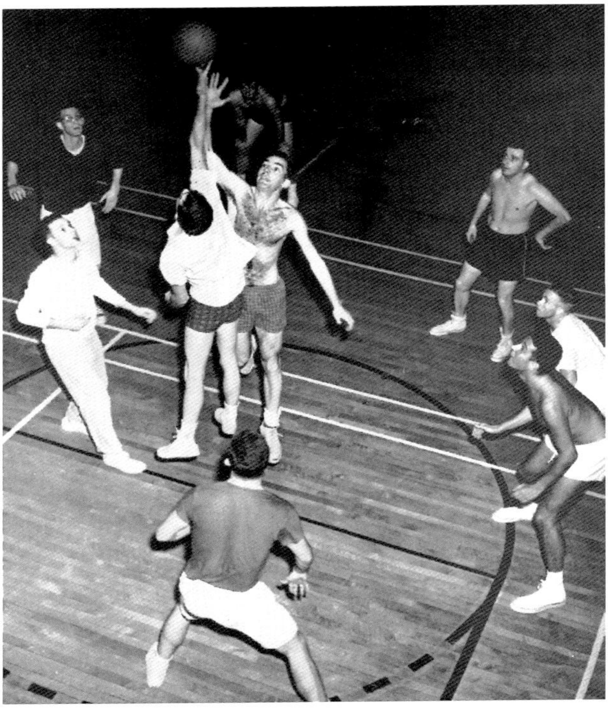

Action in an intramural game at Duke in 1956. The long tradition of Duke basketball among its men's and women's teams has led to increased interest in intramural games and fan attendance at games.

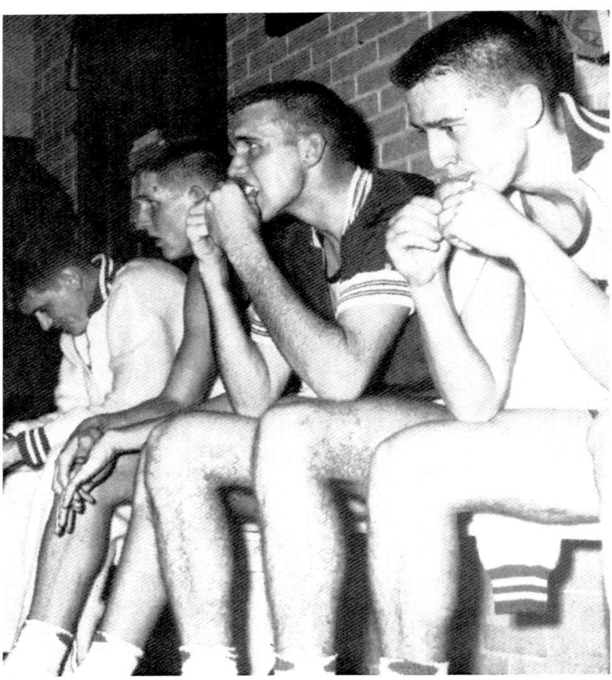

Shown from left to right during halftime of a 1959 game are Larry Bateman, Doug Kistler, Carroll Youngkin and Merrill Morgan. A couple of them are eating oranges.

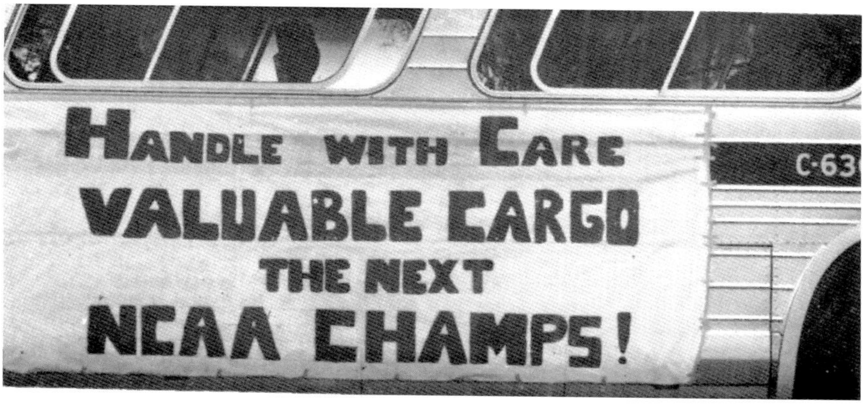

Valuable cargo indeed, the 1962–63 team, coached by Vic Bubas, won 27 and lost 3 while winning the ACC Tournament Championship and reaching the Final Four. Duke lost to Loyola, Illinois, in the semifinal of the Final Four, despite Art Heyman scoring 29. Heyman won national player of the year honors and scored 24.9 points per game, while Jeff Mullins also made All-America and averaged 20.3 per game.

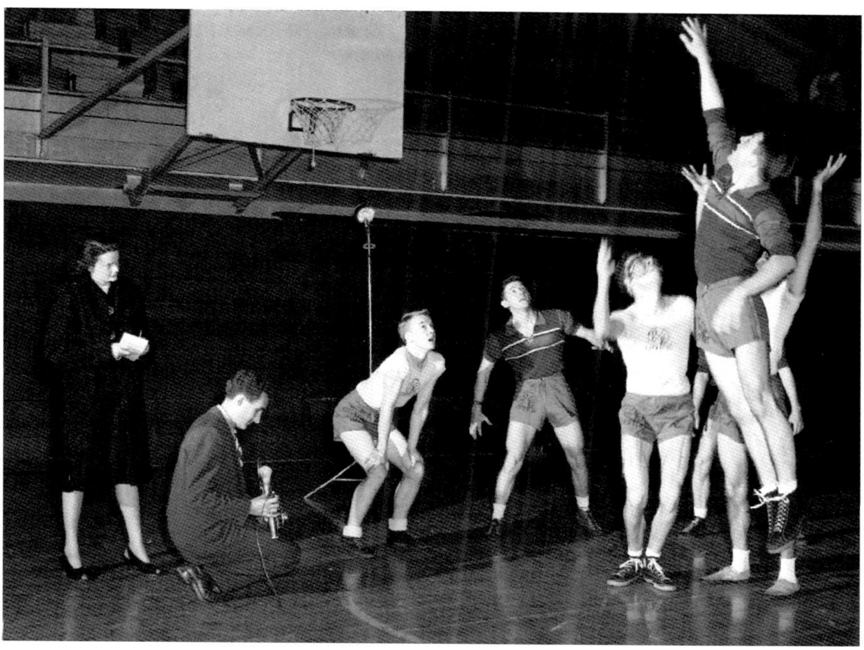

A *Life* magazine photographer takes some pictures on the Duke campus in the 1940s.

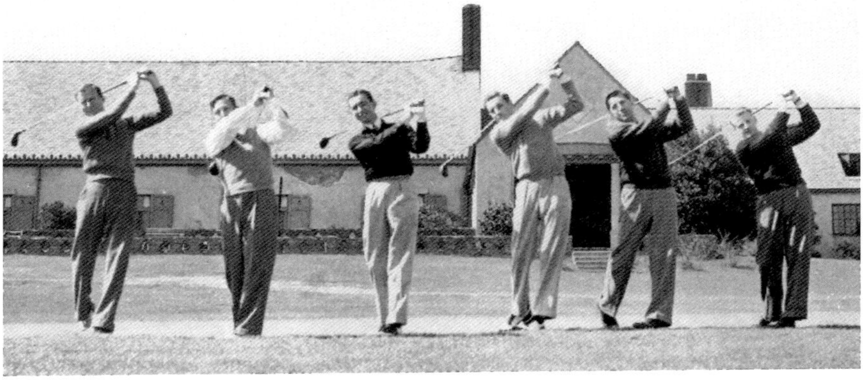

Basketball certainly is not the only sport Duke has excelled in through the years. Here is the 1937 golf team.

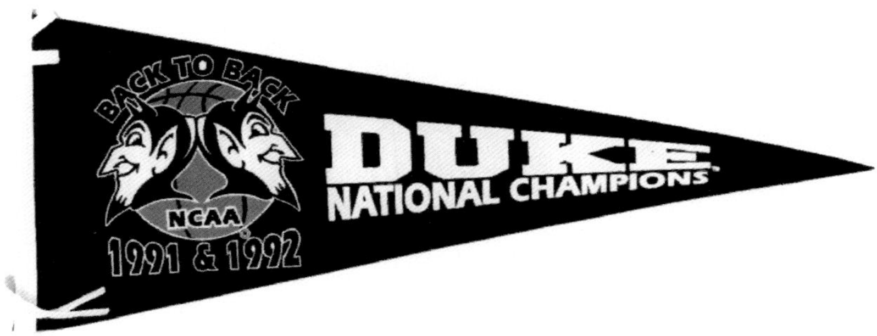

The Duke men's basketball team won back-to-back national titles in 1990–91 and 1991–92. The 1990–91 team was 32 and 7, as Christian Laettner led in scoring with 19.8 points per game, while Thomas Hill averaged 11.5, Bill McCaffrey 11.6, Bobby Hurley 11.3 and Grant Hill 11.2. In 1991–92, Duke was 34 and 2 as Laettner averaged 21.5, Thomas Hill 14.5, Grant Hill 14, Bobby Hurley 13.2 and Brian Davis 11.2. Duke beat Kansas for the national title in 1991 and Michigan in 1992.

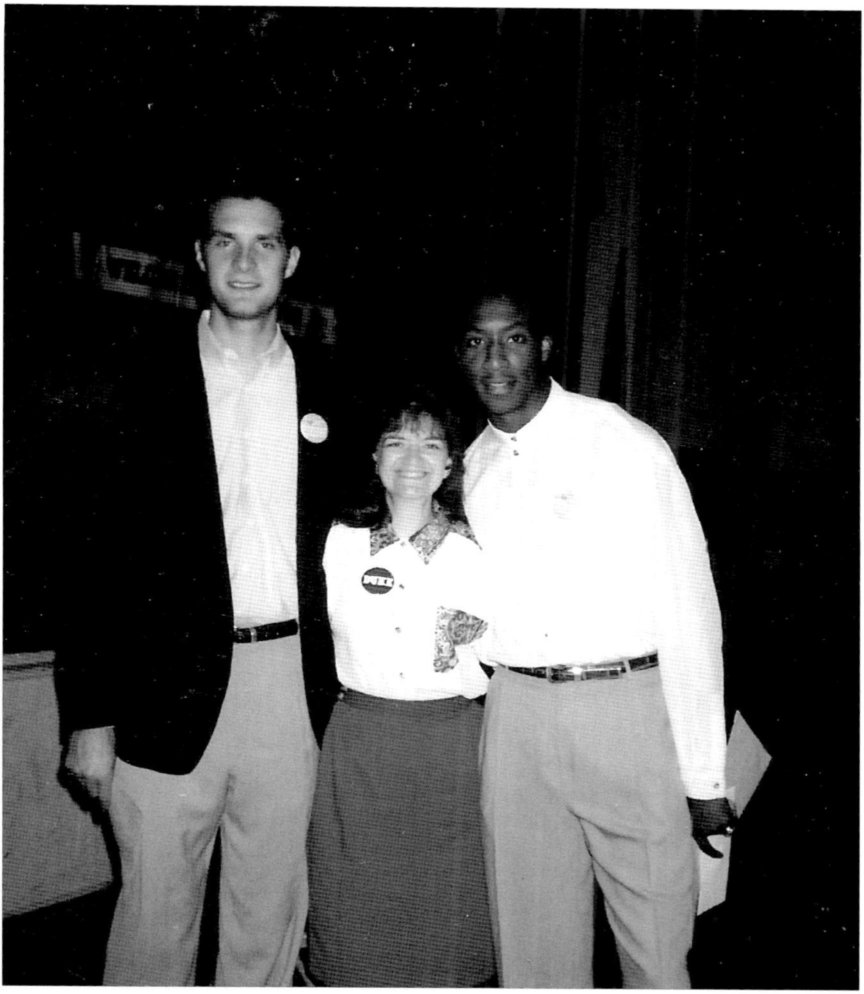

From left to right are Christian Laettner, Beth Harward and Brian Davis. Laettner and Davis, members of the 1991 and 1992 national championship teams, are visiting Hawley Middle School in Creedmoor, North Carolina, at the invitation of teacher Beth Harward. The players spoke to the students about the importance of academics and working hard to achieve goals.

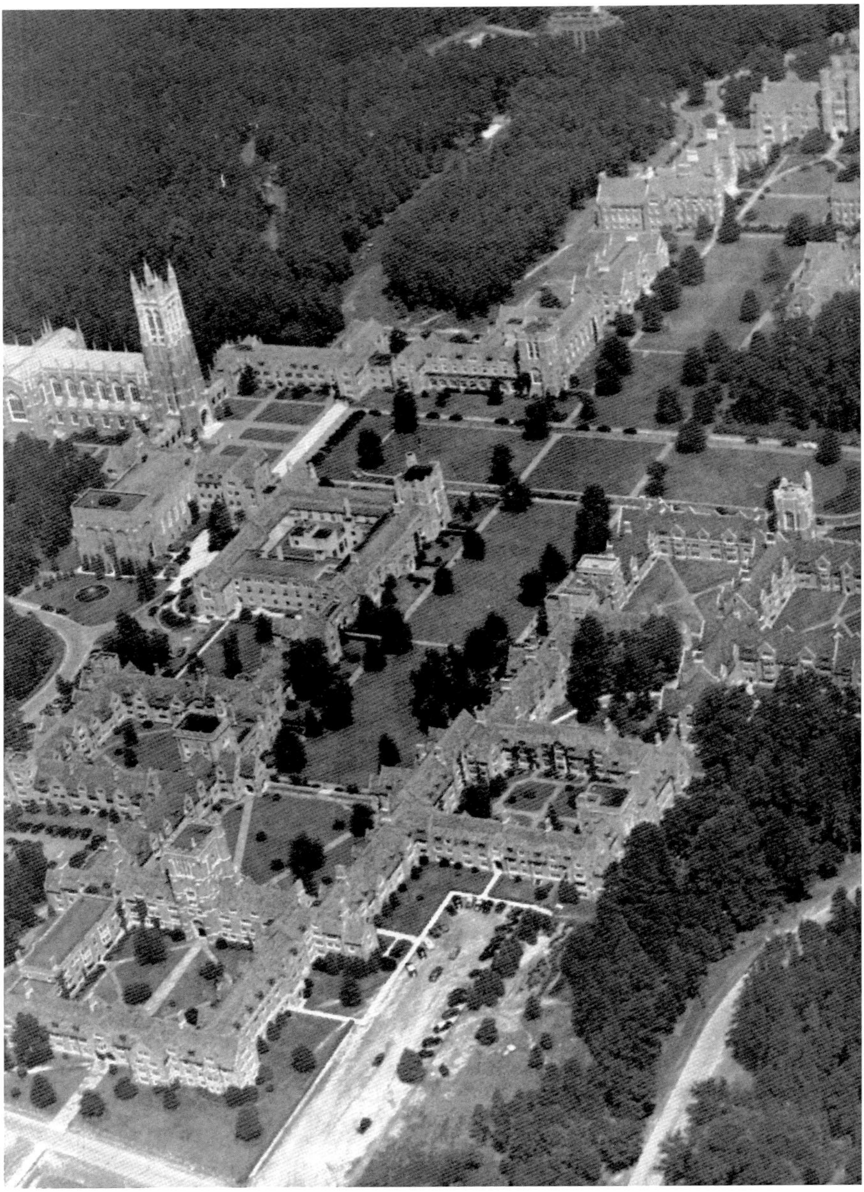

This is an aerial view of the Duke University West Campus. The Duke Chapel is in the upper left of the picture. Along with Cameron Indoor Stadium, Duke Chapel is one of the most visited buildings on campus. Construction on the Duke Chapel began in 1930 and was designed by Julian Abele, America's first African American architect of national acclaim.

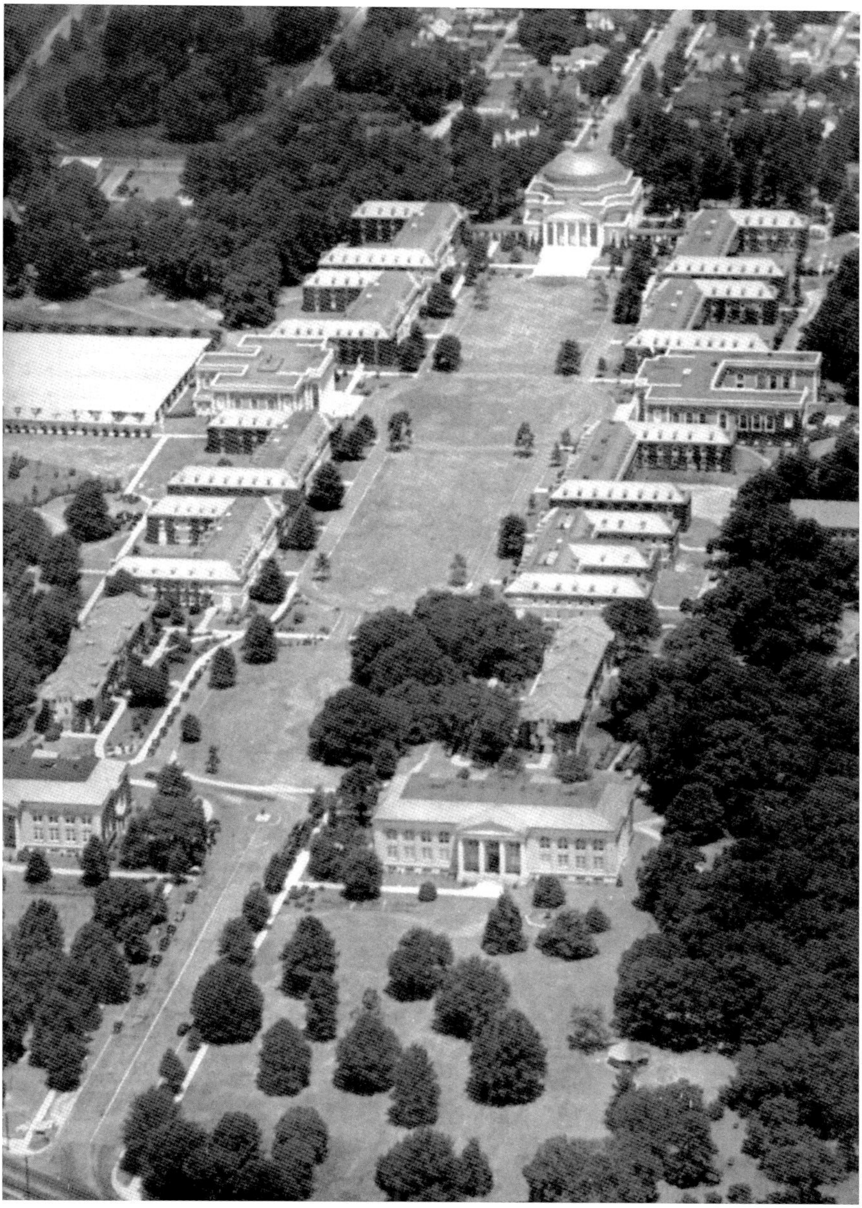

This is an aerial view of the East Campus of Duke University. The domed building in the top center is Baldwin Auditorium, named for Alice Baldwin, the first dean of Duke's Woman's College. The nine-hundred-seat auditorium is the site of musical performances ranging from jazz to chamber music.

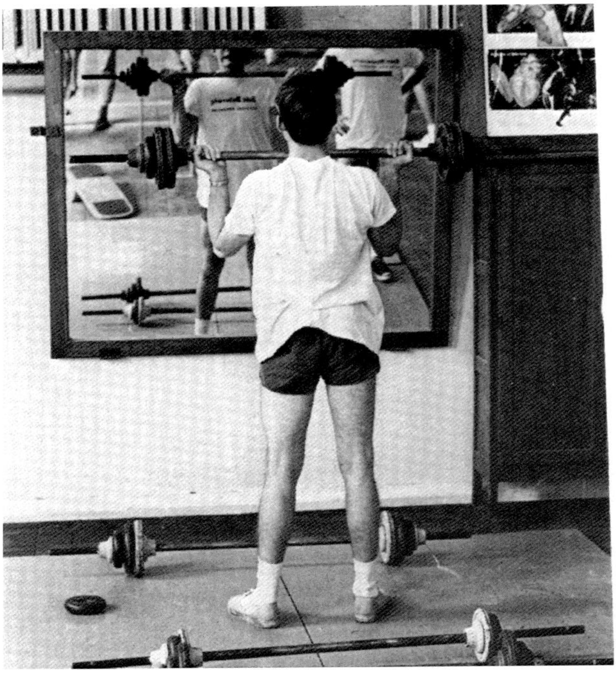

Left: Perhaps this young man, who is lifting weights on the Duke campus, is dreaming of some day running the court in Cameron Indoor Stadium as a member of the Blue Devil basketball team.

Below: Mike Gminski and Gene Banks are being interviewed by Billy Packer, on the left, and Al McGuire, on the right. Packer is a former Wake Forest player who is now recognized as one of the best television broadcasters of college basketball, and McGuire was a former head coach at Marquette.

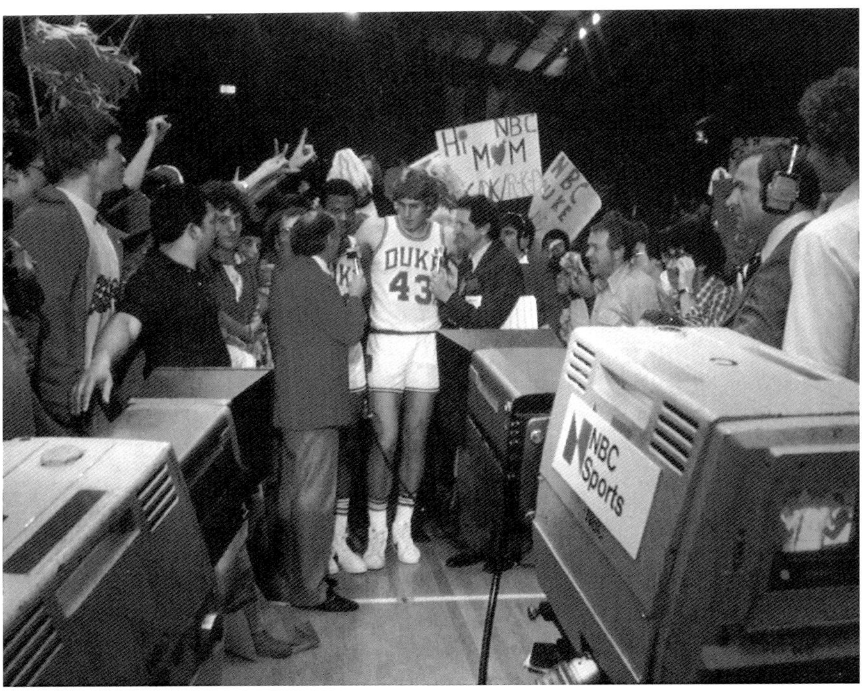

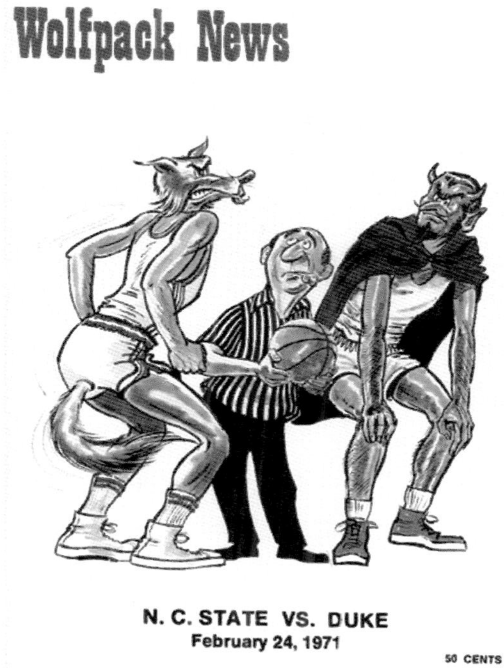

Shown is a program featuring a game between Duke and NC State in 1971. NC State, at that time, was coached by Norm Sloan, who led the Wolfpack to a national title in 1974. Duke was coached by Bucky Waters. Waters was a successful coach everywhere he worked. As an assistant coach at Duke in the 1960s, Duke went to 2 Final Fours while Waters was on the staff. As head coach at West Virginia, he posted a 70–41 record, and as head coach at Duke from 1969 to 1973 Duke was 63–45.

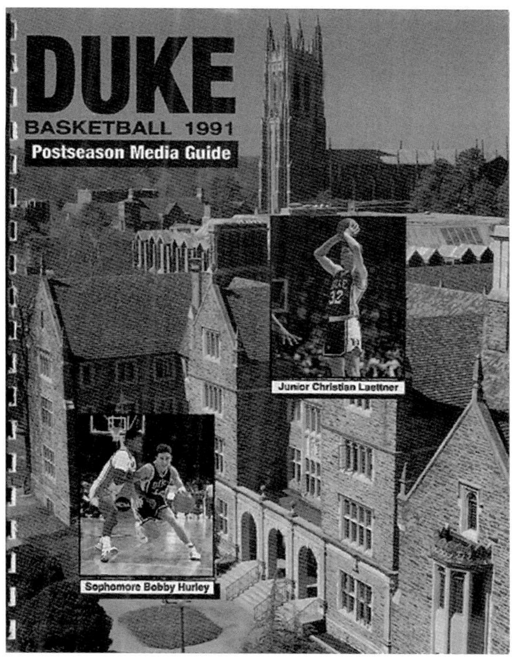

Here is the 1991 Duke basketball media guide, with Bobby Hurley and Christian Laettner on the cover, along with the majestic tower of Duke Chapel on the top.

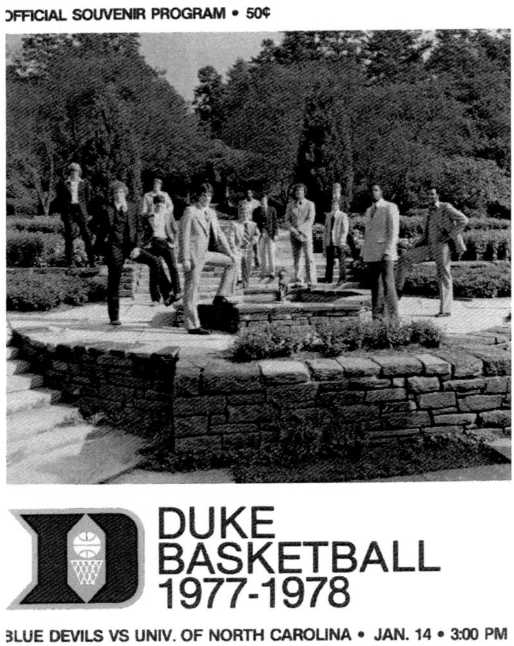

This 1977–78 Duke basketball program has the team posing in the tranquil serenity of Duke Gardens.

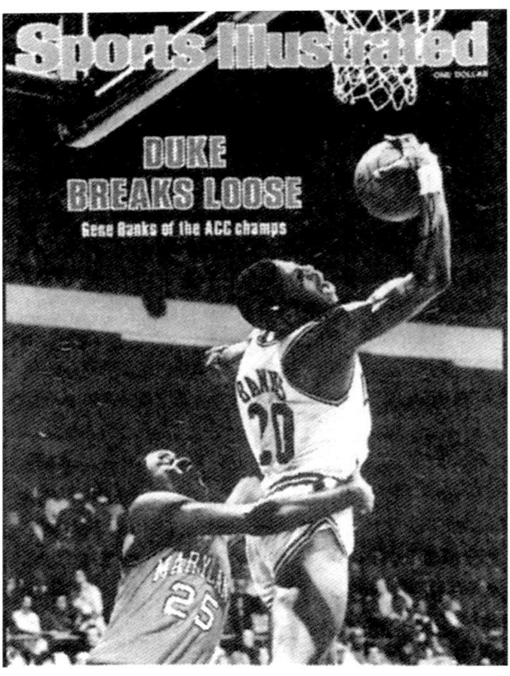

Gene Banks was on the cover of *Sports Illustrated* in 1980 after Duke beat Maryland for the ACC Tournament Championship. Banks scored 21 points in the victory over Maryland. Duke finished 24 and 9 in the 1979–80 season under coach Bill Foster. After winning the ACC Tournament, Duke went on to beat Pennsylvania and Kentucky before losing to Purdue in the NCAA tournament.

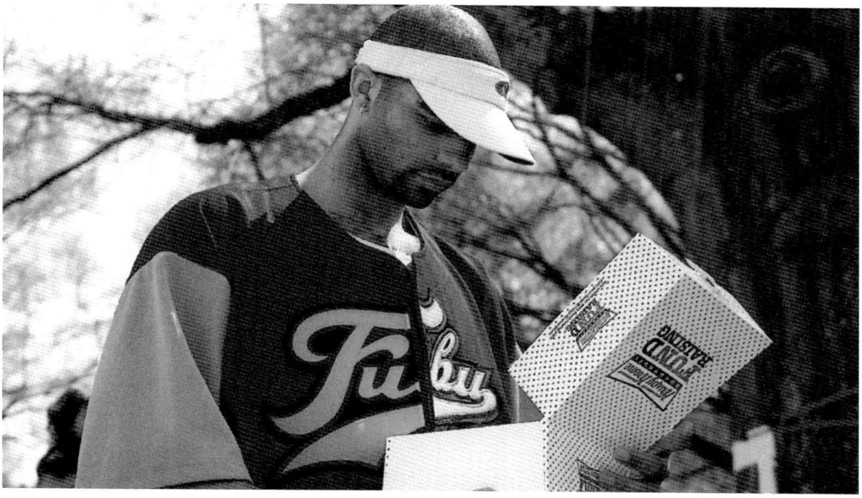

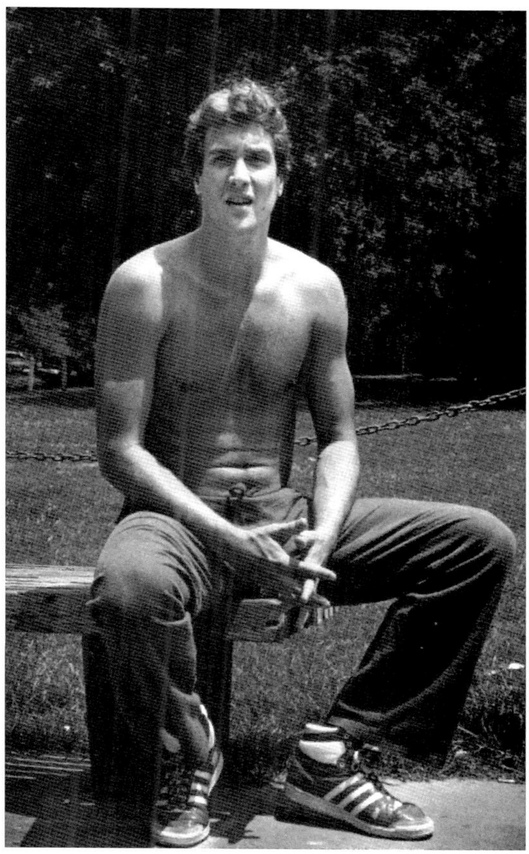

Above: Carlos Boozer was the most accurate shooter in Duke history, connecting on 63.1 percent of his shots during a career that spanned the years from 1999 to 2002. He once made 11 of 11 shots in a game against Portland in 2000, and made an astounding 33 of 39 shots in three games versus NC State in the 2002 season. Duke won 3 ACC Tournaments and 1 national title in Boozer's three years. Boozer is now recognized as one of the premier players in the NBA, starring for the Utah Jazz.

Right: Kenny Dennard is shown relaxing and soaking up a little sun in this photo. On the basketball court, however, Dennard was known for his tenacious play during a Duke career from 1977 to 1981. Dennard's senior season was Mike Krzyzewski's first season at Duke, and Dennard averaged 10.6 points and 7 rebounds a game. Dennard went on to play three seasons in the NBA.

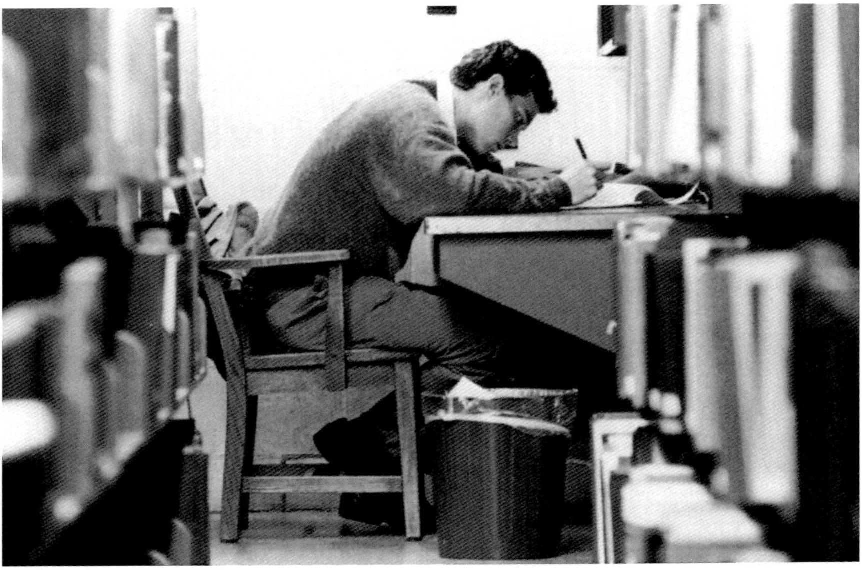

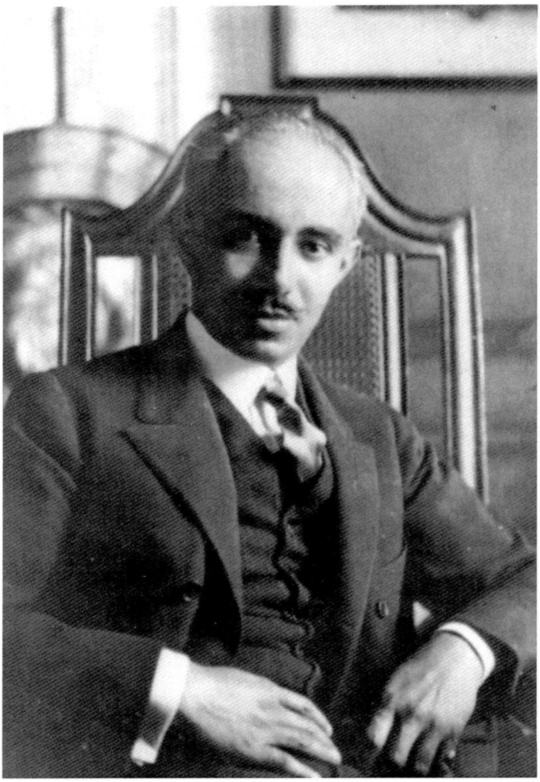

Above: As you can see, Quin Snyder did more than play basketball while a student at Duke. Snyder was an Academic All-American and won the Duke team's academic award three times during his career. After serving as an assistant coach on Coach K's staff from 1995 to 1999, Snyder became head coach at Missouri, compiling 126 wins against 91 losses before resigning. His 2002 Missouri team reached the Elite Eight of the NCAA Tournament.

Left: Julian Abele was the first black architecture graduate of the University of Pennsylvania, and designed much of Duke University, including athletic facilities. Abele also designed Harvard's Widener Library and the Philadelphia Museum of Art.

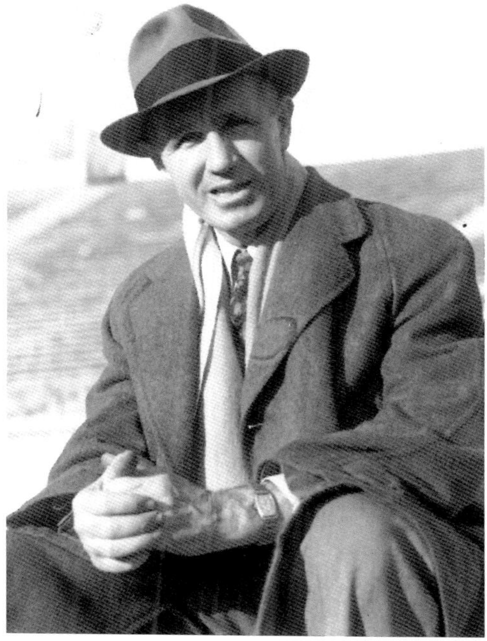

This picture is on the cover of another book the author has written, titled *Wallace Wade: Championship Years at Alabama and Duke*. The book covers the career of Wallace Wade, legendary Duke football coach. Coach Wade's football teams paid for much of the construction of Cameron Indoor Stadium.

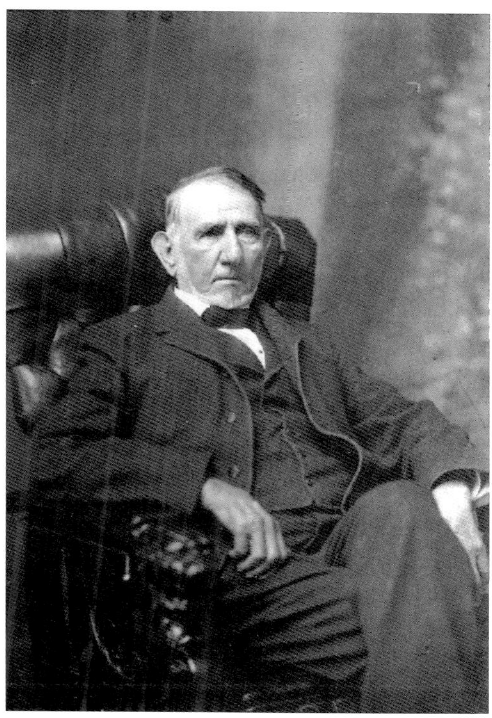

Washington Duke started a tobacco business that eventually led to the naming of Duke University. His sons James B. Duke and Benjamin N. Duke were also enormous benefactors of Duke University. Washington Duke lived from 1820 to 1905, and a statue was dedicated in his honor in 1908 at the entrance to Duke's East Campus.

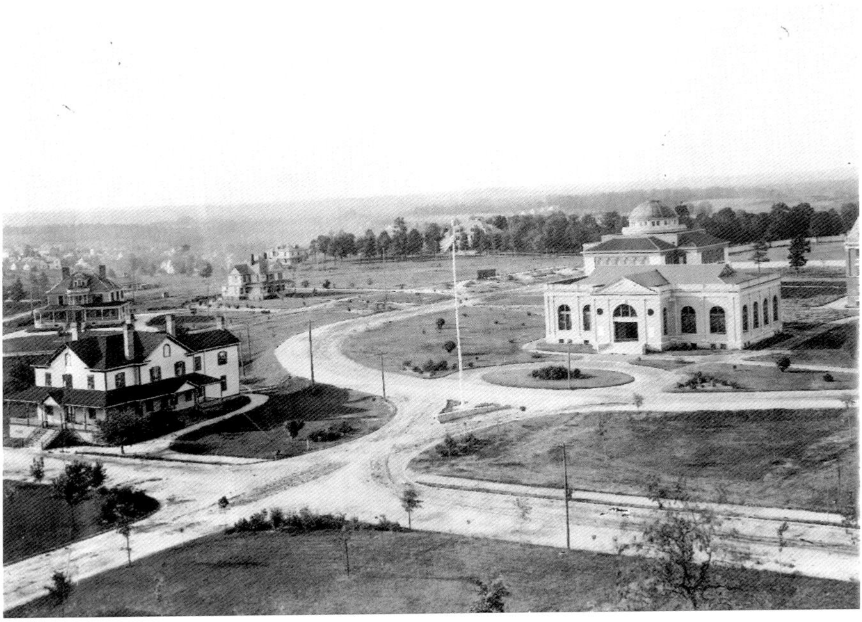

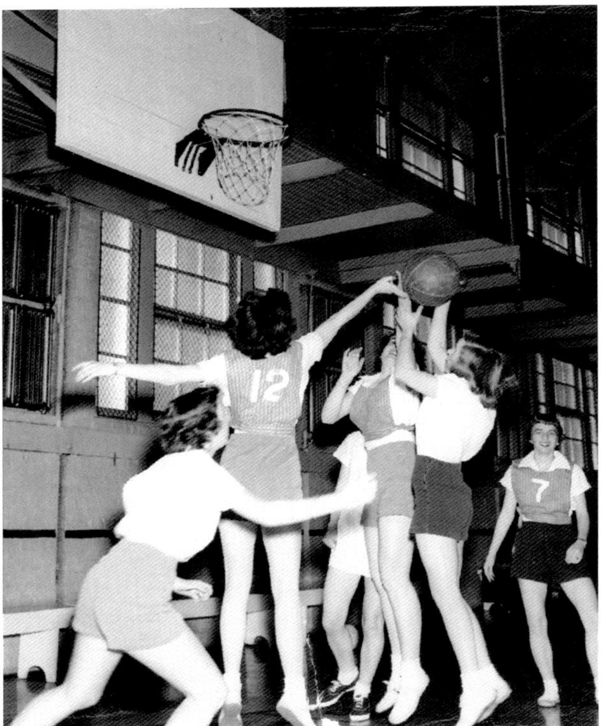

Above: The Trinity campus is shown here in 1910. Trinity was renamed Duke University in 1924.

Left: Some Duke female students play basketball during a physical education class.

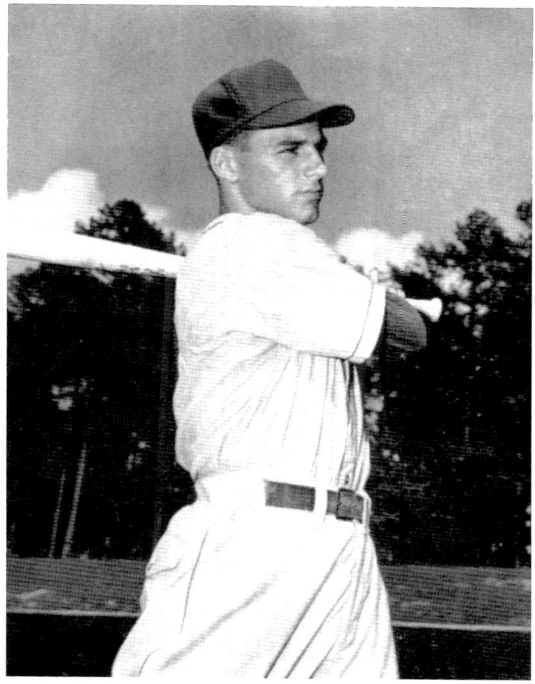

Here is Dick Groat, the baseball player, at Duke. Groat batted .386 in 1951 and .370 in 1952 and took the Blue Devils to a College World Series. He went on to win a National League MVP award with Major League baseball's Pittsburgh Pirates.

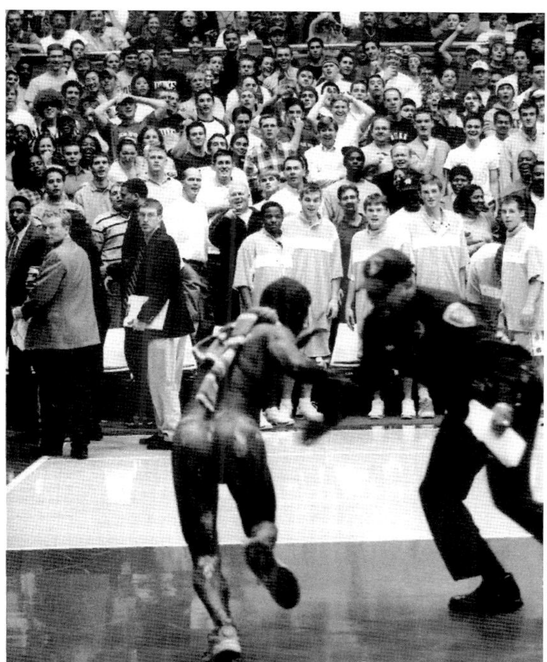

A little extra entertainment takes place during a 2003 home game at Duke, as a fan gets a little too exuberant. By the expressions on the faces of the crowd and players, they seemed to enjoy the diversion.

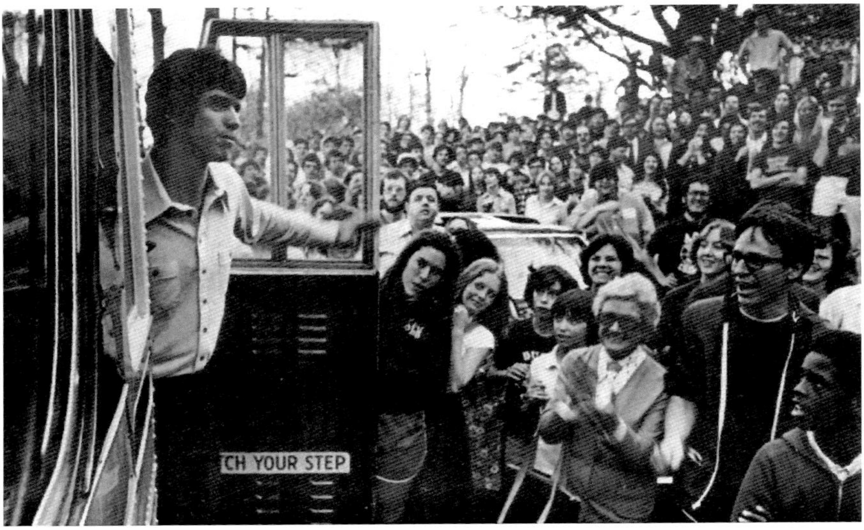

Jim Spanarkel steps off the bus in Durham to a huge welcome after Duke beat Villanova in Providence, Rhode Island, for the Eastern Regional championship, earning Duke a trip to the Final Four in 1978. Duke would beat Notre Dame in the Final Four behind Mike Gminski's 29 points, and then lose to Kentucky in the final.

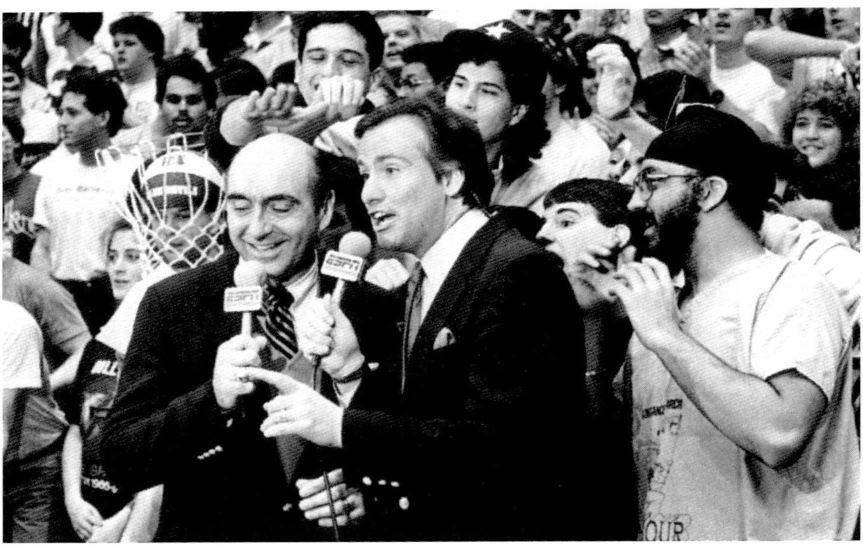

Dick Vitale is one of the top college basketball television analysts in the nation, and is a favorite of Duke fans. Vitale has a special relationship with Duke fans; sometimes the Duke students will hold Vitale over their heads and pass him through the bleachers. Vitale is a former head coach at the University of Detroit and the NBA's Detroit Pistons. He called ESPN's first college basketball game in 1979. He is shown at a Duke game in this picture in 1988.

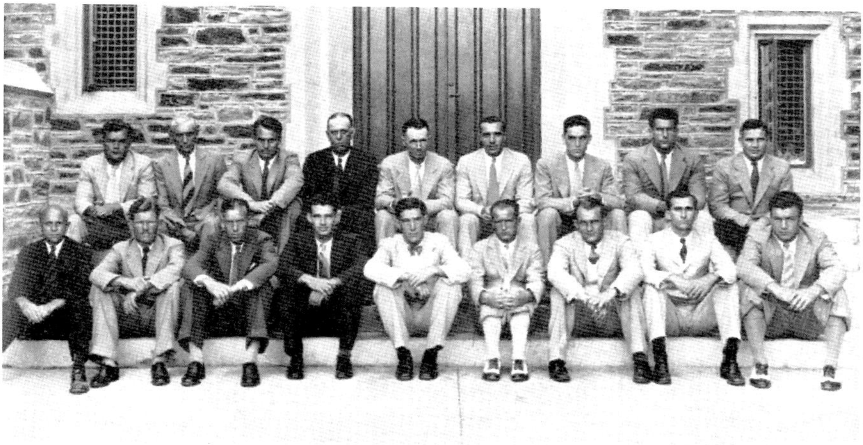

The Duke athletic coaching staff posed for this picture in 1932. *Front row, left to right*: Coaches Gregory, Tuttle, Caldwell, Dean, Persons, Crichton, Gerard, Allen and Warren. *Back row, left to right*: Coaches Hagler, Card, Cameron, Coombs, Wade, Voyles, Baker, Sington and Waite.

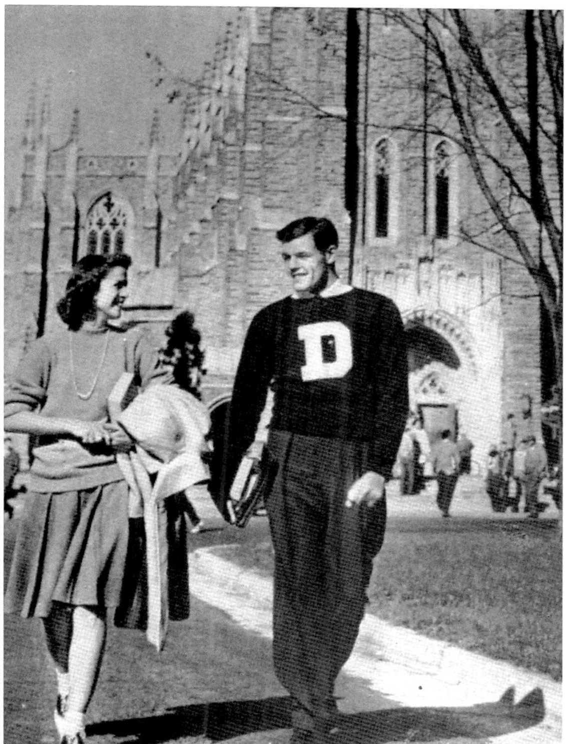

Bob Gantt walks the Duke campus with a pretty coed. Gantt was an All-American in football at Duke, and also played a good game of basketball for the Blue Devils in 1941–42 and 1942–43. Gantt became Duke's first NBA player when he performed for the 1947 Washington Capitals.

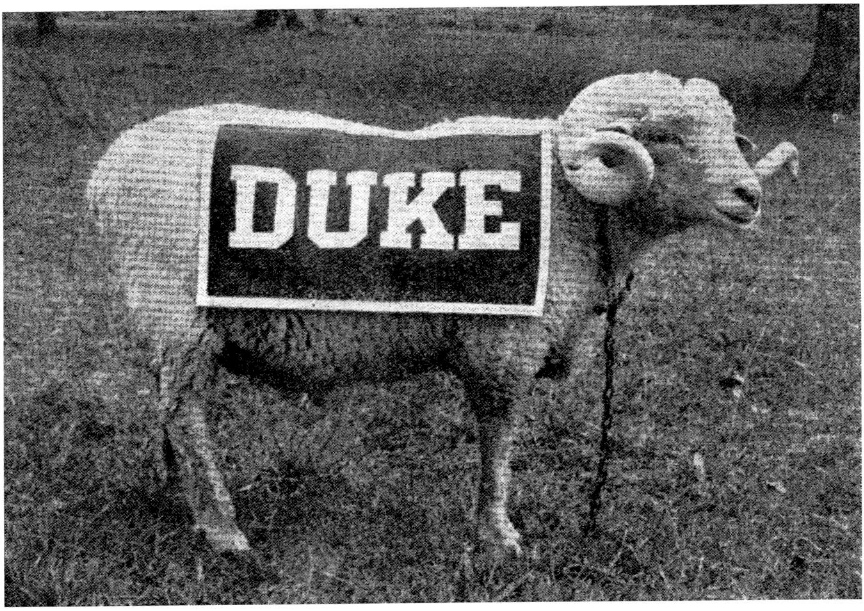

North Carolina's mascot, Rameses IX, was abducted and adorned with a Duke sign in 1977. The five Duke students who performed the heist left a note signed, "With best wishes for a glorious Carolina defeat, we are, Sincerely, The Men of Operation."

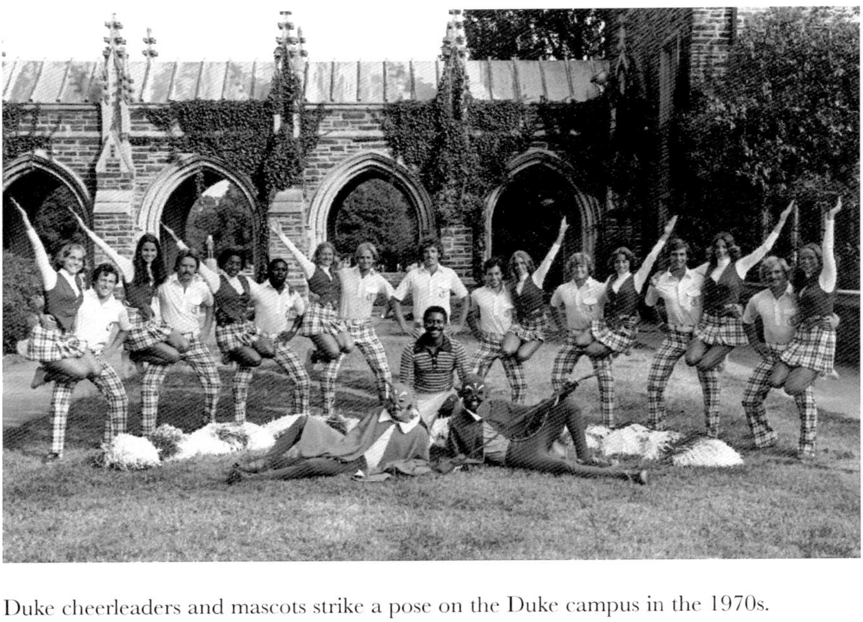

Duke cheerleaders and mascots strike a pose on the Duke campus in the 1970s.

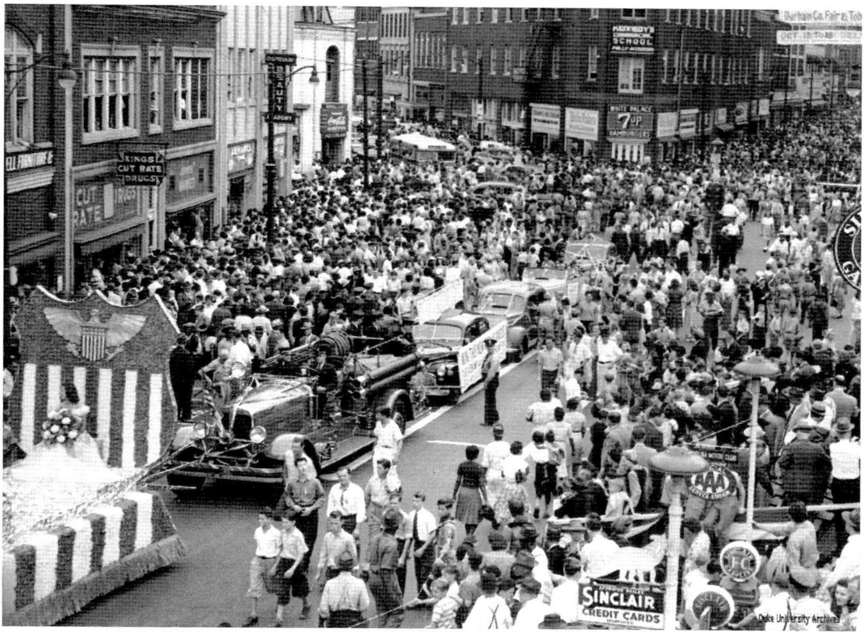

This picture of a Duke homecoming parade in downtown Durham in 1942 demonstrates how at one time football was the dominant and most popular sport on campus.

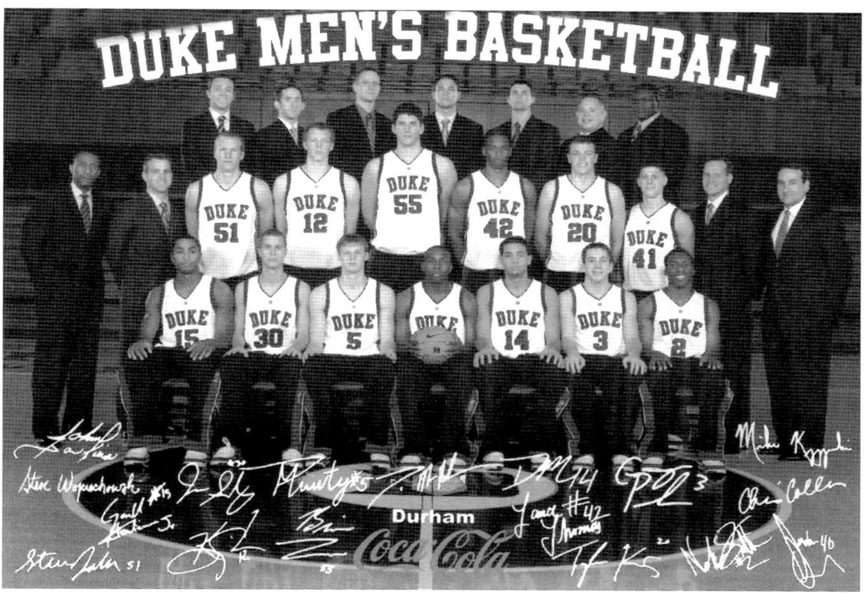

The 2007–08 Duke men's basketball team. *Courtesy of Duke Sports Information.*

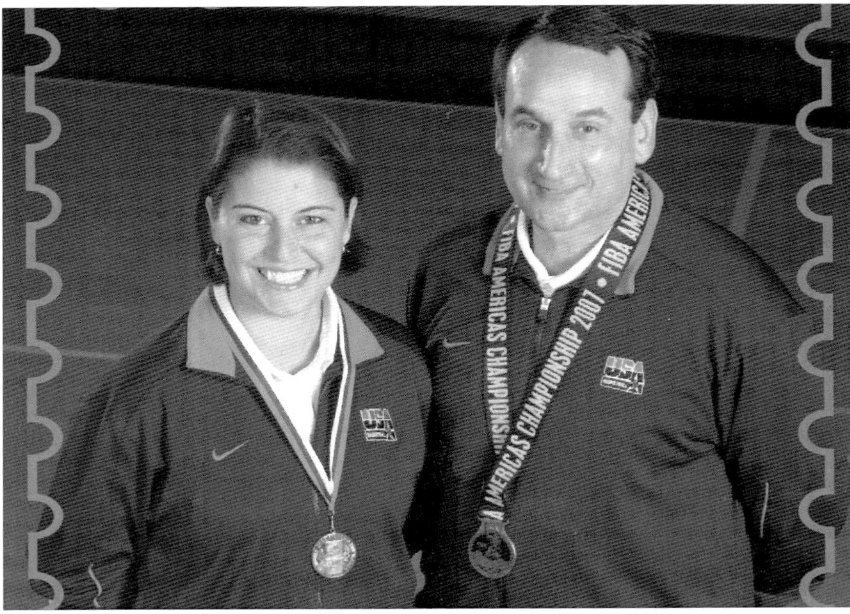

Women's basketball coach Joanne P. McCallie and men's basketball coach Mike Krzyzewski stand in unison as they lead Duke basketball into the future. *Courtesy of the author.*

ABOUT THE AUTHOR

Lewis Bowling teaches in the physical education departments at North Carolina Central University and Duke University in Durham, North Carolina. He has authored four history books on his native Granville County, and writes a history column called "Looking Back" for the *Oxford Public Ledger*. Bowling has also authored *Wallace Wade: Championship Years at Alabama and Duke* and *Resistance Training: The Total Approach*, and is a contributing author to *Lifetime Physical Fitness*. Additionally, he writes a weekly fitness column for the *Durham Herald-Sun* and is a contributing writer to *Blue Devil Weekly*. Contact Lewis at lewis_bowling@yahoo.com or 919.477.7046 for comments.